Charles Marvin

The Russian Advance Towards India

Conversations with Skobeleff, Ignatieff, and other distinguished Russian generals

and statesmen, on the Central Asian question

Charles Marvin

The Russian Advance Towards India
Conversations with Skobeleff, Ignatieff, and other distinguished Russian generals and statesmen, on the Central Asian question

ISBN/EAN: 9783744754606

Printed in Europe, USA, Canada, Australia, Japan

Cover: Foto ©Suzi / pixelio.de

More available books at **www.hansebooks.com**

THE
RUSSIAN ADVANCE TOWARDS INDIA.

Conversations

WITH SKOBELEFF, IGNATIEFF, AND OTHER DISTINGUISHED
RUSSIAN GENERALS AND STATESMEN, ON THE
CENTRAL ASIAN QUESTION.

BY

CHARLES MARVIN,

LATE SPECIAL COMMISSIONER IN RUSSIA OF THE "NEWCASTLE DAILY CHRONICLE;"
AND AUTHOR OF "MERV, THE QUEEN OF THE WORLD," "THE DISASTROUS
RUSSIAN CAMPAIGN AGAINST THE TURCOMANS," "GRODEKOFF'S
RIDE TO HERAT," "OUR PUBLIC OFFICES," ETC.

"I consider the Central Asian Question all humbug."—SKOBELEFF.

London:
SAMPSON LOW, MARSTON, SEARLE, & RIVINGTON,
CROWN BUILDINGS, 188, FLEET STREET.
1882.

[*All rights reserved.*]

DEDICATED TO

SIR WILLIAM P. ANDREW,

AS A MARK OF THAT APPRECIATION OF HIS EMINENT SERVICES IN CONNEXION WITH INDIAN RAILWAY ENTERPRISE—MORE PARTICULARLY ON BEHALF OF THE EUPHRATES VALLEY SCHEME OF OVERLAND COMMUNICATION—WHICH ALL MUST ENTERTAIN WHO HAVE AT HEART THE STRENGTHENING OF THE TIES BETWEEN THE EUROPEAN AND ASIATIC PROVINCES OF THE ENGLISH EMPIRE.

PREFACE.

It is obvious that a writer who records the conversations of his contemporaries is liable to be unintentionally indiscreet, particularly when they place themselves under no restraint in expressing their opinions to him. Nothing would pain me more than to find I had in any way been guilty in this respect, in describing my interviews with the leading Russian authorities on the Central Asian Question; and if any opinions have been published, which their authors would rather have had treated as private, I trust the difficulty of the position in which I was placed will be taken into account, and a generous pardon be accorded to my indiscretions.

In several instances I have supplemented the conversations, as originally published in the *Newcastle Daily Chronicle*, with matter taken from previous articles of mine on Central Asia, which I thought might add to the value of the text. If I have not always quoted the source from which these extracts have been taken, it should be remembered that I should probably have exposed myself to a counter-charge of egotism in doing so. As it is, as the only current English writer on the Turcomans, I have had to speak so often of my own books that I can hardly hope to escape having this charge pressed against me.

With regard to the opinions expressed, it should be clearly understood that they are solely and exclusively my own, and are not put forward either on behalf of Mr. Joseph Cowen, M.P., or the *Newcastle Daily Chronicle*. This should be clear enough from the context, but I give prominence to this caution that there may be no doubt whatever upon the subject. At the same time, I would have it with equal clearness understood, that the opinions expressed are not merely the heedless and ephemeral views of an irresponsible journalist, but the deep convictions of one who is conscious that they may some day be called up against him in other spheres than that of journalism or literature.

PLUMSTEAD, KENT,
June, 1882.

CONTENTS.

CHAPTER I.

HOW THE JOURNEY TO RUSSIA CAME TO BE UNDERTAKEN.

PAGE

General Skobeleff's speeches at Paris—Omission of English correspondents to interview him on the Central Asian Question—Enterprise of the *Newcastle Daily Chronicle*—Mr. Cowen's decision to send a correspondent to Russia to interview him there—The origin of the map of the Russo-Persian frontier—Russia not wrong in annexing Akhal—Superfluous criticism of Mr. O'Donovan—Russophobes and Russophils—A broad view of Imperialism—Councillor Davidoff's opinion of Russophobia—The *Newcastle Chronicle* and Prince Krapotkin—In advance of the Embassy—Suspicions of Nihilist intrigue—One effect of "Merv and the man-stealing Turcomans"—Davidoff's views on the Central Asian Question—Journey from London to St. Petersburg—The Skobeleff fever—Excitement at Berlin—Possibilities of a German invasion of Russia—Superiority of the German railways over those of France or Russia—German migration to Poland—Affluence on one side of the Russo-German frontier, poverty on the other—Luxurious travelling—"An Englishman or a lunatic"—Anxiety at the frontier—Troops guarding the line from Gatchina to St. Petersburg 1

CHAPTER II.

THE RUSSIAN FOREIGN OFFICE AND BARON OSTEN-SAKEN.

Interview with Baron Osten-Saken—Shabbiness of the Russian Foreign Office as compared with our own—My map already received from London—Personal appearance of Baron Osten-Saken and his present position at the Foreign Office—The map a good letter of introduction—Optimist tone of the Baron—Agrees with Councillor Davidoff in disbelieving that a junction will soon take place of the English and Russian empires in Central Asia—Decadence of the Central Asian agitation—The change of base of operations in Central Asia—His opinion of Sir Henry Rawlinson — The best-informed man in Russia as to the Perso-Turcoman region—The new frontier beyond the Caspian—Deep interest of M. de Giers in Persia—The Chinese barrier between Russia and India — Chinese assimilation of the Jews—Jewish outrages exaggerated—Sir Charles Dilke's declaration as to the recall of General Skobeleff from Geok Tepé—Skobeleff's journey home—Was Russia guilty of duplicity in annexing Akhal?—Points for and against her—Verdict   23

CHAPTER III.

THE "RUSSIAN BURNABY" AT HOME.

General Grodekoff's history of Skobeleff's siege of Geok Tepé—The Russian Burnaby and the English Burnaby compared—Grodekoff of nomad proclivities—Facts about Skobeleff's great siege—Russia never meant to occupy Merv in 1881, as repeatedly announced by O'Donovan—The alleged recall of Skobeleff in disgrace — Grodekoff against the annexation of Akhal—Merv not the key of Herat

—Change in the Russian base of operations—Merv overrated—Arrival of the first Russian caravan at Merv—Grodekoff not an astute man—A manufacturer of false Russian news at Berlin—The new school of writers on Russia—List of military officers acquainted with Russian—Opinion of the *United Service Gazette* on the study of the Central Asian Question — The sack of Geok Tepé — Captain Butler's Allegation that he helped to fortify Geok Tepé—Grodekoff's view of the railroad to India—Loss of guns at Geok Tepé—Grodekoff's opinion of General Roberts—The Russian Burnaby an Anglophil—Russian maps of Central Asia—One million maps in store ready for hostilities—The history of the Russian corps of military topographers—The old processes of map-making and the new—Achievements of Russian map-makers—Colonel Baker and the secret English maps—Grodekoff's map of his ride to Herat sold for fourpence halfpenny . . 39

CHAPTER IV.

A DISCUSSION AT THE GENERAL STAFF OFFICE ON THE POSSIBILITY OF INVADING INDIA.

General Soboleff and the Asiatic department of the Russian General Staff—His career and acquaintance with the Ameer Abdurrahman Khan—A review of his "Anglo-Afghan Conflict"—A Russian staff officer on the war in Afghanistan—Our want of skill—Feebleness of the Indian army—Balkh to be a future outpost of Russia—Russian humanity and English cruelty in Central Asia—Soboleff on English inability to take Herat—Relative positions of the English and Russian outposts in regard to the "Key of India"—Description of the General Staff—A Russian official account of the last Afghan war—Enormous amount of English information on the subject—Russia able to invade India—The map discussed—Russian concessions—Arrival of Colonel Stewart's map from England—English policy towards our travellers in Central Asia—The Conservatives as bad as the Liberals in their concessions to Russia—General Soboleff's opinion of English travellers in the East—Captain Butler the cause of the annexation of Askabad—Kaufmann's intended march on India in 1878—The Oxus or the Hindoo Koosh as a frontier?—Discussion about Persia and Bokhara—Tchernayeff's policy . . 60

CHAPTER V.

SKOBELEFF ON THE CENTRAL ASIAN QUESTION AND A RUSSIAN ATTACK UPON INDIA.

Grodekoff's note to Skobeleff's adjutant—Ensign Abadzaeff and his share in the fighting at Geok Tepé—Numerous callers at Skobeleff's house—His military career—Seventy battles and sieges in nineteen years—Probability of his being the equal of Wellington—Description of Skobeleff—His fascinating manners—His opinion of the annexation of Akhal—Why he was recalled from Askabad—His view of the efficacy of slaughter—The massacre of the 8000 at Geok Tepé—The mowing down of women—Persian traffic in Turcoman girls—Skobeleff's criticism of the executions at Cabul—His opinion as to the different standards needed for soldiers and civilians—What he thinks of General Valentine Baker—An invasion of India not feasible—The difficulties explained—His opinion of the Afghans—The Central Asian Question all humbug—He would fight us at Herat—Russia has no desire to occupy Afghanistan—Captain Butler and Geok Tepé—Opinion of Maiwand—His art of war—His account of the battle of Makram—Twenty thousand men drowned like flies—Skobeleff's assurances regarding Central Asia—Skobeleff not the Russian Government 90

CHAPTER VI.

THE MINISTER FOR FOREIGN AFFAIRS ON THE NEW RUSSO-PERSIAN CONVENTION.

A visit to M. de Giers—His personal appearance—The charges of evasion brought against him by the English press—Ignorance of the English Embassy at St. Petersburg — The best way to negotiate foreign affairs is to know nothing about them— Career of M. de Giers—His services—Opinion of the new frontier beyond the Caspian—Mr. Ashmead-Bartlett's Question in the House of Commons— The new Russo-Persian frontier a permanent one —The Atabai Yomood difficulty—Merv not likely to be annexed—Liberation of Kidaeff, the Russian captive at Merv—Opinion of M. de Giers of the situation in Central Asia—Russian influence in Khorassan and English influence in Afghanistan —The future of Bokhara—An interview with the Tsar impossible 113

CHAPTER VII.

GENERAL TCHERNAYEFF ON THE FUTURE OF BOKHARA.

Tchernayeff's appointment as Governor-General of Turkestan — Description of him — Comparison between him and Skobeleff—His views on the elevation of Servia to a Kingdom—The difference between Turkestan and Turkmenia—The railway to Khiva—The fate of Bokhara—The Cossack on the Oxus—Are mountains or rivers the best frontiers?—No fear of an annexation of Merv— The frontier policies of England and Russia in

Central Asia — Khorassan safe from seizure—
Russian influence in Persia—The duty on Indian
tea—The caravan trade between India and Turkestan—The Afghan barrier not worth breaking down
—Uselessness of defining a Russo-Indian frontier
in Asia—A Russian invasion of India practicable—
Opinion on the annexation of Candahar—Russia
likely to be drawn to Herat—His view of the Jewish
atrocities—His opinion of Sir Henry Rawlinson—
Assurances respecting Russia's friendliness towards England—" Tashkent—*c'est mon ouvrage* " . 122

CHAPTER VIII.

THE VICE-PRESIDENT OF THE RUSSIAN IMPERIAL GEO-GRAPHICAL SOCIETY AND THE ADVANCE UPON KHORASSAN.

A morning with Gospodin Semenoff—An ideal naturalist
—The Central Asian Question misunderstood—
Difference between the enmity between Russian and
German and between Russian and Englishman—
Impossibility of a fusion of the Slav and Teuton
races—The time too early yet for the establishment
of an understanding in regard to the partition of
Central Asia—The new Russo-Persian border a bit
of the future permanent frontier — The Atabai
Yomood difficulty surmountable—Frontier arrange-
ments in Central Asia — Misrule in Persia no
concern of Russia—Why Russia's interest is greater
in Turkey than in Persia—Russia and the Slavs
—She cannot abandon her historical mission—
Nomads must be kept in order—Russia will some
day occupy Merv—Russia the future mistress of the
whole of the Turcoman tribes—England must
establish greater control over the Herat tribes, or
Russia will advance to the "Key of India"—
English and Russian policy in Central Asia—

Chinese rule only temporary in Kuldja—Lessar's exploration of Sarakhs—Ancient books found at Geok Tepé—Semenoff's view of Sir Henry Rawlinson—My own policy in regard to the Central Asian Question—The Duke of Argyll's patriotism—Semenoff's admiration of Skobeleff—The future of Hungary 137

CHAPTER IX.

GENERAL GRODEKOFF AND CAPTAIN MASLOFF DISCUSS THE RUSSIAN VIEW OF THE CENTRAL ASIAN QUESTION.

A second conversation with the "Russian Burnaby"—Captain Masloff's brilliant sketches in the *Novoe Vremya*—Grodekoff insists on the impossibility of a Russian invasion of India—His opinion of General Soboleff—Difficulties at Geok Tepé—300,000 troops needed for the invasion of India—Khorassan never to be absorbed by Russia—Fanatic character of the people—The Atabai Yomood difficulty not a solitary one—Major Napier and Kari Kala—Masloff's opinion of a march from Askabad to Sarakhs—Grodekoff and O'Donovan—Krapotkin's view of the Russian advance—Parallel between Russia's operations in Central Asia and ours in South Africa—The importance of Merv overrated—Misconception regarding "keys"—Skobeleff's mission—England thinks more of the Central Asian Question than Russia—Useless for Russia to try and persuade England against Rawlinson—Grodekoff's decision to write a book on the Central Asian Question—Lord Lytton's "mad" scheme for invading Central Asia—Kaufmann's dubious march in the direction of India—Afghan hatred of Russia—Grodekoff and the Treaty of Berlin—A greater danger than the Russian invasion of India—English and Russian generals—Final assurances . 150

CHAPTER X.

ENGLAND TO INDIA IN NINE DAYS.

PAGE

General Annenkoff's scheme for constructing a railroad to India—His Transcaspian line—Lessar's journey to Sarakhs — Comfort in Russia — Annenkoff's knowledge of the literature of the Central Asian Question—Skobeleff and the "Disastrous Russian campaign against the Turcomans"—Invitation to occupy the whole of Afghanistan—Annenkoff's view of the Central Asian Question—The Russian Government and the passage of English troops through Russia on their way to India—An account of his scheme—Rival routes to India—The new Russian railways bringing the Cossack closer to the Sepoy—Russia's aim to tap the overland trade to India — Effect of Annenkoff's scheme upon the Euphrates Valley railway—Evil of English suspicion of Native loyalty in India — Anecdote of Skobeleff—Annenkoff on Khorassan and Sarakhs—Ignorance of the English public regarding the Central Asian Question — His opinion of the evacuation of Candahar and of General Roberts—Annenkoff's wound at Geok Tepé — The present garrison in Akhal — Kouropatkin's march from Samarcand to Geok Tepé—Cultivation of esparto grass in the Transcaspian region — Why Lessar chose to survey the route for the railroad to Sarakhs—Refusal of the English authorities to let him have recent maps of Afghanistan—English policy towards exploration in Central Asia . . . 165

CHAPTER XI.

REFUSAL OF PERMISSION TO PROCEED TO ASKABAD.

An offer from an important Russian personage to pay a visit to Askabad · A second call upon General

Soboleff—Arrival of an officer from Geok Tepé—
The recent expedition, under another general than
Skobeleff, might have ended in disaster—Soboleff
refuses to give me permission to proceed to Akhal
—His opposition to English exploration of Central
Asia—Lessar's journey towards Herat—Fewness of
Russian travellers visiting India—List of Russian
explorers in Central Asia since 1854—Disfavour
shown by the English Government to exploration
of Afghanistan—Apathy and want of patriotism of
the Royal Geographical Society—Effect of Burnaby's "Ride to Khiva"—Russian indignation at
the publication of Schuyler's "Turkistan"—The
Krijanovsky frauds at Orenburg and their bearing
upon Russian corruption in Turkestan—The Yomood massacre, the Lomakin massacre, and the
massacre at Geok Tepé—Opinion of Soboleff on the
subject—Frightful scenes during the pursuit after
the fall of Geok Tepé—Murder of sixty Russians
by the Tekkes—Mr. Gladstone left to deal with
the three massacres 188

CHAPTER XII.

PROFESSOR MARTENS AND RUSSIAN INTERESTS IN HERAT AND AFGHANISTAN.

The position which the various Russian authorities on
Central Asia occupy to one another — Influence
exercised by General Soboleff and Professor
Martens — The bargaining feature of Russian
policy—"The catspaw of the wily Gortschakoff"
—How Martens' brochure on Central Asia came to
be written—His opinion that England ought not to
have Herat, and that we ought to keep out of
Afghanistan—Lord Hartington's declaration of
English policy—Baron Jomini's threat—Proposition to turn Herat into an Asiatic Switzerland—

Russian claims to Afghanistan—A red rag to English Russophobists—Necessity for deciding upon a clear and consistent policy for England to pursue in Central Asia—England much to blame for the Central Asian agitation—Professor Martens and Sir Charles Dilke's declaration anent the evacuation of the Akhal Tekke region—The secret Cabul correspondence—Kaufmann's policy in Central Asia—General Stolietoff in digrace . 201

CHAPTER XIII.

COUNT IGNATIEFF ON "MISREPRESENTED RUSSIA."

Count Ignatieff at home—A Tuesday reception at his official residence—Curious commingling of cocked hats and sheepskins—Waiting to see the Minister—Ignatieff's mode of dealing with place-hunters—Worked to death—His attitude towards newspaper correspondents—How he humbugs them—A second interview with his Excellency—His cabinet—The disclosure of the Anglo-Russian Agreement—His opinion of Lord Salisbury and his inquiry as to the cause of his enmity—"We were such friends at Constantinople"—Ignatieff on the cause of the war with Turkey, and the Treaty of Berlin—Austria and the Southern Slavs—Russia misrepresented by Europe—Ignatieff's indignation at the European press for trying to make him out to be a fool—Russia did not provoke the occupation of Bosnia by Austria—Ignatieff's admiration of Mr. Gladstone—His view of a Russian occupation of Constantinople—"Russia the victim of English party misrepresentations"—The Jewish outrages—The Russian Government unable to prevent the expulsion of Jews—Something worse than a Parliament—Ignatieff as a reformer—The manufacture of official Russian news—Ignatieff and Lord Salisbury's portrait . . 213

CHAPTER XIV.

A SECOND INTERVIEW WITH SKOBELEFF, AND A SURVEY OF THE RUSSO-INDIAN QUESTION.

General Skobeleff and his Paris speeches—His admiration of General Roberts and his march from Cabul to Candahar—His opinion of long and short service—A campaign conducted by young men—His view of the Channel Tunnel; of the English army; of our native forces in India; and of our frontier policy on the borders of Afghanistan—England's ability to engage in a European war—Her chances in 1878—Russian opinion of Austria and the Austrian army—Skobeleff's mission—Russia compelled to advance in Central Asia—Her designs against India — The new frontier beyond the Caspian—Russia and the occupation of Merv—Prospective annexations—Double movement upon Merv—Russian claims upon Herat and Afghan Turkestan—How to deal with them—Divergences of opinion in Russia upon the Central Asian Question—One mode of dealing with Annenkoff's Indian railroad in the event of a war—Calming effect of Russian assurances—No Sir Henry Rawlinson in Russia—The rival merits of English and Russian policy in Central Asia — Our shiftless mode of dealing with frontier tribes—List of frontier wars—Duplicity of Sir Charles Dilke—Gladstone the deceiver, not Russia 236

APPENDICES.

RUSSIA'S NEW PROVINCE IN CENTRAL ASIA	257
HAS ENGLAND LOST HERAT?	274
THE RUSSIAN FLEET IN CENTRAL ASIA	286

	PAGE
LETTERPRESS ACCOMPANYING THE MAP OF THE RUSSO-PERSIAN FRONTIER	302
SKOBELEFF'S PARIS SPEECHES	306
SKOBELEFF ON WARFARE IN CENTRAL ASIA	313
CAPTAIN BUTLER'S CLAIM TO THE FORTIFYING OF GEOK TEPÉ	319
CONVENTION RESPECTING THE RUSSO-PERSIAN FRONTIER	324
GENERAL KAYE ON THE NEW RUSSO-PERSIAN FRONTIER	330
THE CENTRAL ASIAN PARTY IN ENGLAND AND RUSSIA	335

THE RUSSIAN ADVANCE TOWARDS INDIA.

CHAPTER I.

HOW THE JOURNEY TO RUSSIA CAME TO BE UNDERTAKEN.

General Skobeleff's speeches at Paris—Omission of English correspondents to interview him on the Central Asian Question—Enterprise of the *Newcastle Daily Chronicle*—Mr. Cowen's decision to send a correspondent to Russia to interview him there—The origin of the map of the Russo-Persian frontier—Russia not wrong in annexing Akhal—Superfluous criticism of Mr. O'Donovan—Russophobes and Russophils—A broad view of Imperialism—Councillor Davidoff's opinion of Russophobia—The *Newcastle Chronicle* and Prince Krapotkin—In advance of the Embassy—Suspicions of Nihilist intrigue—One effect of "Merv and the Man-stealing Turcomans"—Davidoff's views on the Central Asian Question—Journey from London to St. Petersburg—The Skobeleff fever—Excitement at Berlin—Possibilities of a German invasion of Russia—Superiority of the German railways over those of France or Russia—German migration to Poland—Affluence on one side of the Russo-German frontier, poverty on the other—Luxurious travelling—"An Englishman or a lunatic"—Anxiety at the frontier—Troops guarding the line from Gatchina to St. Petersburg.

My journey to Russia originated in the following manner. On reading in the *Daily News* of Monday, February 20, an account of an interview the previous day between the Paris correspondent of that paper and General Skobeleff, the idea struck me that it would be an interesting matter to ascertain the views on Central Asia of a commander, who had only recently arrived home after a successful and brilliant campaign on the confines of Persia and Afghanistan, and who was rumoured to regard it as his mission to fight England for supremacy in India. Believing that a report of the interview would be readily accepted by the *Newcastle Daily Chronicle*, and fearing lest some other journalist might anticipate my project, I did not wait to communicate with the editor, but hastened immediately to Mr. Cowen, the proprietor, in London.

The idea was favourably received, and I should have set off at once, but for the report circulating in the papers that Skobeleff was hourly expected in London. On Wednesday night Mr. Cowen wrote to me that he considered it inadvisable to wait any longer, and I accordingly prepared to start for Paris the next morning. Before I could carry my intention into effect, Skobeleff had already left the French capital, in obedience to a summons from the Emperor to return home, and without any hesitation Mr. Cowen asked me to follow him to St. Petersburg, and discuss the

Central Asian Question there. My journey would have been considered a successful one if I had only furnished a report of the Skobeleff interview to the *Newcastle Chronicle*; but events conspired in my favour to render it possible for me to see at St. Petersburg nearly a dozen other personages interested in the problem of the East. The sole instructions I received on setting out were, to report, as impartially as possible, the actual state of feeling in Russia regarding Central Asia, and I did my utmost to accomplish this, although many of the Russian opinions noted are dead against those which I had previously expressed in my books.

A few brief words will explain the origin of the map. The morning after my interview with Mr. Cowen (Tuesday, February 21), I received the *Official Journal* (*Praveetelstvenni Vestnik*) from St. Petersburg with my other Russian newspapers, describing in a letter from Teheran the course of the new Russo-Persian frontier. On tracing the line upon General Petroosevetch's map of Akhal and Merv, which is appended to my "Merv," I was struck with the moderation displayed by Russia in relinquishing territorial claims, that had not only been put forward by her Central Asian writers, but even promulgated on government maps. My researches among the blue books and "Hansard's

Parliamentary Reports" for my history of Skoboleff's siege of Geok Tepé, had already established the fact that Russia had been innocent of any duplicity in annexing Akhal; and the rough map I had made of the new frontier proved the falsity of the charges of fresh aggressiveness against her, that were then being formulated by the English press. So far from having annexed territory south of the River Atrek, as announced in a telegram to a leading London daily paper, she had relinquished territory to the north of it; while so far from having approached within fifteen miles of Sarakhs, she had stopped short 150 miles from that Persian fortress. As a deal of vague alarm prevailed regarding the new frontier, I thought I should be doing a service to both countries if I issued a map to Parliament and the Press, indicating approximately the course of the new frontier. To have drawn a new map of the region, containing the latest Russian and English researches (as Mr. O'Donovan hinted in the *Daily News* I ought to have done) would have been superfluous, and defeated the main object I had in view—namely, that of acquainting the public *at once* with the actual state of affairs in Transcaspia. Such a map would have taken weeks, perhaps months, to compile, and in the interval would have been superseded by the Russian official map of the new frontier. Petrooscvitch's sketch map answered every purpose required by the politician. The lithograph stone was lying ready at the publisher's; it was easy to trace the new frontier-line upon it; and by Friday night copies of the map, with descriptive letterpress appended,[1] were already in circulation. By the following Monday every prominent Member of Parliament and every important English newspaper had received a copy of the map.

No Russophil feeling of the Bulgarian atrocity character prompted me to issue the document. I was guided simply by a principle that I have laid down in my books, and constantly enunciated in the Press—namely, that we can be just to Russia without being unjust to ourselves, and that it is a political folly not to give credit where credit is due. The indiscriminate wolf-cry of certain English writers on Central Asia has done more harm than good to the cause they espouse, and has provoked public distrust against their opinions. I myself take no side. I seek to be impartial. I know I have a greater love for Russia, the country of my youth, and a better appreciation of the Russian people than the so-called Russophil traders in politics, who lauded her indiscriminately in 1877 from motives of self or party interest, and aban-

[1] Inserted in the Appendix at the end of the book.

doned her afterwards to false attacks; and the public know from my writings that I am a vigilant and anxious observer of the Russian advance towards India. I am both a Russophil and a Russophobe. As for my local opinions, my youth was passed in a country which has no political parties corresponding with our Liberal and Conservative factions, and does not want them; while my studies have led me to survey politics from the standpoint of one who considers himself more in the light of a citizen of the English Empire—of that great empire that embraces the five empires of England, of Canada, of Australia, of South Africa, and of India—than merely a Liberal or Conservative Englishman of Lesser England only. Being, in this sense, an Imperialist, and a non-party writer, I claim immunity from any charge of unduly favouring Liberal or Conservative policy in my remarks on the Central Asian Question.

Through an oversight on the part of the agents to whom I had entrusted the getting of my passport, that document was not in order when I called for it a few hours before my intended departure on Saturday, February 25th, and I therefore found myself under the necessity of either troubling the Embassy for the *visa*, or else waiting until the Russian Consulate reopened the following Monday morning. Nobody was to be found at the Embassy when I called, and it was not until it was already too late to catch the night mail for Russia that the Councillor, Gospodin Davidoff arrived at Chesham Place, and gave me an opportunity of asking some one for the *visa*. The Councillor occupies the post of assistant-ambassador; he has been a number of years in England; and he entertains a rooted belief that we are so hopelessly hostile to Russia, that centuries must elapse before any change can be expected in our sentiments.

In reply to his question why I could not wait till Monday for my passport, I stated I wished to proceed to St. Petersburg without delay, to ascertain the state of feeling there regarding Central Asia, and to obtain from Skobeleff information for my new book on the siege of Geok Tepé. Eliciting that I should represent the *Newcastle Daily Chronicle*, he said drily, "Ah, that is the paper to which the Nihilist leader, Prince Krapotkin, contributes." On my hastening to remove any bad impression by stating that I should represent Mr. Cowen personally more than the *Chronicle*, he rejoined in a still drier tone, "Ah, that is the friend of Prince Krapotkin!"

I had a copy of my new map in my pocket. I

drew it out to explain more clearly the nature of the information I desired to obtain at St. Petersburg. He scanned it with interest. "You are in advance of the Embassy," he said, forgetting all about Krapotkin for the moment. "We ourselves know nothing about the new frontier arrangements."

"But my information is taken from a source accessible to the Embassy, the Russian *Official Journal*," I pointed out.

"Unfortunately we do not take it in, and thus we do not know the nature of the negotiations that have been in progress at Teheran." His conversation then became of a personal character, and ended by a promise on his part to let me have the passport with the *visa* at eleven o'clock the following morning.

When I called upon him at that hour his first remark was a repetition of the suspicions he had expressed the previous evening. "We still believe, Mr. Marvin, that you must have some other aim in view besides obtaining information regarding Central Asia. We can hardly believe that the *Newcastle Daily Chronicle*—a mere provincial paper—would send you out on that mission alone."

"In plain language, you think my journey is connected with the revolutionary movement in Russia."

"Yes."

I earnestly repudiated any such mission, and was relieved to find that he was unaware I had spent the Thursday evening in the company of Prince Krapotkin, discussing the Central Asian Question. My protestations prevailed. The councillor gave me my passport, and the conversation turned from Nihilism to the Russian advance towards India. Gospodin Davidoff expressed it as his opinion that I should not be able to obtain any more information at St. Petersburg about Central Asia than I should in London. "I can understand your going to Krasnovodsk or Tashkent for information," he said, "but not to the Russian capital." The reader will decide whether he was correct or not in his prediction. He also again repeated his belief that the English people have been written into such a distrust of Russia, that no amount of Russophil literature will write them out of it. This I questioned. I admitted that the Russophil rant of Gladstone, Malcolm McColl, the Duke of Argyll, and other writers of the atrocity school, had failed to promote any genuine feeling in favour of Russia, while provoking a strong Russophobe reaction; but I pointed out the improved impression of Russia England had derived from Mackenzie Wallace's writings; and the conversation becoming personal, I mentioned, as an illustration of literature not having yet lost its force, the fact of my "Merv" having extinguished the sentimental notion of regarding the man-stealing Turcoman in the light of a warrior patriot, or Central Asian Pole. Discussing afterwards the Russian advance towards India, Davidoff ridiculed the opinion of Burnaby and others, that Russia has any designs upon our Eastern Empire, or that Russian military men entertained the idea of one day fighting us in Central Asia. He thought the Afghan settlement would be of a permanent character. Referring to Annenkoff's scheme for constructing a railway to India, he doubted whether it would ever be seriously entertained by the Russian Government, and he confidently expressed an opinion that neither he nor I would witness in our time the junction of the two empires in Central Asia. These views, he said in conclusion, I should find general in Russia. Here, again, the reader will decide whether he was correct or not.

One good result attended the delay in my departure for Russia. I was able to supervise personally the despatch of the maps, which occupied the whole of Sunday; and when I took my seat in the eight o'clock mail in the evening, I had the satisfaction of knowing that the whole of them had been posted at Charing Cross, to be transmitted during the night to all parts of the metropolis and the provinces.

I arrived at the Russian capital on the 2nd of March, in advance of General Skobeleff, and will commence my narrative from that point.

ST. PETERSBURG, March 3.

The sensation produced by General Skobeleff's utterances anent the Panslavist mission has been prodigious throughout Europe. I arrived here last night from London, by way of Paris and Berlin; and the whole distance, from what is really one end of Europe to the other, the main topic of everybody was Skobeleff. On my way to Paris, I overheard snatches of conversation at the railway stations in which his name was prominent by repetition. On leaving Creil for Cologne the Paris express was charged with passengers more or less animated with discussion as to the rival merits of Slav and German; at Cologne everybody was reading or talking about the hero of Plevna; and at Berlin his name was being uttered everywhere, from the Unter den Linden to the stuffy but comfortable little *bier* and *butterbrod* shops outside the town. Happening at Berlin to stop before a shop-window, in which a fine map of Russia and Germany was displayed, a horde of little boys rushed up, fresh from school and full of guttural chatter, and at once began discussing the topic of the hour. "That's the way, Herman, we shall go," shouted one, pointing to the Warsaw Railway, "up that railroad there; and when we get to St. Petersburg, won't we teach that fellow Skobeleff a lesson!" "Ah, but if they try and come to Berlin?" rejoined another dubiously. "Phoof," shouted half a dozen at once, "come to Berlin! Look how long they were fighting the Turks before they beat them. The Russians are only good at fighting savages. And what is that Skobeleff himself but a bragging barbarian?" Then off the youngsters ran, shouting excitedly what they would do if Russia invaded the Fatherland, and their places were taken by less boisterous, grown-up folk, sobered by years of beer and tobacco, who expressed in curt monosyllables their contempt for the Slav and Skobeleff. There was not a newspaper in Berlin on Tuesday which was not more or less full of bitter comment on Russia. Happening to stand near the Guard House at the aristocratic extremity of the Unter den Linden, I heard the soldiers, young but smart and intelligent linesmen, talking in a most warlike strain about Russia. Having lost on the way a button from my overcoat, and entering a tailor's shop in the Friederich Strasse to have a new one sewn on, the worthy tailor exclaimed at once,

"Ah, Mein Herr, your coat is like Skobeleff—he has also got a button loose." These are but a few of many instances coming under my notice at Berlin, proving how widespread the excitement was and is throughout the German capital at the words of hatred against the Teuton dropped by Skobeleff at Paris. In my journey through France the principal phase of the conversation on the subject was, the possibility of a Franco-Russian war against Germany, and the general approval which was accorded to the idea showed that the statesmen of Paris and St. Petersburg would incur no disfavour whatever in promoting such an alliance, which is, further, much advocated in Russia. It would be taking up too much time to go into the various combinations to which such an alliance might give rise, in the opinion of Russians and Frenchmen; but the leading impression would appear to be that Germany, attacked on one side by France, and on the other by Russia, would be compelled to succumb, particularly if a well arranged Slav rising throughout Austria paralyzed the action of the statesmen of Vienna. It is noteworthy that in the discussions on this point I heard little or no mention of England. We are, in fact, considered of no account in European politics.

How far a joint attack from Paris and St. Petersburg against Berlin would be successful is a matter of pure speculation. I have just traversed almost every inch of the road—for Criel is within an hour's sharp run of Paris—and have thus had an opportunity of gauging somewhat the chances of such an enterprise. From Paris to the Belgian frontier the road runs through a succession of prosperous villages and cosy provincial towns, the whole of them having an air of comfort and content, and affording indications of surplus supplies that would charm the heart of any commander. On nearing Belgium the mining districts begin, and from St. Quentin almost the whole way to Cologne, through Belgium and Rhineland, there is nothing but a succession of large industrial centres, connected by iron mines and iron works, and manufactories of every description. Beyond Cologne, in the direction of Berlin, agriculture and the industrial arts go hand in hand, manufactories being constantly in sight, and the intervening fields being tilled to the highest degree of excellence. Of course, in the vast industrial area, extending from Northern France to Berlin, a considerable share must be apportioned to Belgium, but in the remainder there is a prodigious reserve of strength, which has no counterpart in Russia. East of Berlin, after quitting the Oder, the country is mainly agricultural, and, with the exception of the district in the immediate vicinity

of the Vistula, its surface becomes more and more
thinly populated as one approaches the Russian
frontier. Still, there are no wastes or barren
expanses of country to any extent; and in this
agricultural area of Pomerania and Baltic
Prussia the sturdy, big-boned men are raised, who
make up for the inferior physique of the industrial population of the Rhine. From the frontier
beyond Königsberg to St. Petersburg, a distance
of some 500 miles, there is little to be seen from
the railway window but marsh and forest. Possessing, then, a large reserve of industrial force on
the Rhine, and occupying a strong offensive position west of it, Germany, with railways radiating
in every direction in her rear, is well disposed for
any conflict with France; while as regards Russia,
she is certainly better able to protect her east
frontier than that country to force it. On this
point both public opinion in Russia and Germany
appears to be united. In spite of the threatening
tone of Skobeleff's speech, no Russian affects to
believe that Russia could invade Germany with
ease, and they even admit the possibility of a
German occupation of Poland. In Berlin I found
people going beyond a mere occupation of Poland,
and talking seriously of annexing a slice of Russia
right up to St. Petersburg. Since 1870 over a
million Germans have migrated and become lost

to the Fatherland. This stream of colonists, deflected towards Russia, would rapidly Germanize the area proposed to be annexed, and would thereby add to the strength of the Empire. Even as it is, within the last few years 100,000 Germans have crossed the frontier into Russia, and have created an alarm lest an extension of their numbers should Teutonize the Vistula province.[1] But Russia would never acquiesce, like France, in a loss of territory. The vastness of her area, and extensive character of her military resources, would enable her to maintain an offensive guerilla war for years. Russians readily admit that Germany could take the Baltic provinces, but they insist that they would retake them again in course of time.

I was very much struck during my journey at the difference between the railways and railway

---

[1] This stream of Teuton migration eastwards does not please the Russian Government, and the recent rumour that it meant to expel all foreigners who, at the end of five years, failed to become Russian subjects, really applied to these German settlers in Poland. Naturally, the Russian Government cannot regard with satisfaction thousands of Germans settling down on Russian soil, and forming a foreign and hostile community inside its European frontier. Russia does not like the idea of being pushed back by Germany into Siberia. Her most prosperous and progressive provinces are those of the Baltic littoral and Poland. Riga and other Baltic ports have become the great outlets for Central Russia. It is precisely those provinces and those ports she fears Germany is desirous of detaching from her.

management in France, Germany, and Russia. In the former country, the looseness of the control and the slovenly character of the stations contrasted sharply with the smartness, precision, and cleanness of the German lines. The railway between Cologne and Berlin has the reputation of being the best-managed in the world; but I was unprepared to find at the various stations, between those points, the officials as numerous, vigilant, and as smart during the sleepy hours of two or three in the morning, as on the occasion of the mid-day stoppage of some great personage. Everything works at these stations with military precision, and if a war broke out to-morrow, an army could be moved along into France without any fear of a break-down of the Staff. In France, on the other hand, it would take weeks before the railway service could be sufficiently organized to move troops without a hitch, and by that time any chance of repelling an invasion would have been lost. On the Russian railway from Wirballen, near Königsberg, to St. Petersburg, there is the same bureaucratic and military aspect visible as in Germany; but the officials lack the intelligence of the Teutons, and the service is so meagre that the Russians would need a long time to concentrate an army on the frontier. A Prussian army advancing into Russia would have a cultivated area at its rear, while a Russian army would have barren marsh land and forest. There is nothing that strikes the traveller more forcibly than the air of affluence worn by the German villages and towns right up to the very frontier, as compared with the miserable Russian hamlets immediately beyond. Considering that a railway always improves the district through which it runs, the condition of the Russian villages further away from the line must be very deplorable indeed. If any candid reader could have a peep at Russian village life from the railway carriage while travelling to St. Petersburg, he would readily admit that the pessimist pictures of Russia which have appeared in the columns of the *Newcastle Chronicle*, from the pen of Prince Krapotkin, have not been unduly exaggerated. Yet the peasants of the forest zone of the Baltic provinces are better off than many I have lived among in East and South Russia.

One thing alone is admittedly good in Russia—the railway travelling. When I left London on Sunday night I shivered all the way to Dover, in my great coat and plaid, in one of the mourning-coach-like carriages of the South-Eastern Railway. Those on the French lines were a little better, and were warmed with the awkward hot-water tins, as used in England. After Cologne, however, the carriages were heated with hot air, and from Berlin to the frontier the carriages had the additional advantage of being furnished with a regulator for adjusting the temperature of the compartment. The Russian carriages are on the American system, with a door at each end and a gangway for the guard from one end of the train to the other. The third-class carriages are little more than pigsties; the seconds are fairly good; but the first-class carriages are really very comfortable, and in some instances even sumptuously furnished. A great advantage is, that they are provided with capital lavatories, although the supply of water is rather meagre. At night the seats can be drawn out so as to form litter beds six feet long, with a pillow at the head. The carriages are heated with hot air, driven through pipes from the locomotive; and, if anything, the defect of the system is, that they are kept too warm. From Berlin to St. Petersburg I only made use of my great-coat when I went on the platforms of the stations, and in the Russian carriages it was so hot that, although in traversing Wilna there was a howling snowstorm outside, I was strongly tempted to wound Russian susceptibilities and seek relief by sitting in my shirt-sleeves. Among the passengers in the train was a character, who would have delighted Jules Verne.

At every station we stopped at, he emerged from the carriage in a thin lounge suit, with a smoking cap on his head and a terrific eyeglass affixed to his eye, and in this summer costume promenaded the platform, or plunged into the refreshment room, while the Russians peeped at him out of their furs and sheepskins in amazement. "That is either an Englishman or a lunatic," I overheard a station-master remark to a subordinate, as he stared at the gaunt, tall figure retreating in the distance; and the guess proved to be not far-fetched, as the individual turned out to be one of the many Englishmen who have settled down and made fortunes in Russia. Throughout the whole distance from Berlin to St. Petersburg, and particularly in Russia itself, the buffets were excellent, and if one can imagine a "Criterion," or some other huge and well-conducted establishment of Messrs. Spiers and Pond, at intervals of every six hours' distance, with a couple of model coffee palaces between, he will have a good idea of the luxurious refreshment arrangements on the Russo-German lines. The dishes are such as would delight an epicure, the wines are good, and prices are about a half less than those that prevail in London. On the Russian lines half an hour is allowed at the buffet stations, and at what may be called the "tea-stations," about ten minutes. There are plenty of waiters, no crowding whatever, and if you do not care to quit the train, the waiters who jump aboard the moment it stops, will bring you all you want in the shape of dinner and tea for the same gratuity you would give them in the refreshment-room itself.

I have already stated that in leaving London, my journey was delayed by the retention of my passport at the Embassy for the necessary *visa*. The Russian Embassy expressed a very strong belief that the *Newcastle Chronicle* must have some other object in view, besides that of Panslav and Central Asian politics generally, in sending a "special" to St. Petersburg. I considered I had exposed the groundlessness of any such impression; but none the less, when I reached the frontier at Wirballen, and was conducted into the examining-room by a Cossack to have my luggage and passport investigated, I awaited with interest and anxiety any fresh development of suspicion. Years ago, before I paid my first visit to Russia, I heard a lecture delivered by a clergyman, who, having been placed in circumstances very similar to my own, was exposed to all manner of annoyances on reaching Russia, and was only too glad to get out of the country again as quickly as possible. There was some little mark made on his passport by the Embassy that rendered him an object of suspicion wherever he went. Luckily, nothing of the kind occurred to me, and my passport was not only very politely returned by the officials, but the contents of my portmanteau, which contained many books and a large number of copies of my new map of the Russo-Persian frontier, tied in a bundle, were merely glanced at; neither the books nor the rest of the printed matter being in the slightest examined, or even disturbed, although they might easily have been a mass of revolutionary literature. Beyond a larger number of Cossacks at each station than there used to be when I visited Poland in 1873, I saw no indication of the terrorist state of affairs till we got to Gatchina, which was literally overflowing with troops. After Gatchina, all the way to St. Petersburg—a distance of twenty-eight miles—there was a soldier with a bayonet fixed standing at intervals of every thousand yards. At St. Petersburg itself, the station was again crowded with troops and police, and I noticed that every effort was made to prevent too many expectant friends assembling together, and that Cossacks were incessantly circulating among the crowd and breaking it up into small proportions.

CHAPTER II.

THE RUSSIAN FOREIGN OFFICE AND BARON OSTEN-SAKEN.

Interview with Baron Osten-Saken—Shabbiness of the Russian Foreign Office as compared with our own—My map already received from London—Personal appearance of Baron Osten-Saken and his present position at the Foreign Office—The map a good letter of introduction—Optimist tone of the Baron—Agrees with Councillor Davidoff in disbelieving that a junction will soon take place of the English and Russian empires in Central Asia—Decadence of the Central Asian agitation—The change of base of operations in Central Asia—His opinion of Sir Henry Rawlinson—The best-informed man in Russia as to the Perso-Turcoman region—The new frontier beyond the Caspian—Deep interest of M. de Giers in Persia—The Chinese barrier between Russia and India—Chinese assimilation of the Jews—Jewish outrages exaggerated—Sir Charles Dilke's declaration as to the recall of General Skobeleff from Geok Tepé—Skobeleff's journey home—Was Russia guilty of duplicity in annexing Akhal?—Points for and against her —Verdict.

St. Petersburg, March 5.

I HAD a preliminary interview yesterday at the Russian Foreign Office with Baron Osten-Saken, who for many years was head of the Asiatic

Department, and in that capacity was the constant exponent of Russian policy in Central Asia. The Foreign Office occupies a wing of the semi-circular building devoted to the General Staff, and known in the vernacular as the *Glavni Shtab*. It immediately faces the Winter Palace. I did not have an opportunity of going entirely over it, but was struck, in passing through what portion of it was necessary to reach Baron Osten-Saken's room, at the meagreness and bareness of the place, as compared with the handsome and sumptuously decorated and furnished English Foreign Office in Downing Street.[1] Leaving my fur coat and over-shoes in the hall, where I entertained a groundless fear that they would get lost among the hundred or more other specimens of warm clothing promiscuously disposed about the place, I followed the directions of the very civil hall-porter, and proceeded up several flights of bare-looking stairs to the top of the building, where an official on duty in the corridor conducted me into a waiting-room adjoining that occupied by the Baron. I sent in my name, and the attendant re-appearing a minute or two later, to ask me to enter, I

---

[1] An account of the English Foreign Office will be found in "Our Public Offices," third and popular edition, illustrated, price 2s. Messrs. Sonnenschein and Co., Paternoster Row, London.

was preparing a terse little speech in Russ to define my mission as briefly as possible, when the Baron anticipated any remarks by advancing to meet me, and saying in English, "I am very glad to see you, Mr. Marvin; we are already well acquainted with you."

With that he returned to the table, and motioning me to sit down, drew from among some despatches a copy of my map of the new Russo-Persian frontier. "We have received this," he continued, "with the despatches from London to-day, and I have just been glancing through it."

"I hope the frontier-line has been correctly traced," I replied, "and that there has been no greater annexation than that alleged."

"I do not know the state of affairs in the region now," rejoined the Baron; "I am no longer concerned in the politics of Central Asia. My position is now that of head of the consular and commercial relations of Russia, and these give me no time to devote any attention to the political affairs of the East. But I know that a map is being prepared in the office showing the new frontier, and this, directly it is issued, will set all disputes at rest."

Baron Osten-Saken was superseded in the Asiatic section by Baron Jomini some time ago, and in a conversation which ensued, of a geographical character, I soon became convinced that his representations of being only slightly informed as to the recent phases of the Central Asian Question were correct. The Baron, who is about forty-five years old, somewhat bald, with a decidedly German face, and a manner more clerical than diplomatic, was exceedingly frank throughout the interview—so much so that I am compelled to respect some of his utterances and suppress them. The map received from London proved to be a better letter of introduction than any I could have brought with me, for he repeatedly drew attention to it, and said: "You have rendered a great service to Russia in showing at a glance that she has not annexed so much as alleged, and in allaying thereby the hostile feeling against us previously prevailing in England." In connexion with this feeling, he expressed very decidedly his conviction that if England knew more clearly the state of affairs in Central Asia, she would not run so often into panics. This led me to point out that I had come to Russia to assist in bringing about the desired enlightenment, and evoked in turn a rejoinder that he would do his best to give me access to information.

I was very much struck with his optimist tone, as compared with the contrary feeling prevailing at the Russian Embassy in London. Councillor

Davidoff had said to me: "Your people are so prejudiced against us, that whatever you write will not remove the bad impressions that prevail. Attempts have failed in the past, and your people will go on for years hating Russia like they used to detest the French. You will get no more information in St. Petersburg than you would get in London, and what you publish from there will have no more effect than what you would issue from here." Quite a different tone was held by Baron Osten-Saken, who maintained that the Central Asian excitement is not so keen to-day as it was a dozen years ago, and expressed a belief that it would disappear altogether in course of time. I could not agree with this. "I wish it to disappear, but it is only now that we have come to the most critical phase of the Central Asian Question—the impending inevitable delimitation of the two empires in Central Asia."

"I do not think it will be in my time," he replied. "I believe the junction will not take place till long after I am dead, but I tell you candidly I am not so well up in the latest developments of the Central Asian Question as you are. During the last five years the question has shifted its base altogether. Turkestan used to be the arena of interest; this it has now ceased to be, and the Caspian excites attention.

Writers on Central Asia, who were clever as to Turkestan, have to confess their ignorance in regard to this new Transcaspian region. Sir Henry Rawlinson used to write wonderfully clever articles on the Oxus, but he has written nothing lately; and I do not think he knows much of this new region beyond the Caspian."

"That may be," I said, "as regards the newest Russian information, but I imagine no one can approach him as to the historical knowledge on the subject." He assented to this, and then went on to say that General Stebnitsky, at Tiflis, has the reputation of being the best-informed man in Russia in regard to the Perso-Turcoman region.

On my reverting to the map again, he said it was a source of great satisfaction for Russia to have at last a settled frontier alongside a State like Persia. I observed that Persia was not a very substantial country for a frontier to rest against, but the Baron, expressing no opinion on this point, said, "Our relations with Persia are very good. We are on the best terms with her. This is due mainly to M. de Giers (the head of the Foreign Office), who was once Russian Minister at Teheran, and retains a deep interest in Persian politics."

"The result of which is," I observed, "that

you are predominant in Persia, and we have no influence there whatever."

Baron Osten-Saken smiled. "You have your influence in Afghanistan," he said. "But will it prevail," I urged; "how long will the present state of affairs in Afghanistan continue?"

"I do not know," he rejoined, "but I think it will last a long time. I regard it as very convenient that Afghanistan should separate England and Russia. It is as with Kashgar. The Chinese have occupied that country, and interposed a barrier between Russia and India. There is no excitement about Kashgar now."

Before I could point out that there was a very essential difference between Chinese rule in Kashgar, and Afghan rule in Cabul and Herat, he went on to say: "I admire one point very much in the Chinese—they are the only people who are able to assimilate the Jews. I wish Russia could do the same in Poland."

"There would then be no outrages," I remarked. "Now, Baron Osten-Saken, what is your candid opinion of the cruelties alleged?"

"The best refutation of the statements in the *Times* is contained in the Consular Reports on the Jewish Outrages, which have just been published in a blue-book in London."

"Yes, but as regards the alleged outrages on

women. So far as the destruction of property is concerned, there is no dispute about that. What is wanted to be known is, whether any women were ill-treated or not?"

"I do not believe that any woman was violated," exclaimed the Baron energetically; "and as to the statement in the *Times* that Russian women held down Jewish women while the men violated them, it is too horrible to be true. It could not be. It is against nature."

An official entered here with some despatches. The Baron stopped a moment to take them, and afterwards proceeded again to discuss the Central Asian Question. At his request I traced the English impressions of Russian policy both before and after the Candahar debate, and pointed out that the famous declaration of Sir Charles Dilke that Russia had recalled General Skobeleff, and had put a stop to the whole of his undertakings in Central Asia, had been accepted by the House of Commons and the country generally, as implying that Russia would fall back upon the Caspian and evacuate the conquered region in the same manner that England had done Afghanistan. He expressed himself surprised that such an impression should have prevailed, and although the ground was too delicate for him to tread upon, except very carefully, he confirmed the only opinion an impartial mind can deduce from the diplomatic and Parliamentary matter associated with the Candahar controversy—that Russia never entertained any intention of evacuating the conquered Tekke region, and never gave any assurance to that effect. On this point M. de Giers is best adapted to express an opinion, and Baron Osten-Saken promised to obtain me an interview with him on Monday if possible. On taking my departure he gave me a copy of a little work in Russ, entitled "Remarks on the Roads to the East, from Meshed to Afghanistan," by F. Bakoulin, the Russian Consul at Astrabad.

Skobeleff's arrival is anxiously awaited here. He was to have reached St. Petersburg the night before last, and I went to the Warsaw Station to meet him. The papers here say "a sympathetic public assembled to receive the general," but the crowd was not any larger than it usually is on the arrival of the Warsaw train. At the utmost not more than seventy or eighty people were to be seen inside and outside the station, and there were not only no preparations on the part of the public to make a demonstration, but the Government itself did not prepare against any. Yesterday morning, the crowd that assembled at eight o'clock was still smaller, and I do not anticipate that there will be any ovation, if, as announced, he arrives this afternoon. The German element is too large in St. Petersburg for any extended Panslavist demonstration to take place ; and, besides, the general has many enemies even in purely Russian society. A certain countess who leads society here, and fills a large space in a clever German work, translated into English, entitled " Distinguished Persons in Russian Society," said yesterday of Skobeleff, " *C'est un homme dementi*," and in repeating this to me, the Russian official to whom she had uttered it pointed out the fact that Skobeleff, although declaring that his utterances had been exaggerated by French journalists, had never attempted to deny them. He was purposely ordered to return home through Vienna, since it was feared that if he came *viâ* Berlin he would be insulted, and Russia provoked into immediate war.

*　　*　　*　　*

As I have already touched upon the matter, and shall have to refer to it again, it will not be out of place to give here, in a concise form, the case of England and Russia, in regard to the annexation of Akhal and the formation of the new Persian frontier. The reader will be able to see on what basis the charges against Russia of duplicity and double-dealing rest.

1. On the 9th of June, 1879, the Marquis of Salisbury, then Secretary of State for Foreign Affairs, wrote to the English Ambassador at St. Petersburg, Earl Dufferin, with reference to a conversation he had had that day with Count Schouvaloff, regarding the truth of the rumour that General Lazareff intended to advance upon Merv:—" The present expedition, he (Count Schouvaloff) stated, was directed against the Tekke Turcomans, and, if successful, probably would have for its result the construction of a chain of posts uniting Krasnovodsk and Tchikishlar by a curved line, of which the extreme point would not be nearer than 250 kilometres to Merv."—*Blue Book, Central Asia* (1880), No. 1, p. 92.

In other words, Russia announced that she intended to occupy territory to within $139\frac{3}{4}$ miles of Merv, which is considerably nearer than Askabad or Gyaoors, and not far short of Sarakhs. The statesman of "big maps" had evidently studied them to such little purpose, that he failed to realize the significance of the declaration. He raised no objection whatever to the advance.

2. On the 16th of July, 1879, the Earl of Dufferin wrote to the Marquis of Salisbury:— " Baron Jomini says the Russian advance is intended to stop at a point some 200 versts ($132\frac{1}{2}$

miles) this side of Merv. This spot forms the easternmost apex of a triangle, in which are contained the various oases where the Tekke Turcomans keep their women and children."—*Ibid*, p. 100.

We thus see that the Russian Ambassador's declaration was no casual one. It was followed up by a similar declaration from the Russian Foreign Office itself.

Lord Salisbury manifested throughout this period extreme uneasiness in regard to Merv, but he did not concern himself at all about Akhal. Russia promised over and over again she would not occupy Merv. She faithfully kept her word. She declared she would annex Akhal. She has kept her word also. There was no duplicity on the one side; there was certainly heedlessness, to use no stronger expression, on the other. If the annexation of Akhal by Russia was dangerous and alarming when Lord Salisbury was out of office, its foreshadowed annexation was equally a matter of importance when that statesman was in office. The time to have arrested Russia's progress was when she was expressing her intention of marching upon Askabad, not when she had already established 5000 troops there.

At the same time, these declarations may be said to cut away from under the feet of the Gladstone

Government any excuse in evacuating Candahar, on the grounds that they did not know Russia meant to permanently occupy Askabad.

It must be pointed out, however, that the Gladstone Government has never sought to be excused on this score. It has also never accused Russia of duplicity. The charge of trickery against Russia has been put forward by the supporters of the Gladstone Cabinet, to cloak the trickery or stupidity of the Cabinet itself. Gladstone, so anxious to shield Russia from hurtful accusations, whether right or wrong, in 1876, has never sought to defend Russia against this most unjust of charges, made by his own followers.

3. On the 25th of March, 1881, the Candahar debate took place in the House of Commons, and Sir Charles Dilke completely broke down the Conservative attack at the very outset, by making the following declaration:—"He was able to make this statement: that the very first act of the new Emperor upon ascending the throne was to recall General Skobeleff to St. Petersburg, and to put a stop to all operations which that general had been conducting in Asia." (Ministerial cheers.)—*Hansard*, Vol. 159, pp. 1852-53.

The recall of Skobeleff did not imply that the Russians would retire from Akhal, and Lord George Hamilton very appropriately pointed out the unsatisfactory character of the assurance the following evening.

4. In reply, the Marquis of Hartington said :— "The right hon. gentleman seems to think that the statement made by Sir Charles Dilke last night with regard to the policy of the present Emperor of Russia, and the order given for the recall of General Skobeleff has been made by the Russian Government for some political purpose connected with this debate. Now, I do not think that my hon. friend attributed any very great importance to the statement which he was able to make —('Oh, oh,' from the Opposition) — but he thought it was one, and I think it was one, which was satisfactory to the House. (Hear, hear.) And it may be an additional satisfaction to the right hon. gentleman to know that the information did not reach her Majesty's Government from the Russian Government, or from her Majesty's Ambassador in Russia, but from a totally different and a totally independent source. I hope, therefore, that the right hon. gentleman will no longer think that that information was given for the purpose of influencing the decision of the House." —*Hansard*, Vol. 159, pp. 1999—2000.

But whether the information was or was not given for influencing the decision of the House, it certainly had that effect. It was that declaration which mainly gained the Government its victory. Treated by itself, the recall of Skobeleff was nothing. His operations were already over, his troops were already preparing to move towards home, and he himself was under recall *before* Alexander II. died. This is supported by incontestable evidence. His recall was an act of the old Tsar, not of the new one. It was the English Government that treated it as a new departure. Its supporters accepted Sir Charles Dilke's declaration in a broad sense—they believed the recall of Skobeleff meant also the recall of his army; they believed the Russians would fall back from Askabad to Krasnovodsk. The Gladstone Government knew this was the belief of the Liberal section of the House, and of many Conservative members also. Whether it was its own belief or not is a point undetermined. But knowing what the belief of others was, it never sought in any way to remove the impression. Out of this erroneous impression arose the whole of the subsequent ill-feeling against Russia.

5. A reference to the published blue books will show, that throughout this period the English Government never concerned itself diplomatically about the fate of Akhal. It was continually worrying Russia about Merv, but it never inquired about the future of Askabad. Even the news of

the "recall of Skobeleff" was not derived from Russia, but from an independent source, which the *Daily News* announced to be Berlin. There is no evidence to show that Russia ever declared that she would retire from Akhal, or that she directed any second party to make any such declaration. If she informed Berlin that Skobeleff had been recalled, and that his operations had been put a stop to, was she guilty of misrepresentation? Certainly not. Skobeleff did not increase the area of his operations an inch after that declaration, and he came home as soon as he could put the affairs of the conquered region in order.

6. When, therefore, the Tsar issued an ukase on the 24th of March, 1881, annexing Akhal, he broke no promises and annulled no assurances. He simply consummated an act, which for two years Russian diplomacy had repeatedly announced would some day be accomplished, and to which the whole of the Russian operations beyond the Caspian had pointed with a clearness that could not be mistaken. Do what I can, as a Russophobe, I cannot discover any duplicity in the transaction, and a love of fair play compels me candidly to admit the fact.[1]

---

[1] These views were expressed in an article in the *Army and Navy Magazine*, July, 1881, entitled "Russia's New Province in Central Asia," which will be found in the Appendix.

CHAPTER III.

THE "RUSSIAN BURNABY" AT HOME.

General Grodekoff's history of Skobeleff's siege of Geok Tepé—
The Russian Burnaby and the English Burnaby compared—
Grodekoff of nomad proclivities—Facts about Skobeleff's
great siege—Russia never meant to occupy Merv in 1881,
as repeatedly announced by O'Donovan—The alleged recall
of Skobeleff in disgrace—Grodekoff against the annexation
of Akhal—Merv not the key of Herat—Change in the
Russian base of operations—Merv overrated—Arrival of
the first Russian caravan at Merv—Grodekoff not an astute
man—A manufacturer of false Russian news at Berlin—
The new school of writers on Russia—List of military
officers acquainted with Russian—Opinion of the *United
Service Gazette* on the study of the Central Asian Question
—The sack of Geok Tepé—Captain Butler's allegation that
he helped to fortify Geok Tepé—Grodekoff's view of the
railroad to India—Loss of guns at Geok Tepé—Grodekoff's
opinion of General Roberts—The Russian Burnaby an
Anglophil—Russian maps of Central Asia—One million
maps in store ready for hostilities—The history of the
Russian corps of military topographers—The old processes
of map-making and the new—Achievements of Russian
map-makers—Colonel Baker and the secret English maps—
Grodekoff's map of his ride to Herat sold for fourpence
halfpenny.

St. Petersburg, March 6, 1882.

Being unable to see M. de Giers, the head of the Russian Foreign Office, to-day, I thought I would call on Major-General Grodekoff, who acted as the chief of Skobeleff's staff in the recent campaign against the Turcomans, and gained great notoriety earlier by a ride through Afghanistan, from Samarcand to Herat and Meshed. He is the last European who has visited Herat since Captain Marsh rode through the place in 1872, and seems likely to retain the distinction for some time to come. He lives in Kononova House, in the Bolshoi Morskoi, one of the most fashionable thoroughfares in the capital, and occupies a room in some residential chambers on an upper storey. It is a large and comfortably furnished room, with one corner screened off as a vestibule; another containing a small bed; while the rest is divided into a sort of sitting-room on one side and a writing-room on the other. The writing section consists of a large table and desk, both piled up with maps and manuscripts, for General Grodekoff is writing an official history of Skobeleff's great campaign, under the supervision of Skobeleff himself. There is a curious absence of books about the place, but Grodekoff lives close to the magnificent library of the General Staff, which contains every book he requires, and plenty of clerks to copy out matter for him.

His man-servant apologized for his master being in an undress, as he helped me to remove my fur coat at the door. He was ill, he said. On entering the room I found myself confronted by a small-made man, with features very little changed from those depicted in his portrait in the work published by Messrs. W. H. Allen and Co., "Grodekoff's Ride to Herat." His somewhat worn and invalid appearance was enhanced by the huge Bokharan khalat, or dressing-gown-like robe, he was encased in, the colours of which formed a glaring forked-lightning sort of pattern, reminding one of a sorcerer's robe in a burlesque. It was difficult to realize that this slight, frail officer had borne the fatigue of three great campaigns, and had accomplished one of the most daring rides on record. Grodekoff was chief of Lomakin's staff when that officer led the Mangishlak column to Khiva in 1873. Skobeleff, who accompanied the column, must have recognised his worth then, as he chose him as chief of his staff in the Khokandese war, and again in the recent campaign in Akhal. From his daring ride through Afghanistan he has gained the appellation of "The Russian Burnaby." But the English Burnaby is a giant in stature, whereas Grodekoff takes after Sir Frederick Roberts.

He gave me a warm welcome, and as we had already been known to each other by letter, we were at once friends. He apologized for being ill.

"I am a nomad," he said; "settled life does not suit me. I am only at home in the steppe. I am unwell when I live in St. Petersburg in a state of inactivity. During a campaign I enjoy the best of health; after it is over I suffer. I was about the only person in Skobeleff's force who escaped being ill or wounded throughout the war. I now experience the reaction."

The impression I myself had formed of Grodekoff, from the "Ride to Herat" I had translated in 1880, was that he was a very astute and taciturn man. This impression was not merely my own, it was shared by others. In a review in a German paper—the *Allgemeine Zeitung*, I believe—Arminius Vámbéry, while bestowing praise upon myself for undertaking the translation, had charged Grodekoff with giving the kernel of his travels to the Russian Government, and throwing only the husks to Europe. To be therefore frank and idiomatic, I expected to get very little indeed out of the General. I thought he would confine himself to common-place remarks. But, on the contrary, he was as candid and as free with his facts and opinions as Arminius Vámbéry would have been with any congenial spirit, and discussed the Central Asian Question in a manner I hope some day to see repeated in a book.

It is a great disadvantage to England and Russia

that the political writers of each country know so little of one another. Occasional intercourse would dissipate many of those erroneous impressions that mar the friendly relations of the two peoples. Most of the English writers on Central Asia are personally unacquainted with Russia, and have no knowledge of the Russian language. The majority of them are good judges of the Central Asian Question from an Indian standpoint, having served in India; but they know nothing of the Russian aspect of the problem, except what they derive from the exaggerated and distorted intelligence appearing in the newspapers. Where this proceeds from Berlin or Vienna sources, it is rare indeed that facts are narrated in the fair and accurate form they should be. There was, up to recently, a correspondent at Berlin of a leading London daily newspaper, who had grossly misrepresented Russia for years. The most innocent acts were twisted by him into guilty deeds, and he had much to do with the development of that spirit of Russophobia, which Councillor Davidoff does not believe will die out for at least another century.

Any speculations on this point, however, would be useless. Much will depend upon the new school of writers on Russia, which is now coming into existence. Ten years ago there were very few persons who knew anything about the country, and still fewer who were well acquainted with the language. Nowadays a knowledge of Russian is becoming common, particularly among military men. It is only recently that Lieut.-Colonel James Brown, R.E., published in *Colburn's United Service Magazine* a very good translation of the *Golos* narrative of the Akhal-Tekke Expedition. Colonel Spalding's translations from the Russian poets are well known. Colonel Burnaby found his Russ of use when he rode to Khiva. Major E. Gowan, of the Indian Army, has in the press a translation of Ivanoff's Russian Grammar. Lieutenant J. J. Leverson, R.E., published a few weeks ago an excellent translation of Skobeleff's official report of the siege of Geok Tepé. Lieutenant Grierson, R.E., has contributed several translations from the Russ to the Transactions of the Royal Artillery Institute. Lieutenant Pemberton, another engineer officer, is at present at St. Petersburg improving his knowledge of the Russ he voluntarily acquired while at the Royal Military Academy at Woolwich. And there is also, I am told, a Major Thompson at Moscow, hard at work mastering the Russian language, having devoted his furlough from India to its acquisition. These are a few names, taken at random, of officers who form the growing school of Russian scholars. In less than a decade the old reproach of England being grossly ignorant of the language spoken by one of the greatest nations in Europe, will no longer have a meaning.[1]

[1] The *United Service Gazette* of Jan. 28, 1882, expressed the following opinion on this point, " What is wanted is a larger and stronger interest on the part of the public in the ' Eastern Menace.' The Central Asian Question should no longer be left to a few specialists like Rawlinson, Vámbéry, Cory, Marvin, &c. The Russian advance should form part of the private study of every officer who cares for his profession and his country. With so many able officers with leisure on their hands, why should it be left to a civilian writer like Marvin to write the various Russian Asiatic campaigns? Russia had her General Soboleff to write an account of our Afghan war, and why have we not our Soboleff to narrate Skobeleff's three weeks' siege of Geok Tepé, and the various incidents of the greatest Russian campaign yet witnessed in Central Asia. But for Marvin's assiduity in piecing together the correspondence appearing in the Russian press, we should have never had a connected and intelligible account of Lomakin's disastrous expedition of 1879. Such a task was one, however, that should have been properly achieved by our Intelligence Department. In the same manner, although the Russian press has teemed with accounts of Skobeleff's campaign, the Intelligence Department has merely published the curt official report of the actual siege of Geok Tepé. Here, again, Mr. Marvin has come to our aid, and in a few weeks' time, the papers announce, he will issue a history of the war, consisting of matter extracted from 8000 Russian newspapers, and illustrated with sixty or seventy maps, plans, and engravings. But why should such a task be left to a non-military author, who but three years ago was a copyist at tenpence an hour at the Foreign Office ? The Russian military movements in the direction of India are of the highest concern to our Government. There should be no better avenue

Moving aside a pile of manuscript on the table to offer me a cigarette, General Grodekoff expressed a hope that I might see my way to translating his "Siege of Geok Tepé" into English; and on my promising to undertake the task, he said, in reply to a series of questions put to him, "When we set out for the war, Skobeleff remarked to me how barren Central Asian history was of great sieges. His siege of Geok Tepé has filled up this gap. It was a great war. It took us a year to conquer the Akhal Tekkes, with 5000 men and 100 cannon, and it cost us 20,000,000 roubles (2,500,000*l.*). We never meant to advance upon Merv. We had not the means to do so. You have seen what it needed to occupy the 400 versts from the Caspian to Geok Tepé: to advance another 400 versts from Geok Tepé to Merv meant a repetition of this. We commenced the war with 20,000 camels; at the close of the siege we had hardly one. When Skobeleff set out for Akhal the late Emperor gave him written instructions, and these were that he was

to promotion for an officer than by making himself an expert in them. We trust that what we have said in connexion with this, and the move upon Saraklis, will have due weight with enterprising officers, and that Marvin's 'Siege of Geok Tepé' will be the last work issued by a civilian on operations which ought to be, and might be, better dealt with by professionals."

only to occupy Akhal. He never made any preparations to do more."

I remarked that I had just completed translating and arranging the whole of the published Russian and English matter dealing with the siege and the Candahar controversy, and that this entirely bore out what he said. Mr. O'Donovan, I observed, was constantly telegraphing that Skobeleff was advancing on Merv; but his telegrams and letters show that he never had any clear notion of the Russian operations beyond the border, and that he was constantly being misled by his Turcoman informants. But, I continued, in connexion with this, there is a point around which the whole of the recent phase of the Central Asian Question revolves. It was represented in the House of Commons that when the present Emperor ascended the throne he abandoned Russia's forward policy in Central Asia, and recalled Skobeleff. Outside the House it was represented that the General was recalled in disgrace, for extending, or wishing to extend, the area of operations. "That is all false," he broke in, interrupting me; "Skobeleff never wished to go to Merv; he made no preparations to do so; he fulfilled the orders given him by the late Emperor, and came home, but not in disgrace. The Emperor was not angry with him for his acts in Central Asia. If he was angry at all, it was for other reasons. Do you know, I was personally against the annexation of Akhal? I did not approve of a permanent occupation of the oasis. But we had no thought of Merv. How could we, when we had no transport? If Geok Tepé, with a smaller population than Merv, and having no guns, was such a difficult place to take, what was the resistance to be expected at Merv, furnished, as the Tekkes were known to be, with over thirty cannon? No, no, all the alarm that prevailed, on that score, was groundless."

Referring to my translation of his ride to Herat, which he said he received during the siege of Geok Tepé, he observed: "You will remember that in this book I express the opinion that Merv is not the key of Herat. In a chapter apart, you contested this view. But I am right. Merv lies off the road to Herat—it is through Sarakhs or Meshed that the road to Herat runs."

I pointed out that the question depended a good deal upon the standpoint from which one regarded Merv. In his "Ride," I dealt with a Russian advance from the Turkestan base upon Herat, in which case I considered that Merv lay on the direct road to that place. Matters, however, had changed since then. The Russian base of operations had shifted to the Caspian. From that base,

Sarakhs or Meshed formed the key of Herat, and Merv was left on the one side. In that sense, therefore, Merv was not the key of Herat.

General Grodekoff thought the importance of Merv was altogether overrated. He did not believe that there would be any early Russian advance on the place. The people were now on friendly terms with Russia, and had allowed caravans to be sent thither.[1] "If they do not raid against Akhal," he said, "we shall have no need to operate against Merv; for we entertain none of those aggressive designs against the place England persists in ascribing to us."

Referring to the siege of Geok Tepé, he observed: "After the capture of the stronghold, Skobeleff gave the troops three days' holiday to sack it. The loot was enormous. It exceeded 6,000,000 roubles. Most of it went to the suttlers. It was no uncommon thing for a soldier

---

[1] A telegram from Askabad, dated March 19—31, 1882, and published in the Moscow *Vedomosti*, announced the safe return there of the first Russian caravan that had visited Merv. The people of Merv received Gospodin Konshin very favourably, and, "thanks to the part taken by our authorities, the caravan succeeded in overcoming all difficulties; establishing commercial intercourse, and obtaining precious information relative to the roads leading to Merv." A Merv deputation afterwards visited Askabad, and was feasted there. Konshin was raised from the merchant grade to that of the *noblesse* for his success in reaching Merv.

to sell a valuable article, worth many months' pay, for a glass of vodky. Hundreds of mules and camels carried off the plunder to Meshed. Skobeleff sent to St. Petersburg a number of ancient books he found inside the fortress, but nothing else. He tried to get some of the jewellery worn by the women, but it was all gone. I had a carpet, but it was stolen. The one you are sitting upon (a very handsome one) was purchased at Meshed."

He made inquiries about Captain Francis Butler, the Turcoman traveller, who claimed in the *Globe* that he had been instrumental in the fortifying of Geok Tepé. "His letter was telegraphed to us from St. Petersburg," he said, "and we received it a day or two after the capture of the place. It amused us very much. We found no evidences whatever of European skill in the fortifications, nor yet anywhere else in the Akhal-Tekke region."

On my stating that evidence appeared to be altogether against the claim, and that I had already expressed this opinion in my manuscript of the Siege of Geok Tepé, he handed me some of the manuscript of his own book to read, in which the matter was dealt with fully. I promised if I came across any information in support of Captain Butler's claim, I would forward it to him, and he promised, on his part, to notice it in his volume. This should appear in September next.

With reference to the projected railway to Herat and India, from Askabad, he said he did not think much of the scheme. " The distance between Michaelovsk and Shikapore is very great, and years must elapse before those points can be connected, even if they ever be connected at all, which I doubt. The railway was of very little use to us during the siege, for it was not finished until the operations were concluded; and it did harm to us in this way, that the conveyance of the *matériel* for making it used up many of the camels we subsequently needed, in our advance from Bami to Geok Tepé."

"The siege," he continued, "was very trying. On one occasion we even lost two guns. Skobeleff was greatly enraged at this."

"But the loss of two small mountain pieces," I said, " was insignificant, compared with the whole batteries we lost at Maiwand and at Isandula. Your campaign was clear of any such disasters. We have had a series of unlucky generals."

"And General Roberts?" rejoined Grodekoff. " What of him? He is a general to be proud of. That was a splendid march of his from Cabul to Candahar. We heard of it in Akhal."

He did not think that we need entertain any

fear of the Russian advances in Central Asia. They were not directed against us. They were inspired by no designs upon India. The allegation was untrue that Russian generals nourished the ambition of some day fighting us in Central Asia. He thought there would be no further move in Central Asia for a considerable time to come.

The English Burnaby overflows with Russophobia. The Russian Burnaby, on the other hand, is full of friendly feeling towards England. He does not insult or reproach her. He holds that if she knew Russia better, there would be an end to the Central Asian Question.

The rest of our conversation was taken up with matters referring to our books on the siege of Geok Tepé. On my departure the general gave me two large maps of Central Asia, and Afghanistan and the adjacent region. Both were very fine specimens of the magnificent maps published by the Russian Topographical Department. England has many things to be proud of, but she cannot beat Russia in the production of maps.

At the present moment there are 1,030,000 maps in store at St. Petersburg, Warsaw, Wilna, and Kieff, ready for any sudden outbreak of hostilities. To a person whose ideas of maps have been derived from the inspection of a score or so of more or less dusty specimens, displayed in the windows of a few map-makers' shops in London, the notion of 250,000 maps collected in a single store at Kieff must seem quite appalling, and he will be disposed to accord the Russians as map-makers that respect which was freely given them at the recent geographical display at Venice. Most of the Russian maps which figured in this display were the production of the " Corps of Military Topographers," whose history has just been published; there being scarcely any maps manufactured in Russia by private individuals. Some idea of the strain which is thrown at times upon this department, may be gathered from the fact that during the Russo-Turkish war more than 200,000 maps were issued to the army in Europe, and 20,000 to the troops in Asia. Owing to various causes, the supply was rather late in reaching the invading forces, but the Corps of Military Topographers has undergone a reorganization of late, and in the interval some wonderful improvements have been made in the reproduction of maps, which would render any break-down in the future almost impossible.

The " Corps of Military Topographers " was founded in 1796 by the Emperor Paul, who paid its expenses out of his own private purse, and ordered that its productions should be at the free disposal of any one who could afford to pay a moderate price for them. Maps in those days were all engraved, and to provide good engravers a school was specially attached to the institution two years later. Under his son Alexander I. the corps made still greater headway, the Tsar allowing 1000 gold imperials out of his own private purse annually, for the purchase of maps and plans abroad for the library of the department. In 1705 a twenty-verst map, which had been several years in progress, was completed of the Russian Empire, consisting of ninety-eight sheets, with an appendix of sixteen sheets of the kingdom of Poland. After the French invasion the corps was fused with the Ministry of War, and became quite a military institution. In 1821 a ten-verst map was commenced of the Russian Empire, and after eighteen years' exertion was completed, and was used as the standard map of the empire up to so late as 1869, when an immense number of copies were struck off, in anticipation of a war with Germany. In 1832 the corps was formed into two companies of topographers, consisting of 120 men—all good engravers—and over forty officers. Lithography was now added to the copper-plate engraving of maps, and after the corps had become accustomed to it the production of maps reached 86,000 annually. Both the engravers and lithographers were very badly paid, and it is officially admitted that a deal of the work turned out by them was unworthy of the department, and can only be excused on the ground that the corps was so indifferently treated by the military authorities. In 1866 the corps underwent radical reorganization, to adapt it to the altered circumstances of map-making, and a large sum was expended in obtaining the best machinery from Europe for reproducing maps and plans. An increase of the sum allotted for the maintenance of the department from 35,000 roubles to 46,000 roubles a year further added to its efficiency, and, with the numerous special grants conferred since, has made it the highly skilled institution it is to-day.

Without any exaggeration the department can now claim to be one of the finest, if not, indeed, the finest map-manufactory in the world. Every process to which the inventive genius of the world has given birth may be said to be represented there; from the early copper-plate engraving, with which the institution started, to the recent wonderful discovery of the art of reproducing engravings by photography, that is now revolutionizing the illustration of books in this country. The tedious character and costliness of hand-engraving is well known, while the coarseness, inaccuracy, and other defects of quicker and cheaper modes of reproducing illustrations, maps, and plans have rendered their adoption for first-class work a matter of impossibility. During the last two years, however, several processes have been perfected for reproducing engravings by photography, which may be said to have practically superseded the engraver, since they not only reproduce the subject more accurately than by hand, increasing or decreasing the size without any difficulty, but effect it with a speed and cheapness that puts hand-labour altogether outside any possibility of competition. A map that would take a fortnight and cost 10*l.* or so to reproduce by means of hand-engraving, can be copied in twenty-four hours for 10*s.* by the direct photo-engraving process; and this, too, with an accuracy so marvellous that no point of difference can be found between the copy and the original. The advantages of the process are obvious, and will explain how it has been possible for Russia to store maps by the million. Every important map made abroad is reproduced by processes of this character, and it being possible to manufacture by them scores of blocks, while the hand-engraver is producing only one, the Russian map-making department keeps a reserve of blocks in hand in readiness for any emergency. At the present moment the department has in stock 211 plates of the latest Russian maps, 748 plates of military maps of Germany, and 456 plates of other countries. Machines are used to work these, capable of throwing off 500 maps an hour. The Slavonic race has been charged with a want of inventive genius, but the discovery of direct photo-engraving is due to a Pole. His invention has none of that woolliness of texture that characterizes other systems of reproducing maps, or the coarseness of the zincographic process employed by our Intelligence Department. The mode of treatment is kept so profound a secret, that, to prevent its becoming known at all, it has never been patented. Favourable specimens of its use in this country, may be seen in the way of reproduced engravings in Percy Thornton's "Foreign Secretaries of the Nineteenth Century," and reproduced maps in Hensman's "Afghan War." It has one great advantage in copying foreign maps, that any alterations can be made during the process of reproduction, thus enabling foreign names to be exchanged for English equivalents at pleasure.

But the Russian Corps of Military Topographers does not base its claim to respect upon the mere reproduction of maps of other countries—that is only a minor part of its functions. In Asia, for instance, it has acquired brilliant and imperishable renown in mapping the whole of Siberia and

Turkestan. Altogether, during the last twenty-five years, the department has produced 3154 original maps, and has engraved 2659. The *chef d'œuvre* of the series is a three-verst map of the twenty-five governments of European Russia, (two miles to the inch), which consists of 534 sheets. This is constantly being improved upon, and only recently a fresh edition of 419 sheets of sixteen governments was issued, showing the railways, &c. Another great map of European Russia is a ten-verst one (seven miles to the inch), which includes Prussia to Berlin, and Austria to Vienna. It consists of 154 sheets, and took eighteen years to produce. Among the more important maps of countries outside Russia may be mentioned one of Turkey, seven miles to the inch, in eleven sheets; a strategical map of Europe on a thirty-mile scale, in twelve sheets; and a military map of Austria, which is considered superior to the latest production of the Austrian War Office itself. These treasures are not hoarded up and kept unknown to the general public, as in the case of our own and other European Intelligence Departments; nor are they sold merely to a few scientists, as may be said to be the fate of most of the productions of the Royal Geographical Society; but are exposed on sale at the General Staff Office, at a price which renders them accessible to the poorest. Colonel Valentine Baker tells us, in his "Clouds in the East," that when he visited the Perso-Turcoman border in 1873, the secret and confidential maps he took with him from the War Office were found to be so worthless, that he threw them away, and made use of the beautiful Russian maps of the country freely given him at Tiflis by the military authorities there. This was no act of ostentatious courtesy; for he could have purchased the same maps at St. Petersburg by the outlay of a few shillings. We are often apt to accuse Russia of secrecy in her military investigations; but the openness with which she displays the work of her topographers to the gaze of Europe should surely mitigate the charge. When Colonel Grodekoff returned home in 1879, after achieving his great ride from Samarcand to Herat, through a country of which we had little or no information, the Russian Map Department set to work to produce a copper-plate map of his march-route, and in a few months offered it for sale for fifteen copecks, or fourpence-halfpenny. Could the same be said of the survey of any English traveller?

CHAPTER IV.

A DISCUSSION AT THE GENERAL STAFF OFFICE ON THE POSSIBILITY OF INVADING INDIA.

General Soboleff and the Asiatic department of the Russian General Staff—His career and acquaintance with the Ameer Abdurrahman Khan—A review of his "Anglo-Afghan Conflict"—A Russian staff officer on the war in Afghanistan—Our want of skill—Feebleness of the Indian army—Balkh to be a future outpost of Russia—Russian humanity and English cruelty in Central Asia—Soboleff on English inability to take Herat—Relative positions of the English and Russian outposts in regard to the "Key of India"—Description of the General Staff—A Russian official account of the last Afghan war—Enormous amount of English information on the subject—Russia able to invade India—The map discussed—Russian concessions—Arrival of Colonel Stewart's map from England—English policy towards our travellers in Central Asia—The Conservatives as bad as the Liberals in their concessions to Russia—General Soboleff's opinion of English travellers in the East—Captain Butler the cause of the annexation of Askabad—Kaufmann's intended march on India in 1878—The Oxus or the Hindoo Koosh as a frontier?—Discussion about Persia and Bokhara—Tchernayeff's policy.

AFTER leaving the Russian Burnaby, I proceeded to the General Staff Office, to pay a visit to Major-

General L. N. Soboleff. He is the head of the Asiatic Department, and controls the relations between the Russian army in Central Asia and the higher authorities at home. He is, therefore, an influential and experienced man, irrespective of a knowledge of our affairs in Afghanistan, in which he is probably unsurpassed by any of his countrymen. I do not know his early career, but he served a long time in Central Asia. He told me he was on intimate terms with the Ameer Abdurrahman Khan at Samarcand for a period of more than two years; and on his return to Russia his services were secured by the General Staff. Early after the outbreak of the Afghan war of 1878, he commenced a series of articles in the official organ of the General Staff, the daily newspaper *Rooski Invalide*, in which he followed our operations almost week by week. These were marked by a great bitterness of tone against England, and Soboleff made a dead-set at General Roberts, for whom he had hardly a good word to say. He insisted on the vast importance of Herat, but doubted our ability to occupy it, and he claimed the Hindoo Koosh as the future frontier-line of the two empires in Central Asia, instead of the Oxus. This would give Russia Balkh and many other valuable posts. I read them separately at the time, and when they subsequently appeared in a collected form, under the title of "Anglo-Afghan Conflict," I was asked to review them for the *Globe*. The review in question appeared May 11, 1880, and at the risk of being charged with padding my book I reproduce it here, because it throws a very great light on the opinions of a man, who has more control over the course of Russia's Central Asian policy than probably any other military officer in the country. I may mention that in the course of one of our conversations, General Soboleff remarked, in reference to his book, "By-the-bye, the *Globe* was the only English newspaper that reviewed it. I received a copy from London, and at once ascribed the article to Mr. Marvin."

"Did you?" I rejoined. "Well, and what sort of review was it? Did I pitch into you?"

"So, so," he replied, with a smile, "you said some things for me and some against me."

Authors have better memories than their critics. Beyond a general impression that I had written unfavourably of the book, I had forgotten all about the article. Very probably, however, Soboleff had not, and on referring to the article shortly after our interview, I was somewhat horrified at the manner I had dealt with him. However, the review was impartially written at the time, and candour compels me to state that I still approve of it. The reader can read it, or skip it, as he pleases.

"A RUSSIAN STAFF OFFICER ON THE WAR IN AFGHANISTAN.

" He would probably be a bold English writer who would attempt just at present to pen a critical account of our operations in Afghanistan. Not that there would be a dearth of material to work upon; the fault would probably lie in the other direction—he would be distracted by the huge mass of conflicting information lying *perdu* in the files of English and Indian papers. At the same time, he would understand that he could not gain access just yet to the secret influences governing the movements of our troops in Afghanistan, and would feel that, in attempting to decide questions of strategy and explain obscure operations of our generals, he would unexpectedly fall into error, and inevitably bring about his ears a hornet's nest of controversy on the part of officers interested in the campaign. Such influences, however, have not operated upon the mind of Colonel L. N. Soboloff, of the Russian Etat-Major, and military critic to the *Rooski Invalide* and *Voenni Sbornik*, and in the work which he has just brought out at St. Petersburg ('Anglo-Afghanskaya Rasprya'—'the Anglo-

Afghan Conflict') we have a critical narrative of events, from the entry of the English into Afghanistan to the courts-martial of General Roberts, subsequent to the capture of Cabul. Many of the chapters appeared originally in the *Rooski Invalide,* and we must confess that Colonel Soboleff would have done better had he published the whole series complete, making alterations only where subsequent information had affected the accuracy of his statements. As it is, however, the more numerous and important of his articles —those referring to the campaign against Shere Ali—have been condensed into a single preliminary chapter, and, in reality, the volume before us deals only with the relatively inferior operations, from the murder of Cavagnari to the calm preceding the affair at Shirpur. Further, as the Colonel boasts that his book is based mainly upon the telegraphic intelligence addressed to the English papers, and displays internal evidence of having been written without careful investigation of more recent and trustworthy correspondence, it is obvious that his criticism cannot be accepted as of a very weighty character. However, we must remember that the 'Anglo-Afghan Conflict' is likely to serve as a text-book to most of the military writers in Russia for the present, and on this account we must necessarily accord greater attention to his opinions than they intrinsically deserve. Let us add that Soboleff served many years in Turkestan, and that, as an established critic in matters pertaining to Central Asia, he carries to his task more authority than would an ordinary writer unfamiliar with Asiatic warfare.

"Colonel Soboleff commences with a short sketch of the political events leading up to the Afghan war, in which he maintains that the Berlin Treaty lowered English interest in the East; and that, to recover our prestige, we undertook the war against Shere Ali. He then quotes from the Press of India to show the spirit of disaffection rife against us among the natives in 1878, and introduces some sentiments from Mr. Malcolm McColl, embodying the opinions of an unimportant clique that, as India is rather a burden to us than otherwise, we have no special interest in the preservation of the Ottoman power at Constantinople. Soboleff's political remarks are interspersed freely throughout the book; and, indeed, it may be said that quite one-third of the volume is taken up with matter which a purely military writer would have omitted. Describing briefly the operations against Shere Ali, he observes, that the English did not display the slightest skill in conducting the campaign; and that, from beginning to end, it was purely negative in the matter of instruction. 'There was an absence of deliberate operations; the generals did not know how to combine vigilance with decision; they did not display any skill in defending the communications, or in organizing the movement of transport. They evinced a want of tact in dealing with the natives; they encumbered the column with numbers of superfluous followers, who lacked means of defence, and trailed after them superfluous transport of their own. Finally, the military operations were made subservient to political considerations.'

"'This latter blemish, we may observe, was hardly an original one, but any hole is better than none in an enemy's garment. It would be an interesting matter if Soboleff could point out any great war, whether Russian or English, where the pen has not interfered more or less with the operations of the sword. Having described the massacre at Cabul, he thus refers to the reinforcements despatched afterwards to India:—'We consider it necessary to draw the special attention of the reader to the appointment of ten battalions, four squadrons, and eight batteries to reinforce the army of India. For two years the English Press has loudly and unanimously, on every possible occasion, declared the military power of the

English in India to be so solid, that the army there could sustain a great war with any European army that might penetrate Afghanistan; to resist which they could easily place 30,000 troops beyond the Indian frontier, not to speak of their ability to engage alone any Asiatic power. We have our doubts on this point. The English public, undevoted to military affairs, may easily have believed this, but persons at all acquainted with the military situation decidedly failed to comprehend the reason why the English Press exaggerated the military power of India. In the instance given, we see that even in a war with Afghanistan—a country already weakened by a struggle with England, and by civil war—such a tension was produced, that the English War Office considered it indispensable to reinforce the Indian army by the despatch of reinforcements from home and South Africa.' Describing the revolt in Afghan Turkestan, the colonel opines that there can hardly be a doubt that the province has severed itself from Afghanistan proper, and has 'formed itself into a self-governing district, or, more correctly speaking, a group of separate Khanates, of which, may be, Maimene will fall to the Emir of Bokhara. *There can be hardly a doubt that the whole of northern Afghanistan, from the Amu Daria to the Hindoo Koosh, will, by force of circumstances, become included within the sphere of the immediate influence of Russia.*' It is well to note this, as the most eminent writers on Central Asia in this country have always held to the opinion that the Oxus, and not the Hindoo Koosh, ought to form the boundary of the two empires.

"Colonel Soboleff admits that General Roberts displayed expertness at the battle of Charasiab, although, at the same time, he says that the fact of 5000 disciplined troops being opposed only by 7000 disorganized Afghans, unprovided with a leader and a plan of defence, made success a moral certainty. He takes the opportunity on this occasion to praise us for the skilful use we made throughout the campaign of the heliograph, observing that the battle of Charasiab showed that the expert use of the heliograph greatly lightened the task of conducting the engagement. In the last two chapters Colonel Soboleff has much to say about the 'War Terror at Cabul,' respecting which we have only to mention that he bases his opinions largely on Mr. Harrison's recent article in the *Fortnightly Review*, to give our readers a general idea of his statements. In comparing our occupation of Afghanistan with Russia's conquest of Turkestan, he speaks very unfavourably of General Roberts. If we are to believe him, Russia has lowered the taxes in Central Asia, refrained from meddling with the religion, displayed great humanity towards the people, and carefully avoided interfering with the native administration of districts only temporarily occupied; while we, on the other hand, have sinned in every one of these particulars. Our space is too limited to show how utterly false all these statements are, even were it necessary, which, with the revelations of Tchernayeff, Schuyler, and others respecting Russia in Central Asia, we hardly consider it to be. But one can scarcely resist a smile when, in indignant language, he asks us to look to the Caucasus for the proper way of carrying on war humanely, and winds up with, ' Russian officers and soldiers are merciful towards the enemy: here lies the secret of our prestige and our strength; and it is with this weapon that we shall conquer the English in Asia!' Surely Colonel Soboleff cannot be ignorant of Lomakin's operations of last autumn, as described in the *Disastrous Russian Campaign against the Turcomans*. His opinions respecting the execution of a few Afghan fanatics—impartially tried, legally executed—would be all the more valuable, if we could ascertain what he thinks of Lomakin's deliberate bombardment of 5000 women and children, after the Turcomans had expressed their desire to negotiate for surrender."

After the appearance of his "Anglo-Afghan Conflict," Soboleff continued to furnish articles to the *Rooski Invalide* on the English operations, and two of his opinions, denying the ability of England to take Herat, and pointing out the decadence of our prestige in Central Asia, may be very appropriately inserted here. The former was expressed in an article published in May, 1880. In this he commenced by quoting a number of newspaper articles and telegrams, to prove that we really entertained an idea of extending our occupation of Afghanistan as far as Herat, and then went on to demonstrate why we could not do it.

"Four reasons operated against the scheme. 1. The events of December, 1879, under the walls of Cabul, showed the English how difficult it was to obtain a decisive success over the militia levies of the Afghans. The negotiations of General Roberts with the various chiefs, after dragging through January, February, and March, resulted in the recognition that it would only be possible to settle affairs by force of arms.

"2. The negotiations with Persia for the simultaneous advance of a Persian and English force upon Herat, encountered such serious obstacles that the desired end could not be attained.

"3. The appearance of Abdurrahman Khan on

the scene, and the possibility of a coalition between him and the other leaders, rendered it imperative that the English forces should be kept in hand to strike at any combination that might be formed.'

"4. Lastly, there was no hope that the Candahar column, by itself, could march to Herat in sufficient force to lead to a decisive subjugation of Western Afghanistan.

"From Candahar to Herat, according to Bradshaw, is about 388 miles. Major David, in his brochure, 'Is a Russian Invasion of India Feasible?' calculates the route as involving a march of twenty-eight days. In order to march upon Herat, without the co-operation of a Persian force, the English, in the first place, intended to have made use of a detachment consisting of 10,000 foot, 3000 horse, and 800 artillery—in all, 13,800 men. Of these, 7000 would inevitably have had to be detached, to guard the line of communications and the district of Furrah. In this manner only 6800 could have arrived at Herat. To carry provisions for two months for this force and for its camp followers, about 60,000 camels would have been required. Let us admit that these could

[1] The charge was made by the English press against Russia at the time that General Kaufmann, aided, or encouraged, the opportune flight of Abdurrahman from Samarcand, in order that the complications his presence in Afghanistan would produce might restrain us from advancing upon Herat.

have been obtained. The people along the route to Herat were in a turbulent condition, and in the passage of the troops it might be expected that they would offer resistance. But let us allow that the population between Candahar and Herat might have preserved a peaceful attitude, and that the only hostility encountered was on the part of the troops and inhabitants of Herat and the adjacent district. Let us also imagine the Herati troops dispersed, the inhabitants pacified, and the English in occupation of Herat. What would have been their position then?

"The detachment would have arrived at Herat, requiring for the march not less than fifty or sixty days, without provisions, without forage, exhausted, and probably encumbered with sick. At first, as at Cabul, the populace would probably have remained quiet, and the English would have been enabled to collect supplies. The detachment would have occupied Herat and the environs; the English commanders would have issued a series of threatening proclamations; and then the people, recovering from their early fright, and seeing the fewness and the weakness of the detachment, would have broken out in revolt, and would have compelled the English to take up a defensive position. The matter would have been quite different could the English have directed towards Herat 20,000 troops, leaving behind at Candahar and along the road to India 15,000 more. But, in the first place, the Anglo-Indian army is not in a condition to set aside, in its present state, 35,000 troops specially for a march to Herat. Secondly, had the southern column been strengthened by troops expressly brought for that purpose from England, the march to Herat would have been attended with innumerable difficulties, since the despatch of 20,000 men in the direction of Herat, on account of the deficiency of transport, would have been almost impossible. On this account, the English were led to project a march to Herat simultaneously with a Persian force; but as the Shah wished to restrict the English from interference in the affairs of Persia, and desired to receive the province of Herat without acknowledging the right of the English to meddle with it, the arrangements made by the General Staff of the Indian Army, for a march upon Herat, fell to the ground."

Such was General Soboleff's impression of the difficulties attending an English march upon Herat, at a moment when the Russians were posted at Krasnovodsk and the English at Candahar. Their relative distance from the "Key of India" was then as follows :—

Krasnovodsk to Herat, *viâ* Sarakhs...........630 miles.
Candahar to Herat................................369 „

Since then the Russians have advanced upon Askabad, and the English have fallen back to Quetta. Their relative positions are now as under :—

Askabad to Herat......................310 miles.
Quetta to Herat ....514 „

Yet the Duke of Argyll pooh-poohed the alarm excited by the occupation of Askabad, and declared the advance to be a mere bagatelle in the series of Russian movements in the direction of India.

In July, 1880, before the disaster at Maiwand, Soboleff expressed the following opinion of our operations in Afghanistan. " We take the opportunity to characterize, as a grave political error, the belief that the Afghan war has increased in Asia that prestige of the English, which was weakened by our successes in Europe and Asia in 1877-78. The war has shaken the position of the English in India, and has given a substantial pretext for the natives to think that they have been borne away by the idea of England's military power. Even among Afghans it fails to inspire alarm."[1]

[1] This opinion was the outcome of a review of General Stewart's march from Ghuzni to Cabul, which Soboleff defined as " one of the greatest strategical errors of the English General

The Russian General Staff. 75

The reader being now familiar with some of the opinions entertained by General Soboleff, I may pass on to describe the interview.

The General Staff Office occupies the left wing of the huge semicircular building facing the Winter Palace, known under its generic name. It is thus opposite the Foreign Office, which occupies the right wing. Outside, the building is imposing enough, but the inside has been completely sacrificed to secure this exterior display, and a more inconvenient public office it would be difficult to find. Passing up four flights of broad stone stairs, flanked by bare, cheerless walls, one reaches the top storey of the structure, where there is a perfect rabbit-warren of rooms and corridors to traverse before one reaches the Asiatic Department.

In spite of frequent directions from officials scurrying to and fro, I got into innumerable difficulties in making my way to Soboleff's room; opening bureaux instead of passage doors, and even coming to a dead halt at one "no thoroughfare" in the bedroom of a minor clerk. At last, after traversing a number of rooms, and catching

Staff," Stewart having abandoned Ghuzni before he had dispersed the Afghans or quieted the country. "In Asia," said Soboleff, "the abandonment of a town once occupied is almost always regarded as a defeat, and the evacuation of Ghuzni has been accepted as such by the natives."

many glimpses of clerks in military uniform, writing at all manner of awkward and inconvenient tables, I reached a dark corridor, the narrowness of which was still further increased by a series of archive cases, with glass doors, stretching along it. A number of soldier-clerks were loitering about here smoking. One of them took my card into one of the rooms, over which was inscribed in Russ, " Asiatic Department."

A few seconds later he returned, and passed me through the room—in which were a number of military clerks—into a section partitioned off. This contained three plain writing-tables, a few chairs, and some maps on the walls. A more ordinary-looking room it would be difficult to imagine. Any barrack-room office in England would probably beat it. But the world is governed by men, not by habitations. England, in all likelihood, would gladly part with the grand and imposing public office in Downing Street, if she could get in return a powerful and consistent foreign policy, such as is pursued by the political officials in one shabby wing of the General Staff Office at St. Petersburg, and supported by the military officials in the other.

The section contained several officers in uniform. The youngest of them advanced, and, shaking me warmly by the hand, introduced me to the rest. Baron Osten-Saken had described General Soboleff as a "young but clever officer," but I was unprepared to find him having such a youthful appearance, considering his rank. He looks but little older than thirty, possesses only a very small moustache, and has the manner of a young man. He is slight, but strongly built; gives one the impression of being very active and energetic; and has a well-formed head, with physiognominal evidences of great intelligence. Russian officers are not always smart—in the English and German military acceptance of the word—but Soboleff is a strikingly smart officer. He is a man who would create a good impression anywhere.

Our conversation began by his telling me that he is just completing an official account of the Afghan war, in six volumes, for the Government. This is compiled from English official reports, newspaper correspondence, and blue-books, and will be shortly issued. "It has occupied me two years," he said, "and has been a very onerous undertaking. The materials were so numerous. In that respect you, who have been writing the history of Skobeleff's campaign, have been better off. You have not been overwhelmed with such a mass of information."

"Will the tone of the work be hostile to England?" I asked.

"Not at all," said he, "why should we quarrel? Why should we not be friends in Central Asia?"

The rest of the officers concurring in this sentiment, he went on to lament the hostile spirit prevailing in England against Russia, and referred to the violent outburst the Jewish outrages had provoked. At this, an old officer—whom he called, I think, Mikhail Efimovitch—came up and protested vehemently against Russia being so much assailed. "You point at the Jews, but look at Ireland. Is there order there? Are there no outrages? We do not raise demonstrations against you on that account. We have no wish to invade India. It is far off. We could not invade it."

"No, no, Mikhail Efimovitch," said Soboleff, "let us be accurate. We could invade India, but we don't want to. But let us admit we could invade it, though."

"Of course," I remarked, "the ability to invade India is one thing: the desire to do so is another. I certainly think Russia could invade India, but we have statesmen in England—such as the Duke of Argyll, for instance—who think Russia could not possibly invade India at all."

"They are wrong, then," said Soboleff, "for if Nadir Shah could march from Askabad to

Bokhara on the one side, and to Meshed, Herat, and Candahar on the other, we could do the same."

"Certainly," said the rest of the officers; and it was accepted as beyond dispute that Russia could invade India if she wished to do so.

Producing my map of the new Perso-Turcoman frontier, I said that there was a desire in England to know if it was approximately correct. "A number of exaggerated statements being in circulation as to the new frontier," I explained, "I was led, as soon as I received the *Official Journal* describing it, to trace it upon General Petroosevitch's map, and issued it in less than four days. A map with fuller details might have been devised, but this involved time; and my wish was to issue at once an approximate representation of the new frontier, so as to allay the excitement prevailing, and dispel the misconceptions and misrepresentations as to the course of the border-line." Before I had half finished uttering this, one of the officers had run his finger over the map, in a manner showing that he knew every inch of the ground, inserting the omitted names as he traced the border, and had expressed his satisfaction at its accuracy. Both he and Soboleff pointed out Petroosevitch's omissions and errors, but they insisted that the frontier-line was accurately drawn. "The main question is this," I said, "rumours have circulated that the frontier runs close to Sarakhs—my map places it between Gyaoors and Lutfabad. Is that correct?" "As near as possible," replied both at once. "The new frontier runs out towards the desert sixteen English miles east of Gyaoors."[1] I was struck at their glibly expressing the distance in English miles, instead of Russian versts. The Asiatic Department had probably been asked to define it for the satisfaction of the English Embassy.

"The second point of importance is," I continued, "whether the map is right in its course from the Sumbar to the Kopet Dagh; this shows that you have taken only a small and obscure angle of Persian territory, containing the Kari Kala and Nookhoor settlements." "That is equally correct," they replied. "Then," I repeated, "for all practical purposes, we may assume in England that you have not annexed any more territory than this, and that the map may be accepted as a good approximate guide till the

[1] According to the map issued with the Blue Book on Central Asia, No. 1, 1882, shortly after this conversation, the frontier is shown to be twenty miles east of Gyaoors or Gavers. The same map confirmed the substantial accuracy of my own, and if Russia was shown to have annexed a little more of the Atrek country than I was aware of, this was compensated for by the slice of territory she had relinquished south of Askabad. The modifications did not in the slightest affect the opinion I had expressed as to the moderation of Russia in drawing the frontier.

Russian official map is issued." "Certainly," they replied; "the course of the frontier-line is completely regular (sovershenna pravelna) throughout." "I am glad of that," I said, "for Mr. O'Donovan has written a letter to the *Daily News*, decrying the map,[1] and I wished to know whether the frontier was well traced or not." "It is very well traced," rejoined Soboleff, "and the map is an excellent one for the purposes designed." "You are quite certain no more territory has been annexed?" I asked. "Yes, we had a discussion with Persia about the Feroze district, but we let her have it. She likewise asked for the territory between the Kopet Dagh and the Atrek, and we gave it her also."

At the back of General Soboleff's chair was one of those "large maps" of Central Asia, which the Marquis of Salisbury insisted should be studied by the English public instead of small ones. On this map the whole of the territory north of the

[1] Mr. O'Donovan ridiculed my statement that the country between the Kopet Dagh and Atrek resigned by Russia was "magnificent." But not having been there, the "Special" of the *Daily News* was no authority on this point. The statement was not my own, but Petroosevitch's, and Petroosevitch knew the region well. During one of my visits to General Grodekoff, I showed him O'Donovan's letter, and asked his opinion, he having traversed the country several times. He said O'Donovan was wrong, and that the country was exactly as Petroosevitch had described it.

Atrek, between Tchat and the source of the river, was painted as belonging to Russia. Yet, by the new treaty of Teheran, the greater part of this country between the Kopet Dagh range and the Atrek river has been relinquished by Russia, although General Petroosevitch describes it as the finest part of the Perso-Turcoman region.

I noticed this while Soboleff tore open a book-packet from England, which an official had brought into the room. The packet consisted of the Proceedings of the Royal Geographical Society, and contained Stewart's lecture on the Akhal and Merv Turcomans, delivered last autumn. Colonel Stewart proceeded to the Perso-Turcoman frontier during the siege of Geok Tepé, in the disguise of an Armenian horse-dealer. He remained there some time unrecognised; but at last the secret got wind, and Russia complained of his presence at Deregez. It is a part of England's policy in Central Asia to always recall her travellers at the bidding of Russia. Conservative Ministries are just as subservient as Liberal ones in this matter. It was the Gladstone Government that recalled Colonel Stewart and Captain Gill from Persia in 1881; but it was the Beaconsfield administration that dragged home Colonel Burnaby from Khiva in 1875, that sent a messenger to stop General Sir C. M. MacGregor from riding to Merv the same year, and that summoned back, in 1878, Captain Butler from the Turcoman region, whither he had been despatched on a very dubious mission by Viceroy Lytton of India. While readily complying with Russia's requests to recall enterprising English travellers, it is another feature of England's policy to never complain at the explorers that Russia herself sends out in the direction of India. Thus, the Beaconsfield administration considered it only natural that Russia should resent Burnaby's presence at Khiva, but it never thought it unnatural that England should not remonstrate, in her turn, at the presence of Grodekoff at Herat. For years the English Government has done its utmost to prevent English travellers penetrating to Merv, so as to avoid giving umbrage to Russia. Yet it does not think that it ought to be vexed or annoyed when Russia reciprocates this kindly feeling by sending a subsidized caravan to Merv.

Shortly after the return of Colonel Stewart, the Gladstone Cabinet did an extremely wise action, in sending him back again to Khorassan, in the capacity of English Agent, to watch from the advantageous centre of Khaf the operations of Afghans and Russians in the Herat district. Before leaving, he sent me a first copy of his splendid map of the Perso-Turcoman region, which guided me in tracing the frontier on Petroosevitch's little sketch map. This was annexed to the "Proceedings" received, and, opening it, Soboleff ran his finger along the frontier-line, and showed me where it ran out east of Gyaoors. Taking up my map to see how it corresponded, his eye fell upon the list of Central Asian works, published by W. H. Allen and Co., printed on the back of it. "Many of these, referring to the Afghan war," he said, "have been published since I compiled my work, and I cannot use them. Indeed, you have published so many works in England on the Afghan war, that it would take a lifetime to compress their matter into a book. Hensman's 'Afghan War' is a splendid book—we have taken all the maps out of it for our official work. MacGregor's 'Journey through Khorassan'[1]—do you know that the presence of such travellers as he on the Turcoman frontier provokes our advances in Central Asia? Do you know that but for Captain Butler we should not be now at Askabad?"

"That is very extraordinary," I said; "how did he cause it?"

---

[1] Performed in 1875, during furlough. General Sir C. M. MacGregor served with great distinction in the Afghan war, and was afterwards appointed Quartermaster-General of India. He is an officer of whom any country might be proud.

"When Skobeleff was besieging Geok Tepé, Butler wrote to the *Globe*, stating that he had helped to fortify three points in the Turcoman region—Geok Tepé, another beyond, and one at Merv. I received the intelligence from London, and telegraphed the whole of the letter[1] (which was extremely long) to Skobeleff at once. On receiving it he immediately set out to find the second fortified point, and so penetrated to Askabad and Lutfabad. But for that letter of Butler's, he would not have gone so far. So you see what evil these travellers do. As regards O'Donovan, I admit he has done good: he has obviated our going to Merv. There was a Russian gunner

[1] The letter will be found *in extenso* in the Appendix, but the portion particularly referred to by Soboleff and other Russian generals may be quoted here. "Travelling in various disguises in 1878, I was enabled to take a rapid survey of the district about Akhal, and I hold a correct military survey of its neighbourhood. Further, I have before me a plan of Geok Tepé, the original one made by me for the Turcomans, and given to them for the defence and strengthening of the post, before which the Russians had to retreat under General Lomakin, and before which they are now fighting. Should the Russians penetrate further east, they will find *two other posts* equally well fortified as Geok Tepé, and defended by a gallant band struggling for life and liberty." This appeared in the *Globe*, January 25, 1881, the day after the capture of Geok Tepé, but before the news was known in England. Skobeleff despatched his troops eastward January 28th, and on the 30th Askabad was occupied without resistance. It will be remembered Grodekoff spoke of the telegram having been received a day or two after the capture of Geok Tepé. No further strongholds were found.

there a prisoner, and by his advice to the Tekkes to liberate him, he has taken away a cause of complaint against Merv."

"But your own travellers also approach India," I urged.

"No," he replied, "none have been in Afghanistan since 1878, and when Grodekoff rode to Herat a state of war was prevailing." Before I could point out that Grodekoff left Tashkent in September, 1878, i.e. long after the Treaty of Berlin was known there, he proceeded—"And we had prepared for a march against India.[1] At Djam, on the Bokharan frontier, we had assembled a force, and we meant to advance with 20,000 troops. In Siberia we had a reserve of 50,000 soldiers ready, and there were many more in their rear."

"What would have been the line of advance?"

"That would have depended on circumstances: probably through Bokhara to Cabul. While this state of war was prevailing we sent Stolietoff to

---

[1] Great reticence has been maintained in Russia with regard to the aim of this expedition and the operations of the columns composing it, although Central Asian campaigns are usually fully described in the military journals of St. Petersburg on coming to a close. In a series of sketches by an officer of the force, that appeared in the Russian *Graphic* (*Vsèmirnaya Illustratsia*) in 1879, the expedition was called "The Russian Expedition to the Frontier of India."

Cabul. In response to this, you sent an army into Afghanistan. That was bad. You made the Afghans your enemies. They will be your enemies for another quarter of a century. They are against you, though they are not for us."

" But they were against us before we fought them; at least Shere Ali was."

" That is true,"he said. " You could not occupy Afghanistan permanently without at least increasing your Indian army by 30,000 troops. I was very much surprised, though, that you gave up Candahar. Why did you do so ? "

Before I could answer, the other officers replied, " You did not like the expense." I did not reject this view, as my interview was drawing rapidly to a close, and I had no wish to waste time in mere discussion. Without replying, I asked, " What do you think will be the future frontier of the two empires ? "

" The Hindoo Koosh," he replied. " The Oxus is a river, and a river is a bad frontier. Herat would be better in Persia's hands."

" But Persia is a rotten State," I urged ; " the Persians are imbeciles."

" I don't think so," he said.

" Well, when the Shah dies, what will be the state of affairs in Persia ? "

" There will be a revolution," he replied.

"Then Herat would be handed over to an anarchic State," I said.

He made no reply to this.

On his observing that General Kaufmann was still very ill, I asked what the Government meant to do with him. "General Tchernayeff will be his successor," he said.

"Is he an Anglophobe?" I asked.

"No, he is particularly well disposed towards England," he replied.

Regarding Bokhara, he said its annexation by Russia on the Emir's death would depend upon circumstances. "Bokhara is a wretched place to live in." According to his account, the Khanate is so unhealthy that a Russian occupation would appear to be only possible by the aid of Eno's Fruit Salt. Referring to Merv, he said that a Russian caravan had recently arrived there. He praised the Ameer Abdurrahman as a very clever man, and when I pointed out that he was now a sensualist, spending his time mainly in his harem and misruling Afghanistan, he shrugged his shoulders, and said, "He is an Asiatic." He strongly defended himself against any imputation of being an Anglophobe, and the rest of the officers joined him in urging that England and Russia should shake hands in Central Asia. "Why should two great European powers quarrel over a few Asiatics?

We ought to be friends. We strongly wish it. It is England's hostility that provokes our advance more than anything else."

It being already past three o'clock, and the officers preparing to leave, I took my departure, expressing a hope that the meeting of England and Russia in Central Asia might be as friendly as our meeting had been that afternoon.

CHAPTER V.

SKOBELEFF ON THE CENTRAL ASIAN QUESTION AND A RUSSIAN ATTACK UPON INDIA.

Grodekoff's note to Skobeleff's adjutant—Ensign Abadzaeff and his share in the fighting at Geok Tepé—Numerous callers at Skobeleff's house—His military career—Seventy battles and sieges in nineteen years—Probability of his being the equal of Wellington—Description of Skobeleff—His fascinating manners—His opinion of the annexation of Akhal—Why he was recalled from Askabad—His view of the efficacy of slaughter—The massacre of the 8000 at Geok Tepé—The mowing down of women—Persian traffic in Turcoman girls—Skobeleff's criticism of the executions at Cabul—His opinion as to the different standards needed for soldiers and civilians—What he thinks of General Valentine Baker—An invasion of India not feasible—The difficulties explained—His opinion of the Afghans—The Central Asian Question all humbug—He would fight us at Herat—Russia has no desire to occupy Afghanistan—Captain Butler and Geok Tepé—Opinion of Maiwand—His art of war—His account of the battle of Makram—Twenty thousand men drowned like flies—Skobeleff's assurances regarding Central Asia—Skobeleff not the Russian Government.

St. Petersburg, March 8.

Having expressed to General Grodekoff, on Monday, my desire to have an interview with General

Skobeleff, he kindly instructed me as to the best time to see him, and gave me a note addressed to his adjutant, Ensign Abadzaeff, worded in Russian thus :—" Mr. Charles Marvin, the author of a number of English works on Central Asia, wishes to have an interview with Adjutant-General Skobeleff.—N. Grodekoff." By name Abadzaeff was already well known to me, as he was one of the most dashing warriors in the recent Turcoman expedition, and was mentioned as warmly in the official despatches as in the narratives of the Russian correspondents, published at the close of the war. When Skobeleff, last autumn, presented the Emperor with a magnificent white Turcoman charger, captured at Geok Tepé, and which was intended for the English general the Tekkes vainly hoped would come and lead them against the Russians, Abadzaeff was the officer chosen to show off the animal's paces before the Tsar, and was specially thanked afterwards. He is a tall, slight young man, with a face that would pass any day among Russians as an English one, and the pleasant smile that is a characteristic of his countenance still further cloaks his Caucasian origin. On calling yesterday morning at the Belozersky Mansion, in the Nevsky, which is situated opposite the Anitchkoff Palace, the St. Petersburg residence of the Tsar, I found Abadzaeff and several other officers, in Kouban Cossack uniform, in the anteroom of Skobeleff's apartments. Having read the note, he expressed his regret that Skobeleff was not at home, having gone to Gatchina, and asked me to call this morning at ten. His visit to Gatchina was probably in connexion with the recent demonstration at Paris, since M. de Giers, the head of the Foreign Office, went down to Gatchina also. In his capacity of Commander of the Fourth Army Corps, Skobeleff's headquarters are at Minsk, but while stopping at St. Petersburg he resides at the mansion belonging to his brother-in-law, Prince Belozersky.

When I called upon him this morning, I found the anteroom crowded with officers waiting to see him. The anteroom is a small but cozy apartment, leading from the courtyard, and is only separated by curtains from the larger chamber in which Skobeleff receives visitors. The walls are decorated with stag-horns and oil paintings of famous horses, while an English open fireplace, in which a blazing coal-fire is maintained, suffuses an agreeable warmth on a nipping cold day like this morning. Here, on certain days in the week, quite a crowd of officers may be found waiting to see the general. Many of them attend on matters of business, for Skobeleff, besides being commander of an Army Corps, is also a prominent member of a number of important commissions. Not a few of the callers, however, are friends or acquaintances of the hero of Plevna. Skobeleff has seen so much fighting at home and abroad in his time, that his circle of friends is exceedingly large. He has friends in almost every country in Europe, not excluding even Germany, whose susceptibilities he touched so keenly in his recent hard-hitting speech on the rival merits of Teuton and Slav.

When only nineteen years old, Skobeleff proceeded to Poland to take part in the fighting there, and witnessed several engagements during the suppression of the revolt of '63. The first conflict he was engaged in was that between the Russians and Poles at Maikhovoi. The following year he got leave from the Government, and proceeded to Denmark to see the fighting between the Danes and their Prusso-Austrian opponents. Studies at the Staff College afterwards occupied him for a time, at the close of which he went to the Caucasus, and took part in Colonel Stolietoff's descent upon Krasnovodsk—the first link in the chain of events, that closed with the capture of Askabad and the annexation of the Transcaspian territory. In the Turcoman region he did a deal of reconnoitring work, and in 1871 pushed out as close to Khiva as Sari Kamish. When the expedition against Khiva took place in 1873, he commanded the advanced guard of the Kinderly column, from the Caspian, and took part in most of the fighting. He was present at what is known as the Yomood Massacre, and afterwards conducted a secret and dangerous reconnaissance as far as Ortakuya, in the direction of Kizil Arvat. The following year, being on leave in Europe, he became a close spectator of the Carlist war. In 1875 and 1876 he took a leading part in the Khokand campaign, the most difficult Russia had yet experienced in Central Asia. At the close of the fighting he was made governor of the conquered region. Shortly before the outbreak of the Russo-Turkish war in 1877 he arrived on business at St. Petersburg, and as soon as hostilities were declared proceeded to the scene of operations as volunteer. His brilliant conduct and splendid success throughout the war are too well known to be dwelt upon here. On his return to Russia he was made Commander of the Fourth Army Corps, and when Lomakin involved the Russian arms in disgrace in Central Asia, he was sent to Krasnovodsk to retrieve the White Tsar's lost prestige. As yet his siege of Geok Tepé is too little known abroad for him to have gained any European reputation by it, but at home it is considered one of his finest laurels. Few men have seen more fighting than Skobeleff. In the course of the last nineteen years he has taken part in seventy battles, sieges, and engagements. In most of them he has been foremost among the fighters.

Lieutenant Greene, the United States' attaché to the Russian army during the war of 1877-78, wrote of him a year ago, " Though he has lived but thirty-five years he has commanded 20,000 men in battle; he has received the surrender of an entire army of nearly 40,000; he has led more assaults than any living man but Grant; and in no one of them has he failed to carry the line he assaulted, though in one case he was subsequently overwhelmed with numbers and driven out. His stupendous military genius is such, that I firmly believe that should he live twenty years more, he will be commander-in-chief in the next war about the Eastern Question, and history will then speak of him as one of the five great soldiers of this century, side by side with Napoleon, Wellington, Grant, and Moltke." [1]

After waiting in the anteroom a short while, Ensign Abadzaeff came and said the general was ready to receive me. I followed him into the adjoining apartment, where Skobeleff was sitting at a large writing-table between two long windows. He

[1] "Sketches of Army Life in Russia," p. 142.

arose as I entered, and shaking me warmly by the hand, conducted me to a seat alongside the window, close to the study-chair in which he had been sitting. My eyes being dazzled by the sun gleaming brightly into the anteroom, his apartment seemed dark and heavy. While explaining the object of my visit, however, the gloom cleared off; but the animated conversation that immediately afterwards ensued, and which lasted till I came away, prevented me from carrying off any other remembrance of the room, than the general impression that it was very handsomely and most comfortably furnished.

The portraits of Skobeleff do not do him justice. The whiskers he wears give him in a photograph a fierce, and even what has been called a barbarous appearance. But in actual life these whiskers lose all their fierceness in the kindliness of his eyes, and the winning smile that is rarely absent from his face. Lieutenant Greene, in his "Sketches of Army Life in Russia," draws a charming portrait in words of the hero of Plevna, but there are many characteristics omitted which give a still greater lustre to the original. As a rule, I have found that important personages are best regarded at a distance, through the medium of portraits and biographies. It shocks one to become acquainted with their "warts." Skobeleff is the only great personage I have met, who has become enhanced in my estimation by personal acquaintance. He has been so very much praised, that it would have been quite in accordance with past experience if a reactionary feeling of disappointment had followed my interview with him. But the contrary was the case. I have never come in contact with any man who has left so charming an impression upon me. Carlyle, in his latter years, seems to have had no appetite for great men—he heaved at his contemporaries. An interview with Skobeleff would have made him young again. It would have revived the extinct fires of his hero-worship. As for Thackeray, I think if he had known Skobeleff he would have made him his ideal of a perfect gentleman.

Our conversation was throughout in English, which Skobeleff imbibed in infancy from his English nurse, and which he speaks with fluency. As briefly as possible I described the state of the Central Asian Question, showed the false position in which the English Government had placed Russia by giving during the Candahar debate undue prominence to his recall from Akhal. "The Government allowed the erroneous impression to prevail that Russia would retire to the Caspian, relinquishing her conquests," I said, "and the version of affairs transmitted from St. Petersburg to London was to the effect, that you were recalled in displeasure for wishing to extend those conquests."

"That is wrong," he answered, "I was recalled because the operations were finished, and because the army, having already been reduced, was far too small to warrant a general of my position retaining the command. It was impossible for us to relinquish Akhal. You could retire from Afghanistan, because there was a king you could leave behind. But there was no form of government among the Turcomans. We had, therefore, to impose one of our own. Had we retired, they would have recommenced their raids as soon as the effect of the defeat had worn off."

Glancing at my map of the new Russo-Persian frontier, he continued, "I know nothing of the new frontier arrangements. They only transpired during my stay in Paris. I do not believe that there will be any more advances now we have secured a frontier. The retention of Akhal is costly enough without our incurring further expense. Merv is quiet, and will be so until the effects of the lesson at Geok Tepé wear off. Do you know, Mr. Marvin—but you must not publish this, or I shall be called a barbarian by the Peace Society—that I hold it as a principle, that in Asia the duration of peace is in direct proportion to the slaughter you inflict upon the enemy. The harder you hit them, the longer they will be quiet afterwards. We killed nearly 20,000 Turcomans at Geok Tepé. The survivors will not soon forget the lesson."

"I hope you will let me publish this opinion," I said, "and for this reason. In your official report of the siege, you say that during the pursuit after the assault you killed 8000 *of both sexes*."[1]

"That is true," observed Skobeleff, "I had them counted. The number was 8000."

"This statement," I continued, "provoked great comment in England, for you admit your troops killed women as well as men."

I may here state that in my interview with Grodekoff on Monday, he said frankly, in reply to my questions: "Many women were killed. The troops cut down everybody. Skobeleff gave

[1] "The pursuit of the enemy flying from the fortress was continued by the infantry for ten versts (6¾ miles), and by the cavalry six versts (four miles) further, and only complete darkness and the thorough dispersion of the enemy caused the chase to be abandoned, and the troops to return to camp. In this pursuit by the Dragoons and Cossacks, supported by a Division of Mountain Horse Artillery, the killed of both sexes amounted to 8000 persons. . . . . The enemy's losses were enormous. After the capture of the fortress 6500 bodies were buried inside it. During the pursuit 8000 were killed." "General Skobeleff's Report of the Siege and Assault of Dengeel Tepé (Geok Tepé)."—*Voenni Sbornik*, April, 1881.

orders to his own division to spare the women and children, and none were killed before his eye; but the other divisions spared no one; the troops used their sabres like a machine, and mowed down all they met." This is admitted with equal frankess by Captain Masloff, an eye-witness, who states in his "Conquest of Akhal-Tekke," that on the morning of the assault orders were given to the troops to spare no one.

Skobeleff replied: "It is quite true. When the dead were counted, women were found among them. It is my nature to conceal nothing. I therefore wrote, in making the report, 'of both sexes.'"

"Were any dishonoured?"

"None at all. The troops did not outrage a woman. I must tell you I was deceived by the Persian agent, Zulfagar Khan. He came to me and said that there were many Persian women among the prisoners, and asked to be allowed to take them and send them home. I gave him permission, and when he asked for money I gave him that also. He thereupon chose the most beautiful women, and sent a number to Meshed, where he sold them into harems. Directly I was told of this, I stopped the permission at once."

On my remarking that it was the great defect

of our last Afghan war that we entered the country without a policy, and never applied his principle (and Wellington's) of hitting the enemy as hard as possible, he said: "Those executions of General Roberts at Cabul were a mistake. I would never execute an Asiatic to strike terror into his countrymen, because you are sure to fail. Whatever punishments you resort to, they can never be so terrible as those inflicted by a Nasrullah, or any other despotic native ruler; and to these crueller punishments the natives are so accustomed, that your milder ones produce no effect. Then, worse than this, the execution of a Mussulman by an Infidel provokes hatred. I would sooner the whole country revolted than execute a man. If you take a place by storm and strike a terrible blow, it is the will of God, they say, and they submit without that hatred which executions provoke. My system is this—to strike hard and keep on hitting till resistance is completely over, then at once to form ranks, cease slaughter, and be kind and humane to the prostrate enemy. Immediately submission is made, the troops must be subjected to the strictest discipline: not one of the enemy must be touched."

Skobeleff adopted this system at Geok Tepé. The troops had full liberty to slaughter the enemy on the day of the assault, and to pillage

Geok Tepé for three days afterwards. They were then subjected again to close discipline, and orders were given to the army to neither molest the natives nor to meddle with their property. A soldier who disobeyed these injunctions was promptly tried by drumhead court-martial and shot.

Regarding our generals, he said, "You have one good general. I have never fought him. He is General Baker. He is a good general."

"Unfortunately, he is lost to the service," I remarked. "In England, we expel from the army an officer who makes a false step; in Russia, you reduce him to the ranks and send him to Central Asia, where he has a chance of recovering his reputation. You had several in your expedition—Captain Zouboff, for instance.[1] I think your plan is the better one."

"Yes," said Skobeleff, "and for this reason.

---

[1] In 1868 Zouboff, while serving as lieutenant on board the clipper "Vsadnik," quarrelled with his superior officer on the quarter-deck, for which he was tried by court-martial, reduced to the rank of a common seaman, and sent to Central Asia. There he served so well and fought so well, that at the close of the Khivan Expedition he was made an officer again, and in 1874 was already a captain. His exploration of the Oxus gave him a great reputation, which was increased by his bravery on the Danube in 1877. Skobeleff made him head of the Naval Brigade during the Turcoman war. He subsequently died of wounds received in one of the engagements.

I have had much experience in warfare, and have found that the men who fight best are precisely those who are apt to be troublesome in time of peace. A Government should be always very indulgent to its troops in time of peace. Those who are most difficult to deal with in time of peace, often prove the best fighters in time of war." Taking up a pair of compasses and opening them, he continued, as he placed them in a measuring position on a sheet of paper: "You need to measure soldiers by a different standard to that which you apply to civilians."

As to a Russian invasion of India, he said: "I do not think it would be feasible. I do not understand military men in England writing in the *Army and Navy Gazette*, which I take in and read, of a Russian invasion of India. I should not like to be commander of such an expedition. The difficulties would be enormous. To subjugate Akhal we had only 5000 men, and needed 20,000 camels. To get that transport we had to send to Orenburg, to Khiva, to Bokhara, and to Mangishlak for animals. The trouble was enormous. To invade India we should need 150,000 troops; 60,000 to enter India with, and 90,000 to guard the communications. If 5000 men needed 20,000 camels, what would 150,000 need! And where could we get the transport? We should require vast supplies, for Afghanistan is a poor country and could not feed 60,000 men, and we should have to fight the Afghans as well as you."

On my urging that the Afghans might be tempted by the bribe of the spoliation of India to side with the Russians, he said: "I doubt it. To whom could we offer the bribe? If we bribed one Sirdar, you would bribe another. If we offered one rouble, you would offer two; if we offered two, you would offer five—you would beat us in this. No; the Afghans would fight us as readily as they fought you."

"But if you occupied Khorassan beforehand and made it a second Caucasus?"

"Why should we occupy Khorassan? We should only get provisions from the province, and we could get them as it is. We derive a revenue from Khorassan now, by its trade with Nijni Novgorod; but there would be a deficit if we occupied the province. I do not believe Russia would ever occupy Khorassan. I think the new frontier will be permanent. Do you know"—here he rose and spoke with vehemence, regarding me with a smile—"I consider the Central Asian Question all humbug."

"But in regard to the possibility of invading India, General Soboleff expressed to me a clear conviction on Monday that Russia could march an army to India if she chose."

"That was diplomacy," replied Skobeleff; "of course, it is possible—all things are possible to a good general; but I should not like to undertake the task, and I do not think Russia would. Of course, if you enraged Russia: if, by your policy, you excited her, if you made her wild—that is the word—we might attempt it, even in spite of all the difficulties. For my part, I would only make a demonstration against India; but I would fight you at Herat." He said this with great animation, but very goodhumouredly. "Do you know, I was very much interested during your war whether you would occupy Herat or not. It would have been a mistake if you had done so. It would be difficult to march an army from the Caspian to Herat to fight you there, but we should be tempted to do it in the event of a war."

He spoke slightingly of the Transcaspian railway. At the very utmost he did not think it would be extended beyond Askabad. He ridiculed the notion of extending the line through Afghanistan to India, and considered its continuation so improbable that he would not discuss the argument I advanced, that its completion to Herat or Candahar would facilitate a Russian march to the Indus. He thought things would remain in

Afghanistan as they are for years to come. He would not agree with me that the junction of the two empires in Central Asia is within measurable distance. He expressed a very contemptuous opinion of Afghanistan in general, referring to it as a country that was not worth the cost and trouble of either empire to govern. He did not see what there was to tempt Russia to occupy it.

After this he entered into some very frank criticisms of his own operations, which I do not think I ought to reproduce, and in regard to Captain Butler's claim to having fortified Geok Tepé, he said, " He can exercise his claim, but he gains nothing by it, for it was a mere mud fortress, in the Asiatic style, and does not redound to the credit of any European constructor." Speaking of Maiwand, he said, "I have never been able to understand that battle. Poor Burrows evidently had no conception of fighting. He made the great mistake of charging Asiatic cavalry. I would never have done so. My maxim in warfare is this—always fight the enemy with a weapon in which he is deficient. If he has good cavalry, do not charge him with cavalry; if his discipline is perfect, do not try to beat him in discipline. You have read my instructions to the officers before Geok Tepé, annexed to my official report?"[1] I assented.

[1] See translation in the Appendix.

"Those were framed with great care and contain my views on the subject. The Asiatic has no idea of manœuvring. Do you know the battle of Makram? That was a splendid battle and redounds to the glory of Kaufmann, whom I admire very much. Poor fellow, his career is finished. Do you know that our operations at Makram were suggested by Sir Hugh Gough's battle at Ferozesha. Shall I bore you, Mr. Marvin, if I describe it on paper? It is a most interesting thing. If you will have patience you will see what a great battle this Makram was."

While I was expressing my interest in the matter, Skobeleff was placing a pad of foolscap before him, and selecting a number of pencils from a series of thirty or forty, of various coloured leads, that were lying neatly on the table, all sharpened and ready for use. Drawing his chair close up to mine, he bent his head over the paper, and began sketching the features of the ground at Makram with wonderful rapidity. Although a mere sketch, he made a scale at the outset, and used the various coloured leads to indicate clearly the positions of the troops and the features of the ground. There was no slurring of details at all; the names of the localities were inserted, and the numbers of the forces noted at the side. When it was complete, it was more finished than many of the sketches that have been published in the recent English military works on our war in Afghanistan. While drawing the sketch, he described the battle-field with great spirit and minuteness; he was never at a loss for a word; he stated his facts one after another without displacing their order; and he never needed to explain his explanations.

Briefly, the battle of Makram was as follows :— The fort occupied a position on the banks of the Syr Daria, sufficiently close to a chain of mountains for the Khokandese to attempt to bar the Russian advance up the valley by running out an earthwork towards it, armed with sixty-eight cannon, all pointed towards the invaders; and by continuing the line of defence to the foot of the hills themselves, by stationing in the intervening ground a huge mass of cavalry. At the back of the fort, the settlement of Makram, with its numerous gardens, was held by infantry; the fort itself was armed with guns, and the hills flanking the position were crowded with skirmishers. On the opposite side of the river, the position was rendered unapproachable by swamps. On coming in sight of this barricade, held by 60,000 Khokandese, General Kaufmann reconnoitred the position with his staff. Although he had only a mere handful of troops, he decided to make an attack the next day, to prevent the enemy overrunning the country. Skobeleff may as well relate, in his own words, what followed: "Having surveyed the position, he turned to his staff and said: 'Who knows anything about the battle of Ferozesha?' I had read all about it, but waited for the other officers to reply. No one knowing anything about it, I described the battle." Here he drew a rough sketch of the Punjab, and said: "As you know, Mr. Marvin, Sir Hugh Gough, the father of the General Gough in Afghanistan during the late war, pitched his camp alongside the enemy's at Ferozesha, without reconnoitring the ground; and when they fired into it, he fought at once and lost several thousand men. The next day he reconnoitred the position, and found a hill on the flank that infiladed it. Marching thither, he inflicted a crushing defeat on the enemy with a loss of only eighteen men." Turning again to the plan of Makram, he said: "There was a hill on the left flank, at the rear of the Khokandese position, which corresponded with that at Ferozesha. It is now called the Peak of Kaufmann. The next day we marched straight in that direction, keeping all the way on elevated ground alongside the mountains, until the enemy's position was outflanked. Then we changed front: turning our back upon the hills and our faces to Makram, and, marching straight towards it, swept the enemy right into the river. The river was quite black with heads. Twenty thousand Khokandese perished. We lost only eighteen men. I commanded the cavalry that day. The account of Ferozesha I read originally in French, but more recently in English. Makram was a splendid laurel for Kaufmann."

Schuyler, in his "Turkistan,"[1] gives an account of this battle, in which he erroneously ascribes the turning movement to the suggestion of General Golovatcheff, who carried out the Yomood massacre in Khiva in 1873, two years earlier. His description is very similar to Skobeleff's, and he also mentions the enemy being driven into the river and drowning "by hundreds." Makram was one of the most decisive battles fought by the Russians in Central Asia. It completely crushed the Khokandese, and put an end to all ideas of a Mussulman rising against Russia.

While the general had been describing the battle, several officers had called, but Skobeleff told Abadzaeff to inform them that he was occupied. At the end he manifested no desire to close the conversation, but unluckily I had an appointment with M. de Giers at twelve, and it

[1] "Turkistan," vol. ii. p. 288.

being now within ten minutes of that hour, I was compelled to cut short the interview. On my expressing a hope that I might have another opportunity of eliciting his opinions, he said, "By all means, Mr. Marvin; give me your address, and I will call on you, or you on me." Here he took up the foolscap pad for me to write upon, and before I could prevent it—I had intended to ask him to give me the sketch of Makram, as a souvenir of our interview—he had torn the sketch into pieces. In conducting me to the anteroom, he expressed an earnest wish that the Central Asian Question might disappear altogether from its present place in politics, and that England and Russia might be friends. On my urging that he should allow me to express his opinion as to the best way of pacifying Asiatics, he hesitated for a moment, but assented at last that I should attach it to his statement in regard to the slaughter at Geok Tepé.

Throughout the whole conversation, which Skobeleff carried on with great animation and good-humour, there was no indication whatever of any attempt at plausibility or desire to make an impression. His manner was so simple, so straightforward, and so transparent, that it would have carried conviction to an Urquhart or an Ashmead-Bartlett. It will be seen that there were many very essential points left untouched, but so far as the ground covered was concerned I think Skobeleff's words should have a calming effect. The limit I would assign to them is this—that Skobeleff it not the Russian Government, and that his friendly feelings and prudence might not always prevail against that diplomacy, which is the curse of every country, not excluding our own.

CHAPTER VI.

THE MINISTER FOR FOREIGN AFFAIRS ON THE NEW RUSSO-PERSIAN CONVENTION.

A visit to M. de Giers—His personal appearance—The charges of evasion brought against him by the English press—Ignorance of the English Embassy at St. Petersburg—The best way to negotiate foreign affairs is to know nothing about them—Career of M. de Giers—His services—Opinion of the new frontier beyond the Caspian—Mr. Ashmead-Bartlett's Question in the House of Commons—The new Russo-Persian frontier a permanent one—The Atabai Yomood difficulty—Merv not likely to be annexed—Liberation of Kidaeff, the Russian captive at Merv—Opinion of M. de Giers of the situation in Central Asia—Russian influence in Khorassan and English influence in Afghanistan—The future of Bokhara—An interview with the Tsar impossible.

I REACHED the Foreign Office just as the clock was striking twelve. Baron Osten-Saken received me warmly, and ascertaining that M. de Giers was in, summoned an official to conduct me to his room, which is on the second storey. I had to wait a short time in an adjoining room while he received one or two visitors, and when these were gone he

I

came out himself and asked me to enter. I knew that the head of the Russian Foreign Office had been over forty years in the diplomatic service, but was surprised to find him so aged. He stoops very much, and gives one the impression of great bodily infirmity, although mentally he is probably as keen as ever he was.

M. de Giers has been called an astute man, but he does not look it, nor do I know anything in his career that would bear out the charge made against him. His answers to English diplomats have been called into question. He has been charged with deliberate vagueness, with equivocation, and with evasion. But what are the true facts of the case? If England sends vague minds to the Russian Foreign Office, she must expect them to come back with vague answers. The recent Blue-books reveal that the secretaries and attachés at the English Embassy at St. Petersburg went repeatedly to the Foreign Office to ask questions, which could have been better answered by a reference to current English geographical and political literature at home. Thus, we find Mr. Hugh Wyndham bothering M. de Giers with questions about Sarakhs, which would have been unnecessary if he had taken the trouble to consult such a well-known work as General Sir C. M. MacGregor's "Khorassan."

This contains not only a survey of the country, made by the present Quartermaster-General of India in 1875, but also a plan of Sarakhs. The whole of the contents of the Blue-book on Central Asia, No. 4 (1881), dealing with the annexation of Akhal, reveal the grossest ignorance on the part of the Embassy at St. Petersburg as to the geography of the conquered region and Khorassan. In one place Mr. Wyndham naïvely admits that it took him a fortnight to find out, that Askabad was not the "most southern town of Akhal" but the "most south-east town;" and in the same despatch (No. 21) he speaks of Akhal as though there were only one Tekke oasis instead of two—the conquered Tekke oasis of Akhal, and the independent Tekke oasis of Merv. How can England hope to successfully negotiate with Russia if she will not make her St. Petersburg Embassy officials study a little more what they are negotiating about? The Blue-book in question shows that M. de Giers gave the best answers he could to the ignoramuses who visited him, and that the vagueness lay all on their side, not on his. M. de Giers was roundly abused by the English press for giving such shadowy answers; but the fault was not the Russian Minister's. It really lay with the Embassy. At the most vital phase of the Central Asian Question—that preceding the annexation of Akhal and during the formation of the new Tsar's foreign policy—Earl Dufferin was withdrawn from St. Petersburg, and with his departure disappeared all skill and cleverness from the Embassy.

M. de Giers—I use the Frenchified title by which he is usually called, although Privy Councillor Giers would be a better approach to his Russian appellation—is an exceedingly experienced statesmen in Eastern matters. He entered the consular service in Turkey before the Crimean War, and occupied important political posts in various parts of the Balkan Peninsula, including Constantinople, up to within a very short period of the commencement of the Russo-Turkish war of 1877. At one time he was Consul-General at Cairo, and we may trace from that the inspiration of the claim which Russia has recently advanced, to share with the rest of Europe the control of Egyptian affairs. At another time he was Minister at Teheran, and this gives him experience in dealing with the newest phases of the Central Asian Question, which is likely to be of immense service to Russia. Already, before I visited him at the Foreign Office, he had been for months controller of Russia's foreign policy, although the world still believed it to be in the hands of Prince Gortschakoff; and his appoint-

M. de Giers and the map.

ment as Minister after my departure, consequently was in no sense an event of the exaggerated importance ascribed to it by the European press.

Owing to an interruption rendering our interview a short one, I was only able to elicit the following views:—Spreading my map of the Russo-Persian frontier before him, he said: "It will be some time before the Russian official map of the new frontier appears; because, as you will readily understand, Mr. Marvin, we cannot issue it until the Teheran convention is ratified." On my remarking that the English Government had promised to issue an official map at the close of the previous week, in response to a request by Mr. Ashmead-Bartlett, he said, "I did not know that. They have received no map from us. It must have been received from Teheran." This subsequently proved to be the case.

Showing him a cutting from the *Times*[1] contain

---

[1] House of Commons, March 2.—Mr. Ashmead-Bartlett asked the Under-Secretary of State for Foreign Affairs whether it was true that a treaty was concluded in December last between Russia and Persia, whereby the fertile territory between Askabad and Sarakhs, up to within ten miles of that town, was ceded to Russia, and would be occupied by the Tsar's forces when the treaty was ratified next month; and whether this cession embraced the Keshef Rud; whether Russian engineer officers had lately surveyed the whole territory up to Sarakhs, and had reported that no obstacles existed to the speedy and inexpensive completion of the railway from the Caspian to that town; whether the Russian

ing the promise, I asked whether, in the event of its not being fulfilled, my map could still be Government had given any assurances that they would now fix a limit to their continual annexations of territory, and, if so, what that limit was; whether he would state if the distance from Krasnovodsk, or the Caspian, to Sarakhs, was 600 miles by road or over; whether he could state to what district he referred when he stated that the question of the appointment of a British officer on the Boundary Commission was under consideration; and whether, as the map showing the Russian advance and recent acquisitions, which was first promised by him last June, had not yet been provided, the Government would, at least, supply the House *with copies of a map just issued by Mr. Marvin.* In reply, Sir C. Dilke said:—"The treaty signed at Teheran at the beginning of January defined the frontier between Persia and Russian Turkestan to a further point eastward, about 150 miles from Sarakhs by road. No cession beyond that point, or embracing any portion of the Keshef Rud was made to Russia, nor have we any reason to suppose that there will be any such further advance of Russian troops as is contemplated by the hon. member. The country between Askabad and Sarakhs has been recently surveyed by Mr. Lessar, a Russian civil engineer, and a translation of a communication on the subject made by him to the Geographical Society of St. Petersburg, which has been published in a Russian newspaper, will be included in the correspondence about to be laid before Parliament. With regard to the limit of Russian advance, I can only repeat that the whole question is now under discussion between the two Governments. (Hear, hear.) I believe the distance from Krasnovodsk to Sarakhs by road to be about 500 miles. When I stated that the question of the proposed presence of a British officer on the Delimitation Commission for the Persian frontier was under consideration, I referred to the boundary generally. No joint mixed commission was appointed; but, as I have already stated, communications are passing with respect to that portion of the frontier not settled by the recent treaty. The map showing the boundary, as settled in the treaty, reached London on Feb. 10, regarded as an approximate representation of the new frontier.

"I read the *Times* daily," he replied, "but had not seen this before." Having read the cutting, he scanned the map carefully, and at the end observed, "Yes, it may be accepted as in the main reliable. It is sufficiently correct as an approximate representation of the frontier."

Repeating several times musingly, "It is sufficiently correct," he afterwards went on to say that General Soboleff would express the most authoritative opinion respecting its topographical accuracy, and when I stated that he had done so in favourable terms, he replied that he thought I might rest content with it. He thanked me for the service I had rendered Russia by the timely issue of the map.

In response to a question, he said he thought that the new frontier would be a "permanent and durable" one. "But the wintering of the Russian Atabai Yomoods south of the line, on Persian territory, complicates matters," I observed. "Yes, it is true," he answered, "but I think we shall be able to satisfactorily arrange all that."

and copies are being printed for presentation to Parliament with the papers. As a large number is required, some delay was unavoidable, but I hope they will be ready by the end of the week. (Hear, hear.)"

"Do you think there will be any further Russian advances for a time," I asked.

"I do not think so," he replied. "I do not see what there is to provoke them."

"But what about Merv?"

"Merv is quiet. The Merv Tekkes have entered into friendly relations with us, and I do not anticipate any trouble in that quarter, particularly now that the Russian prisoner Kidaeff has been liberated."

On my mentioning that fears were entertained of further Russian annexations in Khorassan, he said that they were groundless. With the cooperation of Persia, he believed that all cause for complaint along the frontier would come to an end. "In the meanwhile," he concluded, "if the new convention has done nothing more, it has at least secured us tranquility in the Transcaspian region. Tranquility prevails there now instead of turbulence. We do not interfere at all in Afghan affairs, and I think the present aspect of the Central Asian Question is so far satisfactory, that you exercise your influence over one portion of it—Afghanistan—and we over another"—sweeping his hand across Khorassan.

Replying to a question, he said, "In regard to Bokhara, the Emir is better again. I cannot say what course would be pursued towards the

Khanate in the event of his death. That would depend upon circumstances."

On my asking whether it would be possible to obtain any direct personal assurances from the Emperor—" You know, M. de Giers, that such assurances emanating direct from the Tsar would have greater weight than those of the Foreign Office"—he said that it would be contrary to precedent for such a course to be followed. "The Emperor expresses his views to his Ministers, and they to foreign States, and I do not see how this procedure could possibly be suspended." Recommending me then to visit one or two authorities on Central Asia whom I had not yet seen, M. de Giers rose, and our interview terminated.

CHAPTER VII.

GENERAL TCHERNAYEFF ON THE FUTURE OF BOKHARA.

Tchernayeff's appointment as Governor-General of Turkestan—Description of him—Comparison between him and Skobeleff—His views on the elevation of Servia to a kingdom—The difference between Turkestan and Turkmenia—The railway to Khiva—The fate of Bokhara—The Cossack on the Oxus—Are mountains or rivers the best frontiers?—No fear of an annexation of Merv—The frontier policies of England and Russia in Central Asia—Khorassan safe from seizure—Russian influence in Persia—The duty on Indian tea—The caravan trade between India and Turkestan—The Afghan barrier not worth breaking down—Uselessness of defining a Russo-Indian frontier in Asia—A Russian invasion of India practicable—Opinion on the annexation of Candahar—Russia likely to be drawn to Herat—His view of the Jewish atrocities—His opinion of Sir Henry Rawlinson—Assurances respecting Russia's friendliness towards England—"Tashkent—*c'est mon ouvrage*."

ST. PETERSBURG, March 9.

I HAD an interview, this morning, with General Tchernayeff, who leaves here shortly to replace General Kaufmann as Governor-General of Turkestan. I called on the general on Tuesday, but the news flashed that day from Belgrade, that Prince Milan had been made King of Servia, had caused so many persons to call upon him, that he begged me to postpone my interview until this morning at eleven o'clock. This narrowly escaped being again put off, for when I called at the Hotel Belle Vue, at the back of the General Staff Office, at the appointed hour to-day, the hall porter, or Swiss, as the term runs here, informed me that the general was ill, and was receiving nobody whatever. I was about to send up my card and ask for another appointment, when an officer entered the hall, and completely ignoring the statement of the Swiss, demanded to see the general's man-servant. This individual appearing at the top of the staircase in response to a summons from the porter, and inviting the officer to ascend, I thereupon followed at his heels. As soon as he saw me the man-servant, who had conveyed to me Tchernayeff's message on the previous occasion, said that the general would be happy to receive me the moment the officer was gone, and asked me to take a seat in the buffet opposite the head of the staircase. I soon understood why the general was occasionally ill, for in less than five minutes half a dozen persons called to see him, and I am afraid many must have gone away disappointed during our chat, extending till long after midday.

The general gave me a warm welcome, and said he was glad to have a conversation upon Central Asia. The impression I had formed of him from works on Central Asia and Servia was, that he was of a gay and sparkling temperament; but this feature—if it ever existed at all—has been sobered by the misfortunes the general has undergone, and the illnesses that have left their mark upon him. The general, however, still retains that simplicity that has always been a particular characteristic of his, and there is plenty of vigour left for any contingencies that may arise in Central Asia. But I should be inclined to believe that the general is no longer an eager adventurer as of yore, and that, when he takes up the administration of the Russian province in Central Asia, we need not look for fresh repetitions of the Tashkent exploit.

If the truth must be told, Tchernayeff did not come up to my expectations. I was disappointed with him. Perhaps Skobeleff had thrown him a little into the shade. Skobeleff is intoxicatingly young: Tchernayeff is in the sere and yellow leaf. Skobeleff is a man of promise; great things are expected of him; he has such uncommon and brilliant parts that it is difficult to assign any limit to his career. With Tchernayeff the case is different—his career lies behind him. Skobeleff may be a Suvaroff, a Wellington, a Napoleon; but Tchernayeff can only be an administrator of the ordinary type, a trifle more honest than the rest, but not more capable than a score of other Russian provincial governors. Skobeleff's past career stamps him as a born hero: Tchernayeff's as a casual one. If you examine the lives of the two men you will find that there can really be no adequate comparison instituted between them— Skobeleff is so utterly ahead of Tchernayeff. Tchernayeff may prove an excellent official, but his hero days are over. The grandest part of Skobeleff's career, on the other hand, lies before him. He is worth a whole army to Russia. What he would do in the event of a revolution in Russia time alone can tell, but his *rôle* would not be an insignificant one.

Our conversation began by my remarking to General Tchernayeff that the elevation of Prince Milan to the dignity of King must be a source of satisfaction to him. He replied: "Of course it is; but the event no longer possesses the significance that would have been attached to it in 1876. Servia was not then independent, whereas she has been free now for some years, and the significance of the event is lessened thereby."

"There is also another feature," I observed. "Then, Prince Milan would have taken his title from Russia; now he apparently takes it from Austria."

"Yes," he answered, "there is that difference. Servia is now completely under the influence of Austria."

"And Montenegro?"

"That is a different matter. It is the Montenegrins who are conducting the present war."

"Will the insurrection be soon suppressed?"

"I do not think so. I think it will last a long time. I see that Mr. Gladstone is said to have proposed a congress, for the purpose of settling the difficulty. It is hard to say what will be the end of it. Russia has no intention of interfering."

Turning then to my map of the new Russo-Persian frontier, he said he was not acquainted with the fresh arrangements beyond the Caspian. The Transcaspian territory is under the control of the administration of the Caucasus; it is governed from Tiflis. The jurisdiction of Turkestan does not extend beyond Khiva, and in this manner Tchernayeff will have nothing to do on his arrival at Tashkent with what takes place at Askabad.

English statesmen constantly fall into the error

of applying the word Turkestan to the Turcoman region. Whatever may be the etymological meaning of the two words, Turkestan signifies exclusively the Russian territory in Central Asia, administered from Tashkent, and Turkmenia (or Turkomania) the country of the Turcomans, administered from Tiflis. There is no Turcoman country whatever in Turkestan, if we exclude the small area under Khivan control, and the two administrations of Turkestan and the Caucasus are so completely distinct, that no excuse exists for confusing the one with the other.

General Tchernayeff told me that a project is now under examination for extending the Trans-caspian railway from Kizil Arvat, or rather Bami, to Khiva, by a line across the desert. This would give Russia direct communication with Turkestan, which province is now isolated, owing to the badness and the desert character of the roads from Orenburg and other Ural points to Tashkent. By means of the canal system and railways, troops and stores would be sent from the Neva to the Volga, whence they would be transported by water to Michaelovsk, to be there placed on the railway and conveyed to Khiva. From Khiva to Bokhara steamboats would ply on the Oxus, and from the Bokharan ferries good roads lead to the principal points in Turkestan.

General Annenkoff's scheme for extending the railway from Kizil Arvat to Herat, to be there joined by an English line from India, he thought a good one; but he added that the line to Khiva would probably have the preference. General Skobeleff, as I have already stated, ridiculed yesterday the notion of running a railway through Afghanistan, and doubted whether the line would advance beyond Askabad. The same opinion was expressed to me, in still stronger terms, by General Grodekoff on Monday.

Referring to the false rumour circulating in the capital last night that the Emir of Bokhara was dead, he expressed an opinion that the Khanate would be eventually absorbed in Turkestan. "Now that we have occupied Akhal, and have opened up communications with Turkestan from that territory, by way of Khiva, Bokhara acts as a sort of barrier. It would be advantageous to Russia to remove this. Fortunately, there is a very powerful party in Bokhara that wishes us to annex the country, and the measure could consequently be accomplished without any fear of a revolt. The matter affects the commercial interests of Bokhara. At present, as an independent state, Bokhara pays duty on the goods she exports to Russia, whereas goods from Tashkent, Khiva, and Khokand enter Russia free."

" The effect of this would be to bring down the Russian frontier to the Oxus."

" Yes," replied Tchernayeff; " that would be a very good and natural frontier-line."

" But General Soboleff told me on Monday that he did not regard the Oxus as a good frontier. He spoke of the Hindoo Koosh as the future frontier of the two empires. He said a river is not a good frontier."

" That's a matter of opinion," replied Tchernayeff. " Many say that a chain of mountains is also not a good frontier."

Referring to Merv, he said that he did not see that there was any reason to fear a Russian advance upon that place, as the Tekkes were quite quiet. He did not think that there was a prospect of any more annexations in Central Asia. On my pointing out that his appointment would probably be regarded in England as an indication of a forward Russian policy in Central Asia, he assured me that his policy would not be an aggressive one. " You may repeat my assurances to England, Mr. Marvin," he said, " that she need have no fear of fresh annexations."

In reply to a remark I made, that the Russians had not yet obtained a firm frontier in Central Asia, and that the Merv Tekkes and other tribes might attack them, he admitted that fresh advances might have to be made by Russia. "If the robbers of the hills attack the people of the plain, we must retaliate to protect the latter," he said.

"The same is the case with ourselves on the north-west frontier of India," I observed. "We have to advance and punish the tribes; but there is this very great difference between ourselves and yourselves: we punish and retire, and have to re-advance the next year, when the effects of the punishment have worn off. You advance and remain."

"Yes," he said, "that is our system; it is the only efficacious system for putting down brigandage in Central Asia." In reply to a remark made by a gentleman, who had entered immediately after myself, and had interested himself in the conversation, I admitted that I myself regarded the Russian system as very much better, and more rational, than our own.

With regard to the new frontier, General Tchernayeff said that he did not think that any occasion would arise for Russia to annex Khorassan. He agreed with me, however, that disorder might prevail in Persia after the present Shah's death, and capped a remark I made that the Persian Government was worse than the Turkish, by saying, "And Persia is, besides, a very much weaker state." I was struck with his expressing, exactly in the same manner as M. de Giers yesterday, the opinion that England enjoys predominant influence in Afghanistan, and Russia on her part predominance in Persia. He added, however, "You exercise influence in South Persia, from the Persian Gulf," but assented to the rejoinder I made that the proximity of the Caucasian army to Teheran gives a greater force to Russia's influence.

With reference to the prohibitive duty on Indian tea, recently imposed by the Turkestan authorities, he stated that the measure was sanctioned to prevent the better tea, brought by Russian merchants from China, being driven out of the market by the cheaper and inferior Indian article. Said he, "It is easier to convey Indian tea to Turkestan than Chinese tea, as our traders have to bring it a longer distance. The effect of the duty has only been to equalize the prices of the two, and, of course, the consumer will now make use of our article." He did not think the duty would be raised any higher, as it had been increased sufficiently to guarantee protection to Russian tea.

Some remarks I made about the advantage of establishing unrestricted trade between India and Central Asia, did not meet with much encouragement. He did not seem to think the caravan trade *viâ* Afghanistan of any importance. He thought the trade of Central Asia might improve with the formation of good communications; but he did not consider any benefit was to be obtained by interfering with the Afghan barrier.

No desire was expressed by him that the two empires should touch in Central Asia. In reply to a question I put him as to where the future frontier should be drawn, he said, "If we continue friends, it is useless to lay down a frontier; if we quarrelled, no frontier would restrain us."

He did not think the invasion of India by Russia impracticable. "The question is not a new one," he observed. "It was discussed so long ago as in the reign of the Emperor Paul, and was afterwards revived at the Tilsit interview of Napoleon and Alexander I., when an arrangement was made to send an army of 35,000 men, *viâ* Persia and Herat, to India. At the present time our more accurate knowledge of the country lying between Russia and India, and the position which we have taken up in Central Asia, give us reasons for regarding as a practical possibility what was once considered a fantastic undertaking. Russia has no intention or desire of invading India; but if you ask if an invasion is possible or not, I must answer in the affirmative, although I admit the task would not be an easy one."

He said an English annexation of Candahar would excite no animosity in Russia. "You can occupy it if you like, notwithstanding that I consider the position too advanced for you, which I take to be the reason why you evacuated the place last year." On my explaining English policy more fully, he expressed it as his firm opinion that it is a fatal error to fall back in Central Asia. "The natives regard any retirement as a sign of weakness, and are emboldened thereby to renew their attacks." No Russian appears to dissent from this view.

He admitted that if Russia annexed Bokhara, and brought her Cossack line down to the Oxus, she might be drawn into crossing that river. "The people of the plain" (of Afghan Turkestan) "are peaceful, but are exposed to the attacks of the hill tribes of the Hindoo Koosh, particularly the Hazares" (belonging to the Herat district, and under the control of the Ameer of Afghanistan). "They might apply to us for defence, and it is impossible for me to say beforehand what we should do under the circumstances."

In this manner, it is possible Russia might penetrate to the Hindoo Koosh; once there, the same attacks of the Afghan tribes would draw her on to Herat and Cabul, and so by degrees to the frontier of India.

He estimated the present strength of the army of Turkestan at over 40,000 men. This is irrespective of the 8000 which, he stated, garrisons Akhal. General Kaufmann is on the point of death; his mind is almost entirely gone. It is impossible to remove him to Russia.

The general's friend making a remark about the bitter feeling prevailing in England against Kaufmann, and referring to the Jews, I asked what they thought of the Jewish atrocities. Both ridiculed them. Tchernayeff said: " The Jewish houses were pillaged and their property destroyed, but there have been no outrages upon women." I pointed out that the refugees arriving in England told a different tale. " Their stories are untrue," he replied; " the mob beat the Jews when the latter defended their property, but the women were not harmed. I see you are helping the Jews to emigrate. You are welcome to the lot—you can take them bag and baggage."

Referring again to Kaufmann, he observed that he himself had been as much assailed in England as Kaufmann for his operations in Central Asia. His friend remarking that nothing would convince Sir Henry Rawlinson of Russia's Pacific desires, Tchernayeff observed that Vambery carried his hatred of Russia too far. "He overdoes it," he said. I noticed that throughout all these references to the Russophobia prevailing in England, he uttered no reproaches against us. The same was the case with Skobeleff. On my rising to close the interview, he said again that I might repeat his assurances respecting his friendliness towards England, and in impressive language, that admitted of no carping criticism, expressed a hope that the two countries might shake hands across Central Asia. "I shall be glad to see you again," he remarked, "and if you will give me your address I will call upon you." I replied that my presence at home was so uncertain, owing to my appointments varying from day to day, that I would not expose him to the risk of finding me absent, and asked that I might have the pleasure of calling upon him again, to which he, with apparent satisfaction, assented. On my observing at the door that he would find himself quite at home at Tashkent again, and would probably be very satisfied to get back there once more, he said, "Every man is fond of his own work, you know, and Tashkent—*c'est mon ouvrage.*"[1]

[1] This interview with General Tchernayeff was afterwards published in an exceedingly bad report in the *Novoe Vremya*. The general, I am told, described our conversation to Krestovsky, a journalist on the staff of that paper, and it naturally suffered in passing through a second person. The *Novoe Vremya* having

described me as a special correspondent of the *Times* (which I had to contradict in the leading Russian papers), so much importance was attached to the conversation, that the correspondents of the German papers telegraphed the report verbatim. As there are a few verbal differences between the *Novoe Vremya* report and that in the *Newcastle Chronicle*, I may anticipate criticism by mentioning that in these conversations I made use of Stokes's admirable system of memory, which enables one to retain them in a perfect form. It would have been impossible to note down the answers in black and white, for the mere sight of pen and paper is apt to repel confidence and make people cautious. Irrespective of this objection, and the loss of time involved by it, the system I adopted enabled me to concentrate my whole attention upon the varying phases of the subject under discussion.

General Kaufmann, to whose illness repeated reference is made in these conversations, died on the 16th of May at Tashkent.

CHAPTER VIII.

THE VICE-PRESIDENT OF THE RUSSIAN IMPERIAL GEOGRAPHICAL SOCIETY AND THE ADVANCE UPON KHORASSAN.

A morning with Gospodin Semenoff—An ideal naturalist—The Central Asian Question misunderstood—Difference between the enmity between Russian and German and between Russian and Englishman—Impossibility of a fusion of the Slav and Teuton races—The time too early yet for the establishment of an understanding in regard to the partition of Central Asia—The new Russo-Persian border a bit of the future permanent frontier—The Atabai Yomood difficulty surmountable—Frontier arrangements in Central Asia—Misrule in Persia no concern of Russia—Why Russia's interest is greater in Turkey than in Persia—Russia and the Slavs—She cannot abandon her historical mission—Nomads must be kept in order—Russia will some day occupy Merv—Russia the future mistress of the whole of the Turcoman tribes—England must establish greater control over the Herat tribes, or Russia will advance to the "Key of India"—English and Russian policy in Central Asia—Chinese rule only temporary in Kuldja—Lessar's exploration of Sarakhs—Ancient books found at Geok Tepé—Semenoff's view of Sir Henry Rawlinson—My own policy in regard to the Central Asian Question—The Duke of Argyll's patriotism—Semenoff's admiration of Skobeleff—The future of Hungary.

St. Petersburg, March 11.

I SPENT this morning with the venerable Vice-President of the Russian Imperial Geographical Society,

Gospodin Semenoff, who is well known in scientific circles in England as an eminent naturalist and geographer, and as the enterprising explorer of many parts of Central Asia. He lives on the Vassili Ostrof, an insular adjunct of the capital, in apartments in Zablotski House, which is situated in the 8th Line. The room in which he received me was remarkable for the number of oil paintings on the wall, and the numerous dwarf palms stretching along in front of the windows. The sun streaming in brightly upon these, and gaining additional lustre from the well-polished oak flooring, gave an aspect of comfort and repose to the place, altogether in harmony with the calmness and benevolence which are the characteristics of Gospodin Semenoff's countenance. The worthy Vice-President has a bright, intelligent face, a high forehead, and a quantity of hair of snowy whiteness. He would harmonize with most people's ideal of an aged naturalist. Usually calm in conversation, he can be very animated in argument, and it is easy to see that behind his placidity there is a reserve of force that may render service to geographical and natural science for many years to come. Semenoff's whole character and career are such as to reject any suspicion of equivocation, that bitter Russophobes might desire to cast upon his utterances. One naturally looks for humbug from a professional politician, and cautious opinions and reservations from an official, but a man of science like Semenoff is too ready to receive and give facts and opinions to mislead anybody conversing with him, and hence, whether we approve of them or not, we are bound to honourably respect his sentiments.

Gospodin Semenoff began the conversation by expressing his satisfaction that I had come to St. Petersburg to obtain information about Central Asia, and said that he should be glad to do all in his power to assist me. "The Central Asian Question," he observed, "is a subject of bitter controversy, because the position of each power in Central Asia is misunderstood. When the position and the aims of each become better known, I think all hostile feeling will disappear. It is not a case of national hatred. Russia does not hate England, and England does not hate Russia. We have rival interests which part us, but a basis exists for agreement; whereas where deadly hatred prevails it is hopeless to attempt to establish a union. Englishmen and Russians can meet and talk over their differences in a friendly spirit. The things that part them are very different from those that part Russia and Germany. We have Germans in Russia, and, on the other hand, Slavs exist in Germany.

The two races refuse to agree. It is impossible to reconcile their differences by a discussion, such as would be possible in the case of England and Russia."

On my expressing a belief that a mutual arrangement between England and Russia for a partition of Central Asia would diminish the friction between the two Powers, Gospodin Semenoff said: "Unfortunately, we do not yet know sufficiently the intervening region to be able to effect any such desirable arrangement. Circumstances must decide where the line shall be drawn, and I do not think it would be possible or desirable to anticipate events. It is very satisfactory that we have the beginning of a permanent frontier in the line running out from the Caspian, under the recent Teheran convention."

"Do you regard it as a permanent one?" I asked. "For instance, the Atabai Yomoods pass the summer on Russian territory north of the new frontier, and the winter on Persian territory south of it. How will it be possible to maintain such an arrangement?"

"I think it will be possible. There are instances of a similar condition of things in Central Asia. In the Tian Shan range, I found races occupying three terraces of mountains. A tribe there passes one part of the year on the top terrace, and a part on the bottom. To go from one to the other, it has to pass through the third terrace, occupied by a different tribe. An arrangement, therefore, commonly exists, by which the one tribe respects the other in the passage through the intervening territory. Quarrels, of course, do occur, and in these the weaker naturally go to the wall. But in the case of the Atrek, it is the Atabai Turcomans who are the weaker, not the Russians or the Persians. It would be impossible to prevent the nomad migrations from one side of the river to the other. The character of the region does not allow the people to settle down. But we have a line of forts up the Atrek, and the garrisons there will keep the Turcomans in order. If we moved south of the Atrek, we should come into contact with the settled population around Astrabad. We do not want to do that. All that we need is to keep the nomads in order, and we shall be able to effect this from inside the present frontier."

"But Persian rule in Khorassan is weak, and the people are as badly governed there as in Turkey. It is believed in England that disorders in Khorassan will lead in time to the annexation of the province."

"Why should it?" exclaimed Semenoff. "Misrule in Persia is no concern of ours. If, say, Khorassan contained nomad Turcomans, who crossed the frontier and attacked us, then we should have to occupy the province. But the people of Khorassan are not aggressive; they will not attack us; and we shall thus have no cause for interfering with their affairs. There is a very great difference between Persian and Turkish misrule. Persia excites very little interest in Russia, and if the Shah rules badly, that is the concern of his subjects, with whom we have nothing in common. But Turkish misrule means the oppression of men of the same race as ourselves. It touches us to the quick. Our interest in Turkey is not a new one. It goes back to the time of the Tartar yoke. After our emancipation from that yoke, we were brought into conflict with the Tartar vassals of the Sultan in the Crimea, and with the Turks themselves. Step by step we relieved of their control the region bordering on the Black Sea. The war of 1877-1878 was but the continuation of a struggle which has lasted for centuries, and which will not end until the Slavs have been freed from foreign control. It has been Russia's historical mission to emancipate these Slavs, and she will undergo any sacrifices rather than resign that mission. She knows that eventually that mission must be accomplished. But we have no such historical mission in Persia. That country excites no interest at all compared with Turkey, and hence the annexation of Khorassan by Russia, because of Persian misrule, is a most improbable event. Our advances in Central Asia have been due to the fact of our not finding a settled and pacific population to rest our frontier against. Until this recent convention was concluded at Teheran, we had no frontier beyond the Caspian. We now have one, and, I think, a good one. Unforeseen events may lead to slight rectifications of it in course of time, but such modifications can only be very slight. They will not interfere with the integrity of Khorassan. As to the country beyond Gyaoors, where there is a nomad population, the alterations will probably be greater. We have no need to meddle with a settled population, but we must keep nomads in order."

" Then, in the event of the Merv Tekkes proving troublesome, Russia would annex up to Merv? You think a Russian occupation of Merv some day probable?"

" Speaking in a private capacity, and not as Vice-President of the Geographical Society, I think that Russia will some day occupy Merv. The Merv Tekkes are quiet now, but we have no guarantee that they will always be so. Merv is not like Sarakhs. Sarakhs is a town with a settled population—we have no need to meddle with that.

But Merv is a camp; and if the nomads make disturbances and raid against us, we shall have no other alternative than to advance and occupy the place. All the Turcomans will some day probably be under our control."

"When you reach Merv," I said, "you will come into contact with the nomad Sarik Turcomans, living higher up the river Moorgab. If they raid against you, you will advance and occupy their territory. You will then come into contact with the semi-nomad Djemshidi and Hazare tribes, dwelling between the Sarik country and Herat. They will raid against you; they will have to be punished; and so you will advance to Herat. How can this be prevented?"

Gospodin Semenoff expressed his opinion that the only way to prevent it, would be for a stronger control to be established at Herat over the Djemshidi and Hazare tribes. To my question as to whether he thought Russia would object to an English occupation of Afghanistan, he replied that he thought not. He did not think that she would object to an English occupation of Herat. He frankly declared that if the Djemshidis raided to Merv—a matter of almost weekly occurrence now—subsequent to the Russian occupation of the place, Russia would have no other alternative, than to advance and punish them.

"There are two modes of dealing with hill tribes," I observed. "Yours, which consists of advancing, punishing, and remaining; and ours, which is made up of alternately advancing and retiring. We are always conducting expeditions on our Indian border. The aggregate cost of these is enormous, the loss of life very great, and the results most unsatisfactory."

"Speaking from a personal knowledge of Central Asia," said Semenoff, "I consider our system decidedly the more preferable. When you advance in Central Asia, it is always a mistake to retire—it is misunderstood by the natives. They regard it as a sign of weakness. The conquest of Central Asia has been very costly, and still entails upon us a deficit, but the outlay would have been larger and incomparably less satisfactory if we had followed your practice."

Smiling benevolently, he continued: "You know, Mr. Marvin, every annexation in Central Asia is a source of satisfaction to our scientific men. Fresh fields are opened up for research, and all this must naturally be of interest to persons devoted to science. The statesman, however, has to regard these advances from a different point of view from that of the naturalist."

Referring to Kuldja, he expressed a belief that Russia would some day have the province again.

He did not think the Chinese would be able to permanently maintain themselves there. It was a mistake, he said, to occupy territory and promise to give it up when called upon to do so. Better not advance at all, or else advance and give no promise. Russia having promised in the case of Kuldja, there was no other course for her but to keep her word.

He said that the Tiflis Branch of the Imperial Geographical Society was fitting out an expedition to explore the newly-annexed region beyond the Caspian. The Russian engineer Lessar, who surveyed the railway route to Sarakhs a little while ago, would probably proceed, with some other person, from St. Petersburg to represent the society itself. He thought the scientific results of the expedition would be most valuable. There are a large number of ruins lying between the Sumbar and the Caspian, and again in the desert between Akhal and the Oxus. I inquired as to the collection of ancient books which Grodekoff told me Skobeleff had found in Geok Tepé, and sent to St. Petersburg. He said they were very ancient, and of extreme interest. An Orientalist is now examining them.

Speaking of Sir Henry Rawlinson, he said: "I know him personally. He is a very clever man, but he has never been in Russia, and does not understand Russia. Men often get into a train of thought, from which it is impossible for themselves or others to extricate them. They look so long in one direction that they cannot see in any other. It has always struck me as strange that Rawlinson, who is a *savant*, should desire to exclude Central Asia from scientific investigation."

I described then the condition of the Central Asian Question in England, and pointed out that Russophilism was as injurious to Russia as Russophobia, on account of the reaction it provoked. "I myself strive," I said, "to be impartial in my writings. If Russia is right I admit it, and if wrong I point it out."

"It is a proper course to pursue," he replied, "and you can render so much service to Russia thereby, for we are in this position: that we have to remain silent to these Russophobe attacks."

On my mentioning that the Duke of Argyll had written a book on the Eastern Question, in which an attempt was made to prove that since the Crimean war Russia had been always right and England always wrong in Central Asian and Eastern affairs, he laughed heartily. "A man's motives may be right and his actions wrong," he said, "and it is the same with nations. They cannot be always in the right."

He spoke in terms of warm admiration of Skobeleff. "He is a most genuine man," he said. "He is quite transparent. There is nothing concealed about him. Then he is so clever, and has had such a brilliant career." This opinion coincided with what was expressed to me a few days ago by one, who has known him for years in all his moods, both heroic and unheroic. He was with him at Plevna, and has seen him incessantly since. "He is really a wonderful man," he said to me to-day. "He always speaks right out. He hides nothing. He may change his opinions, but they are always genuine ones."

Discussing then the Eastern Question, Semenoff expressed a strong conviction that the annexation of the Balkan Slavs to Russia would be a misfortune. "It would lead," he said, "to the disruption of the Russian Empire. It would be impossible to control the Southern Slav region from St. Petersburg, and the result would be that the empire would break in two, and Russia would lose all the territory south of the Dnieper." He traced, in a very clear and impartial manner, the development of the Russian empire, and, closing the *résumé* with a description of affairs in the Balkan Peninsula, expressed the opinion that the Slavs there would emancipate themselves from foreign yoke. "If Austria touched Montenegro," he said, "Russia would go to war at once, even though she knew she would be beaten. A nation like Russia cannot resign its historical mission. We were defeated at Sebastopol, but we achieved our aim twenty-five years later. It would be the same again. It is useless for Europe to be hostile. The Slavs are there—in the Balkan Peninsula—and they and their aspirations will have to be recognised." Respecting Austria he expressed an opinion that it would some day dissolve, and that Hungary would find itself in the position of a second Switzerland in a great Slav State, or series of States. It was a mistake for Hungary, little as she is, to attempt to domineer over the Slavs. It would be better if she recognised her position, and played the quieter and more natural *rôle* of a second Switzerland.

On rising to leave, Gospodin Semenoff invited me to attend a meeting of the Geographical Society next Wednesday, and repeated his offer to do his utmost to assist me. "I shall be very happy," he said, "to forward the transactions of our society to you in England."

CHAPTER IX.

GENERAL GRODEKOFF AND CAPTAIN MASLOFF DISCUSS
THE RUSSIAN VIEW OF THE CENTRAL ASIAN QUESTION.

A second conversation with the "Russian Burnaby"—Captain Masloff's brilliant sketches in the *Novoe Vremya*—Grodekoff insists on the impossibility of a Russian invasion of India—His opinion of General Soboleff—Difficulties at Geok Tepé—300,000 troops needed for the invasion of India—Khorassan never to be absorbed by Russia—Fanatic character of the people—The Atabai Yomood difficulty not a solitary one—Major Napier and Kari Kala—Masloff's opinion of a march from Askabad to Sarakhs—Grodekoff and O'Donovan—Krapotkin's view of the Russian advance—Parallel between Russia's operations in Central Asia and ours in South Africa—The importance of Merv overrated—Misconception regarding "keys"—Skobeleff's mission—England thinks more of the Central Asian Question than Russia—Useless for Russia to try and persuade England against Rawlinson—Grodekoff's decision to write a book on the Central Asian Question—Lord Lytton's "mad" scheme for invading Central Asia—Kaufmann's dubious march in the direction of India—Afghan hatred of Russia—Grodekoff and the Treaty of Berlin—A greater danger than the Russian invasion of India—English and Russian generals—Final assurances.

ST. PETERSBURG, March 13.

AT the close of the Turcoman war last year, society in Russia was deeply interested by a series of brilliant sketches which appeared in the *Novoe Vremya*, describing the siege of Geok Tepé. These were written by some one behind the scenes, who had followed the operations throughout, and was an admirer of the general commanding the expedition. The narrative was not an elaborate or systematic one; it consisted merely of a series of word-pictures of the operations; but these were so vividly penned, as to surpass anything that I had previously read in the Russian press, and fell not far short of the productions of Mr. Archibald Forbes. A few weeks ago these sketches—which I had already translated for my forthcoming work on the siege of Geok Tepé—appeared in a collected form, under the title of "The Conquest of Akhal Tekke: Sketches of Skobeleff's late Expedition" ("Zavoevanie Akhal Teke," &c.), and the author then stood revealed as Captain Masloff, of the Engineers. Calling on General Grodekoff this morning, I was extremely pleased to find this officer present. He is a tall, thin, pallid man, very little over thirty years of age, extremely intelligent, calm, and self-possessed. He accompanied Grodekoff in his foraging mission through Khorassan before the siege, and again the advanced column sent by Skobeleff towards the Tedjen, in the direction of Merv, after the occupation of Askabad. The opinions of such an officer are valuable, and those which he and Grodekoff expressed on the invasion of India merit every respect.

The question as to the possibility of an invasion of India by Russia was one of the earliest topics of our conversation, and both officers pronounced a strong opinion against it. Grodekoff stated with vehemence that Russia could never invade India from the Caspian. On my quoting General Soboleff's opposite opinion, he said: "Soboleff has never served in any campaign in Central Asia. He does not know what warfare in Central Asia is. He lived a time at Samarcand, but Samarcand is a town, and a journey thither alone in a carriage is very different from a march with an army on foot. He regards the subject more from a civilian than a military point of view. Look at the enormous difficulties we encountered in overcoming Geok Tepé. We killed 20,000 camels during that campaign, in which only 5000 troops were engaged. We should need a good 300,000 men to invade India, and where could we obtain the transport and supplies for such a number? It would be impossible for us to march such an army to India. Rest assured that a Russian invasion of India is an impossibility."

I pointed out that the belief was entertained in England that Khorassan would be absorbed and made a base of operations. "Never," said

Captain Masloff. "You and I will never see Khorassan annexed by Russia; and if it were annexed, the difficulties attending an expedition to India would be equally great. The new frontier beyond the Caspian is one that will last."

Mentioning that the people of Khorassan were stated to be anxious to pass under Russian rule, Captain Masloff said that the feeling was exaggerated. "I have lived in Khorassan, and my opinion is that the people, who are extremely fanatical, would oppose a Russian annexation of their territory. They would not willingly accede to an Infidel ruling them. The notion of a Mussulman province asking to be governed by the Giaour is too ridiculous to be entertained."

"Quite so," observed General Grodekoff, "Persian misrule would not provoke annexation, as it is no concern of ours. If we went to war with Persia we should attack her through Azerbijan, not through Khorassan. If we occupied Khorassan I think England would fight us, but we have no such idea whatever." Here Captain Masloff stated privately some facts connected with the new administration of Akhal, tending to prove that Russia had no thought of extending the area of the recently annexed Turcoman territory, and these, I must say, were of a very reassuring character.

I mentioned that the annual migration of the Yomood Turcomans from Persian to Russian territory, and *vice versâ*, across the Atrek part of the new frontier, would prove a serious complication. "Not so serious as you imagine," said Grodekoff, "since the same state of things prevails on the Azerbijan frontier of Persia. In the district of the river Kour, I believe about 40,000 nomads cross periodically from one side of the frontier to the other, and there is no thought of annexation there. Too much importance is attached by England to these matters. For instance, years ago Major Napier" (who was sent as English agent to the Perso-Turcoman frontier in 1876) "declared that the settlement of Kari Kala, which has been annexed under the new convention, was a most important point. I don't know why he considered it such. It was abandoned some time ago by the Goklan Turcomans, and is now unoccupied.[1] I see you print on your map Fort Tchat (at the junction of the Sumbar and Atrek rivers) in large letters. We have abandoned that place now; it was a frightful locality to live in."

I mentioned the belief in England that Russia would advance on Herat by Sarakhs or Meshed. Both officers ridiculed the idea. "I have been to

---

[1] It was abandoned at the close of Lomakin's disastrous campaign in 1879.

this region," said Masloff, pointing to the expanse between Askabad and Sarakhs, "and know what a frightful country it is for an army to traverse. It would be a most difficult matter to march an army even upon Merv in this direction."

I quoted the contrary opinion of Mr. O'Donovan. "He is not a soldier," rejoined Masloff, "and did not look at the country with a soldier's eye. It is one thing for a solitary man, without baggage, to scamper over a country; it is quite another thing for an army to traverse it, weighted with artillery, baggage, and all manner of impediments."

"O'Donovan's book on Merv should be interesting," remarked Grodekoff, "although he writes in an exaggerated style."

"You mean in the sense pointed out by a London paper, that in his description of Merv he calls a 'crimson banner,' what others would have termed a 'bit of red rag.'"

"Yes, in that sense; but now we have established communications with Merv we shall be able to dispense with his descriptions. O'Donovan is a Russophobe, because Tergoukasoff turned him out of the camp, and Skobeleff refused to allow him to proceed to Geok Tepé. The matter did not rest with Skobeleff, but with the Russian Government."

"I also applied," I said, "for permission to

accompany Skobeleff, but could not obtain it. I shall make another attempt, however, to see the country before long. If I fail I trust I shall not turn into a hater of Russia. Personal grievances ought not to be allowed to influence public opinions."

Captain Masloff here sketched the Russian advance in Central Asia from the earliest times, showing how the raids of the border tribes had compelled her to keep on moving, in order to restrain their turbulence and obtain a quiet frontier. The argument is not a new one; its validity has been admitted by many English writers. Prince Krapotkin, who lived some time in exile on the Chinese border, supported it as strenuously in his conversation with me as any Russian official.

The Russian advance in Central Asia has its counterpart in the movement towards the Zambesi River, which is observable in our South African empire. Tribal attacks on the border settlements constantly lead to an extension of the English frontier in that region. There is, however, an essential difference between the two cases. The Russian advances in Central Asia mostly take place with the consent of the home authorities. The English advances in South Africa, on the other hand, are carried on in defiance of the Colonial Office. But then this is also susceptible of explanation. In Russia everything is done by the Government; in England everything by the People. In Russia the Government is the State, in England the State is the People.

When Masloff had finished, Grodekoff repeated the arguments, published in his book, against Merv being regarded as the key of Herat. "The importance of the place is altogether overrated," he said. On my mentioning that Merv was not so much thought of now as Sarakhs, both officers energetically protested against that place being regarded as the key of Herat. "The fact of the matter is," said Masloff, "you give so much attention to the fact of certain centres being what you call "keys," that you altogether overlook the vast distances separating them from the places they are supposed to protect. We have no desire to advance upon Herat; England can occupy the whole of Afghanistan if she likes; but, in occupying Herat you would expose yourself more to being attacked than where you are now."

It being agreed, in the opinion of both officers, that Russia has no designs either upon Afghanistan or Khorassan, an advance upon Merv was discussed. Grodekoff did not believe that the Merv

Tekkes would occasion Russia any more trouble. Neither he nor Masloff considered that anything would arise to cause Russia to advance on the place. A campaign against Merv would be more serious than even Skobeleff's recent one, they said. They did not believe that Skobeleff would ever be sent to Central Asia any more. As to a statement in the *Times* a few days ago, that Skobeleff considered it his mission either to fight England in Central Asia or the Germans in Europe, they laughed at it altogether. I stated that the impression I had gained from my recent interview with Skobeleff was, that he was quite sick of Central Asia. They said that this was a fact.

Captain Masloff expressing some surprise that his little sketches of the siege of Geok Tepé should have been thought worthy of translation into English, I pointed out that the English public was sated with mere English opinion on Central Asia, and was only too anxious to have fresh Russian facts. "England would be only too glad to have also your opinion, for it is years since any authority spoke out in Russia on the Central Asian Question."

"The fact of the matter is," said Masloff, "England thinks a deal of the Central Asian Question, and hence a deal is written about it. But in Russia less importance is attached to it. The public does not think much of it. On this account few books appear on the subject."

"Besides," exclaimed Grodekoff, "what is the good of Russians writing, the English will not believe us. Rawlinson expresses an opinion, Vámbéry confirms it, the English public believe it, and all that we may say is ignored."

"No, no, no," I said. "We English like fair play. Rawlinson is a great *savant*, but he is not everybody. If you write, you will find plenty to listen to you. It has been Russia's misfortune that for years no competent Russian authority has written on Central Asia. We have had to take our impressions of your views from the *Golos* and *Novoe Vremya*, which I do not believe always correctly represent them. Let me urge upon you, General Grodekoff, or you, Captain Masloff, to write a book on the Central Asian Question, from a Russian point of view, and I will translate it, and lay it before the English public."

"I will do it," exclaimed Grodekoff. "I will write a book, Mr. Marvin, for Englishmen to see what we Russians think of the Central Asian Question."

"I am glad to hear your decision," I said. "You may rely upon its having fair consideration."

He then questioned me about Lord Lytton's

scheme, expressed in his Minute in 1876, for moving an Anglo-Indian army into Turkestan, and driving the Russians out of Central Asia by means of this and a revolt among the Mussulmans. The scheme was officially divulged during the Candahar controversy last year, and I gave particulars of it. They laughed very heartily when I had finished. "What a mad scheme," said Grodekoff. "Its deviser had no idea at all of Central Asia. It would be just as easy for Russia to invade India as for England to invade Turkestan. A Mussulman revolt in Central Asia is a most improbable event." When he and Masloff had sufficiently ridiculed the scheme, in the absurdity of which I concurred, I said: "But General Kaufmann also meditated an advance towards India in 1878, for he collected a force at Djam, on the Bokharan frontier. What was his plan?"

Grodekoff shrugged his shoulders. He said that the force did not exceed 15,000 men, and what could they do? He laughed at the idea of their penetrating to Cabul. I said Soboleff had declared Cabul to have been a probable objective point. Grodekoff replied: "Ah, he only said it was a *probable* one." I remarked that we believed that if he had advanced, the Afghans would have co-operated with him against India. "Mr. Marvin," he answered earnestly, "I travelled through Afghan Turkestan in 1878. The Afghans told me that they were quite as ready to fight us as you. They said they would fight any infidel. Look at our envoy to Cabul, Stolietoff. During the whole time he was at Cabul, he dare not show himself in the street for fear of being murdered. And a march across the Hindoo Koosh, too! An impossibility for an army."

"But what was Kaufmann's aim," I asked; "the troops were assembled at Djam?"

Grodekoff again professed his ignorance. He said vaguely that when nations expect war to break out, they do many things. Masloff observed that in Russia very little importance was attached at the time to the expedition. He was right there. From their manner, I assumed that they did not care to discuss this question. It would have been improper for them to have criticised Kaufmann's scheme, more especially Grodekoff, as he still belonged to the Turkestan army, and Kaufmann was his superior officer. But I derived an impression, that if Kaufmann intended in 1878 to march upon India, they disapproved altogether of the undertaking, and regarded it much in the same light they did Lord Lytton's. I have no right to claim this impression as an accurate one, for they treated the matter with extreme reserve, and I gathered my impression, not from any words they uttered, but from their manner. Barring this point, on which it was quite right that they should avoid discussion, they were frank enough. Thus, when I put the question direct to Grodekoff—" Did you leave Tashkent for Herat knowing the Treaty of Berlin to be already signed?" he answered, without hesitation, "Yes." He therefore merits belief when, in reply to my next question—" Did Stolietoff know of the existence of the Treaty of Berlin when he set out on the final stage of his journey from Mazar-i-Sherif to Cabul?"[1] he said "No; he was not aware of it."

During the previous interview, Grodekoff had expressed his disbelief in a junction taking place of the English and Russian frontiers in Central Asia during his lifetime. The railway to India from Kizil Arvat he laughed at altogether. I brought up what General Annenkoff, the designer of the railroad, had said in an article, as to the practicability of throwing 100,000 troops into Herat. "Annenkoff is not a military man," said Grodekoff; "he says that in order to give importance to his scheme. No practical Russian general believes in the possibility of an invasion of India.

---

[1] Grodekoff visited Mazar-i-Sherif while the Russian Embassy was still at Cabul, and stayed some time there.

You are educating the natives—there is your danger. Will they tolerate your presence when educated? Do not fear a Russian invasion of India. We shall never disturb you there; but beware of educating the natives.

On my rising to take my departure, for we had been conversing more than an hour and a half, and I felt tired of talking, Grodekoff asked me whether I now believed in the impossibility of a Russian invasion of India. I did not wish to express an opinion on this point until I had completed my inquiries, so as to be able then to express it with greater weight. I therefore said: "I am quite satisfied that you cannot at present invade it. But your position may change. You may by degrees annex Meshed and Herat, and your position would be better in that case for invading India from those points."

Grodekoff seemed very disappointed at this reply. Both he and Masloff earnestly protested against England believing that Russia has designs against Persia or Afghanistan. They would not admit that she has any desire of advancing along the Tedjen and Heri Rood to Herat. They insisted on the present and prospective impossibility of invading India. To my remark that Russia might have a Skobeleff to make an advance, and England a Burrows to repel it, Masloff said: "But you have other generals besides Burrows. Take Roberts. What a magnificent march he made from Cabul to Candahar. And Stewart, too. And Napier of Magdala. You have good generals, and your troops fought well in the Afghan war. What have you to fear? In what condition would a Russian army arrive at India?"

"The Millennium will take place before Russia invades India," added Grodekoff.

There was no doubting the earnestness of these two men. I know well when I meet an astute or plausible Russian. It was impossible to entertain any suspicion as to the sincerity of their opinions. I felt pained that I should have taken up an incredulous attitude. I therefore told them heartily that I was quite satisfied with their assurances, and with those I had received elsewhere, and that I felt persuaded their opinions would clear the atmosphere very considerably in England.

CHAPTER X.

ENGLAND TO INDIA IN NINE DAYS.

General Annenkoff's scheme for constructing a railroad to India
—His Transcaspian line—Lessar's journey to Sarakhs—
—Comfort in Russia—Annenkoff's knowledge of the literature of the Central Asian Question—Skobeleff and the "Disastrous Russian campaign against the Turcomans"—Invitation to occupy the whole of Afghanistan—Annenkoff's view of the Central Asian Question—The Russian Government and the passage of English troops through Russia on their way to India—An account of his scheme—Rival routes to India—The new Russian railways bringing the Cossack closer to the Sepoy—Russia's aim to tap the overland trade to India—Effect of Annenkoff's scheme upon the Euphrates Valley railway—Evil of English suspicion of Native loyalty in India—Anecdote of Skobeleff —Annenkoff on Khorassan and Sarakhs—Ignorance of the English public regarding the Central Asian Question—His opinion of the evacuation of Candahar and of General Roberts—Annenkoff's wound at Geok Tepé—The present garrison in Akhal—Kouropatkin's march from Samarcand to Geok Tepé—Cultivation of esparto grass in the Transcaspian region—Why Lessar chose to survey the route for the railroad to Sarakhs—Refusal of the English authorities to let him have recent maps of Afghanistan—English policy towards exploration in Central Asia.

St. Petersburg, March 16.

"London to India in nine days" sounds incredible, but such is the rapidity possible if General Annenkoff's scheme for continuing the railway from

Kizil Arvat to the Bolan Pass ever be carried out. The scheme has caused a good deal of talk in Russia, and has even ruffled official placidity in England; but little is known to the English public of the details of the project, and still less of the original and daring promoter of it. When Annenkoff put forward his plan in 1880 for constructing a railway from the Caspian coast to the edge of the Akhal Tekke oasis, it was laughed at; and in a not-yet-forgotten answer to a question put by Mr. Ashmead-Bartlett, the Marquis of Hartington scoffed and scouted the idea. Undismayed by opposition at home and ridicule abroad, General Annenkoff steadily worked at his project, and notwithstanding difficulties of the gravest nature completed his railway to Kizil Arvat last summer. Then the English public, ever ready to pass from excessive self-confidence to agonies of alarm, imagined all manner of dangers arising from the advancing locomotive, and became as anxious about any development of the scheme as it had been callous before to it. Rumours of the most exaggerated character circulated as to the progress and terminal point of the line. In a bitter speech Lord Salisbury declared the Russian locomotive to be already at Askabad, instead of being very little more than half-way there; and when Lessar, the engineer, turned up at Sarakhs, whither he had proceeded to survey the route, some alarmists saw the railway already rushing on at a rapid rate to the " Key of India." I learned last night from the Vice-President of the Imperial Geographical Society, while conversing with him after the usual fortnightly meeting, that Lessar had set out again for the Turcoman region, to continue his investigations, and this morning the news was confirmed when I paid a visit to General Annenkoff himself.

The general occupies a handsome suite of rooms, richly furnished, on the first floor of one of the newer houses in the aristocratic Bolshoi Morskoi. We are apt in England to consider that we alone possess notions of comfort, and that foreigners, while surpassing us sometimes in magnificence, fail lamentably in providing for cosiness and convenience in a mansion. This is a great mistake so far as the Russians are concerned. Russians share with the English people their love of home, and it is probably owing to this that Charles Dickens is better known and more widely read in Russia than in any other country on the Continent. I have seen country houses in the interior of Russia built and fitted up with a most astonishing regard for comfort; and there is this to be said of all Russian houses— uncomfortable as well as comfortable—that an equable temperature is maintained throughout them, and that they are completely free from draughts. The room into which I was ushered this morning was perfect in these respects, and in the interval that elapsed before the general was disengaged, my time was divided between admiring the elegance of the furniture, the crowded oil paintings on the walls, the handsome vases, and the bookcases crammed with books; and the snugness with which the furniture was arranged in the spacious apartment. But the library into which the general conducted me, and in which our conversation took place, was still more to my taste. Arranged in one huge carved bookcase, occupying the greater part of a wall, were some thousands of books, in various languages, dealing with Central Asia, with railways, with war, with exploration, with literature and politics, and other subjects. The window-sills were heaped up with books. Spare tables, disposed about the room, groaned under them; and they even encroached upon the limited space left for working purposes amidst the handsome and curious knicknacks on the library table. I knew that the general was an assiduous reader of foreign works on the East, for in some articles he published in the *Vestnik Evropi* (*European Mercury*) some time ago, the quotations and references he made indicated a knowledge of the most recent books on the Central Asian and Eastern Questions; but I was unprepared to find him possessing such a large number of English works, and giving a wide space in the bottom of his bookcase to the cumbrous blue-books issued by the English Government. The general tells me he has long entertained the idea of publishing a work on the Central Asian Question, from a Russian point of view, and should he carry out this intention, which, it is very probable, he will do shortly, his opinions will bear all the more weight from the fact of their being based upon such extended knowledge. He speaks very good English, has pleasant reminiscences of visits to England to hunt there, and has an unaffected admiration for the English people. Neither of us needed any formal introduction to the other, for he had only recently reviewed my "Merv" in his brochure, "The Akhal Oasis and Roads to India," and I had also noticed his project for a railway to India in the *Army and Navy Magazine*. He told me afterwards that he and General Skobeleff read my "Disastrous Russian Campaign against the Turcomans" together, while making the final preparations for the siege of Geok Tepé, and that General Skobeleff, expressing approval of an opinion embodied in my criticism of Lomakin's operations, that that general ought to have left a good officer of rank behind to look after the communications, instead of taking all the general officers with him to the front, appointed him to the command of the line from the Caspian to Geok Tepe.

"I do not understand," he said, at the outset of our conversation, "why the two countries should be kept so wide apart. There is nothing to separate us except the Central Asian Question; and that is no question at all. Why cannot we come to some understanding, and be friends? We can both be of help to one another. Occupy the whole of Afghanistan, occupy Herat, if you like—we will not grumble at it. If Merv is of such importance, occupy Merv also. At any rate, let us do something to dissipate the misconceptions prevailing. Every Russian will tell you that we do not wish to invade India, and if England could rid herself of this idea, there would be no Central Asian Question left."

"And the Eastern Question?"

"Here again there are misconceptions. Russia does not want to annex the Balkan Peninsula. Let the people there govern themselves, and form themselves into States like Servia and Montenegro. As for Constantinople, give it to Bulgaria, or form it into a free port under a European protectorate. You fear that we should swallow up the Balkan Peninsula by degrees, but it would be most difficult for us to do so. Accustomed to different institutions, the people would be impatient of Russian control. I wish that England could understand what our real aims are. There is nothing between the two countries to prevent friendship, such as prevails between Russia and Germany. Personally, I do not share the warlike feeling against the Teutons which exists in some quarters. I hate war. But it is impossible to ignore the fact that the conflict between Slav and Teuton in Germany and Austria is such, that we cannot be friends. The matter is different with England and Russia. A railroad to India would promote friendship. If Russia completed the present Transcaspian line to Herat, and England prolonged the Bolan Pass railway to the same point, your troops could then proceed to India from London to Sukhur, on the Indus, *viâ* Calais, Berlin, Warsaw, and the Russian system to the Caspian; thence *viâ* Michaelovsk, Askabad, Sarakhs, Herat, and Candahar, in the space of nine days. The whole distance would be accomplished overland, except the portion of sea from Calais to Dover, and the twelve hours' run across the Caspian."

"Do you think that the Russian Government would consent to the passage of English troops through its territory?"

"I think so. I do not speak, of course, officially, but I think no difficulty would arise. At any rate, the line could be used by officers and merchants."

Whether England would care to send troops through Russia to India, and whether the Russian Government would object to it, are points that cannot be determined, but so far as the possibility of transporting the troops such a distance by rail is concerned, Annenkoff's affirmative belief is of value, since he speaks with the experience of a man who supervised the whole of the arrangements for conveying the Russian army to Turkey in 1877, and again controlled the despatch of the force from the Caspian to Geok Tepé in 1880. In excess of the abnormal experience arising from the transport of a million and a half of men and 600,000 horses during the Russo-Turkish war, he is fortified in what he says by the knowledge derived from the almost daily movement of large bodies of troops in Russia. Maintaining the vast army that Russia does, and requiring constantly to move men and *matériel* from one part of the empire to another, traversing enormous distances, a controller of military transport must naturally be exposed to all manner of difficulties. On this account, his opinions as to the transport of troops must be very different from those of a light-hearted, irresponsible enthusiast.

When he therefore says that Russia could arrange for the quick despatch of English reliefs to India *via* Afghanistan, in preference to the Suez Canal or Euphrates routes, he speaks with an authority which few will care to question.

Whether his scheme be adopted this side of the twentieth century or not, there is this to be said about it: That it is the shortest, quickest, and most feasible project that has yet been presented to the public. This will be seen by an extract from his brochure referred to—" The Oasis of Akhal Tekke and the Roads to India"—which excited so much attention in Russia, when published last year.

"At the present moment there are only two routes by which Indian goods proceed to Europe, or rather, to the docks of England—those immense reservoirs of the products of the Far East—namely, the Cape route, mainly for sailing vessels, and the steamer route *via* Suez.

"I. The Cape route, from Falmouth to Bombay, *via* St. Helena, is 10,400 miles long, and occupies forty-two days.

"II. The Suez Canal route, from Falmouth to Bombay, *via* Malta and Alexandria, is 6000 miles long, and occupies twenty-four days.

"The progress which the latter has made may be seen from the following figures :—

Year.	Number of Ships traversing the Canal.	Dues levied.
1869	10	49,600 francs.
1870	486	5,048,394 ,,
1877	1663	32,554,548 ,,

"But, however short a road may be, there is always a desire to find a shorter one. Hence a number of projects have been brought forward for establishing a still shorter and quicker route to India than by sea, *viâ* Suez.

"I. Paris to Calcutta, *viâ* Brindisi, Alexandria, Suez, Aden, and Bombay. Distance, 6164 miles.

"II. Scutari to Bombay, by two rival routes to Alexandretta, then *viâ* Aleppo, the Euphrates, and Bagdad to Busorah, and afterwards by water to Bombay. Distance, 3380 miles.

"III. Lessep's route. Paris to Calcutta, *viâ* Orenburg, Tashkent, Balkh, and Peshawur, overland the whole way, instead of partly by land and partly by water, as the case with the others. Distance, 5783 miles.

"IV." (Annenkoff's route). "Paris to Sukhur on the Indus, *viâ* Warsaw, Moscow, Baku, Michaelovsk, Kizil Arvat, Sarakhs, Herat, Candahar, and Quetta. Distance, 4326 miles.

"The final route is the shortest and most convenient. It has further this signal advantage, that it only traverses 125 versts (eighty-three miles) of desert, the whole of which has been already constructed, while there are 740 versts (490 miles) of desert to Lessep's Orenburg route, and 720 (477 miles) to the Euphrates Valley Railway."

Such is a brief abstract of General Annenkoff's route to India. When the Baku-Tiflis Railway is completed in the course of the summer, there will be *direct railway communication the whole of the way from the Russian capital to the latest annexation in Central Asia*, from St. Petersburg to Kizil Arvat. Thus :—

St. Petersburg to Odessa by rail	3 days.
Odessa to Poti across Black Sea	2 ,,
Poti to Baku by rail	1 ,,
Baku to Michaelovsk across Caspian	$1\frac{1}{2}$,,
Michaelovsk to Kizil Arvat by rail	$\frac{1}{2}$
Russian capital to Central Asian outpost	8 days.

This is a rough outside estimate, taking no notice of the continuous accelerated service forming part of Annenkoff's projected rapid journey to India. England is severed from India by sea; she cannot quicken her steamship communication with her eastern empire very much beyond its present point. On the other hand, Central Asia is simply a continuation of the south-east Russian steppes, and every verst of railway constructed brings Russia closer to India. There is a significance in this that should not be lost sight of by English politicians. They should remember that they govern the Empire, not only on behalf of themselves, but for those who will come after them.

I have shown that the Russian railway system extends to Kizil Arvat. From this point to Sarakhs no difficulties whatever exist, according to General Annenkoff, and it is not believed that any will be found between Sarakhs and Herat. Estimates that have been framed show that the line could be cheaply constructed, owing to the level character of the country and the absence of rivers of any size. Irrespective of the military and political considerations that have governed the construction of nearly every mile of railway in Russia, there exists in this case in excess the almost irresistible temptation to seize upon the overland trade of India. In his brochure, General Annenkoff points out that in every age the countries through which the trade of India has freely passed, on its way to the west, have become enormously enriched by it. This is the prize he seeks to secure for Russia. He says it is hers geographically. He asserts that there is nothing in the construction of the railway that should cause uneasiness to England.

Personally I believe the construction of the line to be more than possible; I regard it as probable. We have seen its feasibility on the Russian side—from Kizil Arvat to Herat. With respect to the English section, plans for the construction of a railway from the Indian system at Sibi to the city of Candahar were approved of during the Afghan war, and the line would have been completed had the Conservatives remained in power. There would have thus been left only the link between Candahar and Herat, which Russian experts say is even less difficult to traverse than the country stretching from Candahar to Sibi. In this manner, the uncompleted links between the Russian and the Indian railway systems, may be arranged as follows:—

Russian section, from Kizil Arvat terminus to Herat 455 miles.
English section, from Sibi terminus to Herat ... 599 ,,

Total ... ... 1054 ,,

"This," said Annenkoff, as he turned round from rummaging on a window-sill for a bundle of blue-books and documents referring to the Euphrates Valley railway, "would be a complete junction of the European and Indian railway systems; whereas the Euphrates railway is but an unconnected link, with a sea passage at either end."

The Euphrates Valley scheme, running from

Alexandretta on the Mediterranean to Grain in the Persian Gulf, would be 920 miles long, and would cost ten millions sterling. The result of its construction would be, to shorten the journey from England to India by 1000 miles, and enable troops to reach Kurratchee in a fortnight. Delhi, Lahore, and Peshawur would take two or three days longer.

The railway from the Caspian to Kizil Arvat cost 30,000 roubles, or 3000*l.* a verst (two-thirds of a mile). Its construction beyond would be considerably less than this. Annenkoff hopes to see it completed to India in his lifetime, but its success necessarily depends upon the attitude that England takes up towards the scheme. There is also an opposition existing in Russia, for, as I have already stated, neither Skobeleff nor Grodekoff favours the scheme. Skobeleff, however, believes the line will be completed to Askabad. Semenoff, the Vice-President of the Geographical Society, on the other hand, approves of the project. General Annenkoff thinks his scheme has swallowed up all others, but there is this to be said, that if Russia runs on her railway to India, we shall need a railway of our own to fall back upon in time of war. In showing me the blue-books and maps dealing with the Euphrates Valley scheme, General Annenkoff spoke of that project as abandoned, but, as a matter of fact his plan really revives it, and brings Sir William Andrew to the front once more. This, however, does not in any way affect the excellence of the scheme for curtailing the journey to India from a month to nine days.

English opposition to his project may be expected to proceed from a fear that the railway will facilitate a Russian invasion. "That cuts both ways," said a Russian officer to me a few days ago. "Once the line is laid down, it will be as simple for you to advance along it from one end as we from the other." On my pointing out that there would be a large Russian army at one end, and a small English force with doubtful native levies at the other, he rejoined, "You may depend upon it, Mr. Marvin, that when matters come to such a pass in India that you cannot trust your own subjects, it won't be a mere railway then that will upset your rule. But apart from this, has England never considered that the very way to make India turn against her is to be always telling the natives that they are not to be trusted. In our recent war, Skobeleff encountered a number of Tekke Turcomans, while out riding a few days after the occupation of Askabad. 'Who are you?' he demanded. 'Friendly Tekkes,' they replied. 'How am I to believe that,' he asked, 'you bear arms.' 'A Tekke never lies,' answered a Khan proudly. 'Very well, then,' said Skobeleff, dismissing his suite, 'fall in behind me, and escort me back to Askabad.' And, without any Russian defenders, he rode off to the fort, surrounded by a lot of wild fellows who had been fighting desperately at Geok Tepé only a few days previous. I say nothing of the bravery of Skobeleff, but it is his trustfulness I would indicate to you as an element you need in India. Men are men all the world over. They are everywhere proud of having confidence reposed in them. Russia, plus the Herat railway, could do nothing against England and India united; but if things were in such a condition that the natives were against you, then Russia would succeed whether she had a railway or not."

Colonel Kostenko would like to see the English and Russian empires touch in Central Asia, in order that there might be nothing left between them to quarrel about. Gospodin Semenoff would like to see a junction, in the interests of science. General Annenkoff, on his part, favours an alignment, because it would facilitate the accomplishment of his pet project. There is no Anglophobia in either of these wishes. They are altogether distinct from what is considered to be the great aim of Russian foreign policy—to take up such a dominant position on the confines of India, as shall render us incapable of being hostile to Russia in Europe.

If the solution of the Central Asian Question rested in the hands of Annenkoff there would be an end to the controversy. He is most generously disposed towards England. He would make any concessions to put an end to the ill-feeling between the two countries. He does not believe in the possibility of a Russian invasion of India, but he refused to argue the question—" Why waste time on this point? What have we got to fight about? We do not want Afghanistan. We shall not try to annex Khorassan. In your book, 'Merv, the Queen of the World,' which, as you know, I have read, you accuse Russia of designs on Meshed, but none such exist. We shall not attempt to take it from Persia—we have no desire for it at all. As for the Turcoman country beyond Askabad, if any troubles arise it can be formed into a territory under Russian protection. In its advance to Herat, the railway need not traverse purely Persian territory at all; it can go through Turcoman Sarakhs. Persian Sarakhs we have no desire to take. It is quite safe."

Referring then to his visits to England, he said that he found everybody there having most violent opinions on the Central Asian Question, without knowing scarcely anything at all on the subject.[1] If they knew the region better, and understood Russia more, he said, they would cease to regard the Central Asian Question as possessing any great importance. He said it was a great mistake in Central Asia to retire from conquered territories. If Russia had resigned Akhal, she would have been compelled to repeat the expedition after a course of years. Our evacuation of Candahar he considered a glaring error. Referring to the Afghan war, he spoke in terms of eulogy of General Roberts's march from Cabul to Candahar. "He is a splendid general," he said. He expressed a strong desire to see India, which has been visited by only four Russians during the last quarter of a century; but, said he, "I am afraid of the howl that would be raised at the arrival of a Russian general." I assured him that, known as he is as the projector of the shortest way to India, he would hardly excite so much alarm as he imagined, and would, on the other hand, be welcomed. He again earnestly expressed a desire to see India, and at his request I wrote down the names of the latest English books on the country for him to add to his library.

Annenkoff took part in Skobeleff's campaign

---

[1] The same complaint was made to me personally by Vámbéry on the occasion of his last visit to England.

against the Turcomans, and was wounded in the arm during the reconnaissance of Geok Tepé on the 30th of December, the day before the capture of Yangi Kala and the commencement of the siege. The bullet went through the fleshy part of the right arm, near the shoulder, and occasioned no trouble at first, but after awhile the nerves began to contract, and he suffered intense pain, which became almost unbearable while on his way home. Even now that he is nearly cured, every change in the weather causes his arm to ache. Although he has had a long and eventful career, he is only forty-five years old. His partial baldness, however, makes him look older.

In conversing with him about the new Transcaspian territory, I referred to the intelligence published in the *Novoe Vremya*, that eight line battalions were to be established there. He said: " This will excite a fresh outcry in England, but it simply means the withdrawal of the present temporary garrison, which is made up of drafts from different regiments, &c., and the formation of a permanent one, as in Turkestan. The total of the eight battalions will be about 8000 men." The explanation coincided with my own previous impressions on the subject, and has since been confirmed by intelligence from the Caucasus.

After lunch we had a long chat about the

recent operations against the Turcomans. Among other things he said: "It is difficult for Skobeleff to have a good chief of the staff—he does so much himself. Kouropatkin, his chief at Plevna, is a splendid officer. He made the march, you know, from Samarcand to Geok Tepé. When he was approaching Akhal I collected water and made all manner of preparations at Bami to meet him, for his column was overdue and we did not know in what condition it might be in. I myself went out three or four marches to meet him, and really it was wonderful to see how he came along. After a spell of twenty miles' marching across the desert, he would arrive at the halting-place with his bands playing, and his troops dressed up as though on a parade. Kouropatkin is now in Turkestan, commander of the Rifle Brigade."

Some years ago Kouropatkin and Kostenko paid a visit to Algeria, and it was doubtless the suggestion of the former, who had noticed that certain plants thrived upon the sandy soil in Lesser Sahara, that led the Russian authorities to endeavour to acclimatize esparto in the Transcaspian region.

In his article on "The French Permanent Camel-Train in Algeria,"[1] Kouropatkin says:—

[1] A good translation will be found in the *Army and Navy Magazine* for Dec. 1881 and Jan. 1882.

"Alfa (*stipa tenassima*) is a grass that occupies the first place in importance, covering as it does hundreds of square versts. *Alfa* serves as the food of camels, horses, sheep, cows, and goats. It possesses a strong fibre, and is used in the domestic life of the Arabs in making cords, baskets, &c. Of late years it has been found possible to make paper out of *Alfa*, and its export for this purpose increases every year, amounting already to ten million francs (400,000*l*.)."

Annenkoff told me that a Russian man-of-war had recently touched at Algiers to get specimens of *Alfa* to plant alongside the railway in the Transcaspian region. Already vast deposits of naphtha and ozokerit have been found close to the line, and should esparto thrive, the Transcaspian steppes will not prove to have been a barren conquest.

* * * * *

I saw Annenkoff more than once during my stay at St. Petersburg, and I found him on every occasion full of the friendliest feelings towards England. He was looking forward to an opportunity of coming to England to discuss the Indian railway scheme with our leading men; and, if possible, of paying a visit to India itself in connexion with his project. He told me he had chosen Lessar as the explorer of the railway to

Sarakhs, "because he was a young man, and young men are mostly honest."

He said that Lessar had just been to England to endeavour to obtain some recent maps, published by the English Government, of the country between Sarakhs and India; but that the War Office had refused to let him have any. I consoled him by saying that Lessar probably lost nothing by the refusal. When Colonel Valentine Baker proceeded to the Turcoman region in 1873, he found the secret and confidential English War Office maps to be obsolete rubbish, and threw them away in disgust. On that occasion, however, the Russian Government acted differently from the English authorities. When he reached Tiflis the latest maps of the Turcoman region— "splendid ones," he describes them—were freely placed at his disposal by the Grand Duke Michael.

He spoke of the restlessness engendered by residence in Central Asia. I have already referred to the nomad proclivities of Grodekoff. Gospodin Serebriakoff, who was present when this remark was made, said: "It is very curious how nomadized people become who visit Central Asia. They want to be always pushing onwards. Lessar, for instance, is infected with it, and is eager to renew his explorations beyond Sarakhs."

I observed that there would be a great outcry in England if he penetrated to Herat. It is not at all improbable, however, that he will not do so. It is a useless matter for English statesmen to desire or expect things to remain as they are in Central Asia. Their present policy of discouraging all intercourse with Afghanistan or beyond it, and of expressing alarm or anger when Russians try to push their way over the few hundred miles of space intervening between the two empires, is as childish as the old exclusiveness of the Chinese towards foreigners. It cannot be defended on grounds of high policy, nor yet on any other. It is almost time a stop was put to it, for it is contrary to our belief in John Bull's pluck that he should skulk behind the Afghan border, and content himself with merely giving vent to an inexpensive yell (nothing more, for fear of the taxpayer) every time he sees a Russian " White Cap " approaching in the direction of India.

CHAPTER XI.

REFUSAL OF PERMISSION TO PROCEED TO ASKABAD.

An offer from an important Russian personage to pay a visit to Askabad—A second call upon General Soboleff—Arrival of an officer from Geok Tepé—The recent expedition, under another general than Skobeleff, might have ended in disaster—Soboleff refuses to give me permission to proceed to Akhal—His opposition to English exploration of Central Asia—Lessar's journey towards Herat—Fewness of Russian travellers visiting India—List of Russian explorers in Central Asia since 1854—Disfavour shown by the English Government to exploration of Afghanistan—Apathy and want of patriotism of the Royal Geographical Society—Effect of Burnaby's "Ride to Khiva"—Russian indignation at the publication of Schuyler's "Turkistan."—The Krijanovsky frauds at Orenburg and their bearing upon Russian corruption in Turkestan—The Yomood massacre, the Lomakin massacre, and the massacre at Geok Tepé—Opinion of Soboleff on the subject—Frightful scenes during the pursuit after the fall of Geok Tepé—Murder of sixty Russians by the Tekkes—Mr. Gladstone left to deal with the three massacres.

ST. PETERSBURG, March 17.

I CALLED on General Soboleff to-day, to make rather an important proposition to him. In discussing the Russian operations in Akhal a few days previously with an influential personage, whose name under the circumstances I had perhaps better suppress, he had said—"We have nothing to hide from you in our new province. What I have told you about our operations there you would find confirmed if you proceeded personally to Akhal. But why not go to Askabad and see yourself what we are doing there? I do not see why you should not get permission to go. If it rested with me you should have it at once, but this does not concern my department, but General Soboleff's. Ask him, and if he allows you to go, as I feel certain he will, I will do all I can to facilitate your journey thither."

Although the main object of my journey had been to have a conversation with Skobeleff, still the *Newcastle Chronicle* had intimated that if I saw my way to extending my mission advantageously, I was at liberty to do so. The offer seemed to meet my instructions, and I was all the more ready to accept it, on account of the exceptional assistance that could be rendered me by the personage, by whom it was made. Moreover, the season was propitious for a journey in the Turcoman region, and Askabad could have been reached in three weeks' time without any particular hardship or difficulty. The personage who wished me so much to go there had been concerned in the recent expedition, and occupied a position that would have enabled him to smooth my way from St. Petersburg itself to the final Cossack outpost at Gyaoors.

His assistance, however, was of no value unless permission could be obtained from the Government to proceed to the newly annexed territory, and it was for the purpose of soliciting this that I called upon General Soboleff this afternoon. I had to wait a little while for him, as he was out of the room, but the interval was pleasantly spent in listening to the description which an officer, who had just arrived from Geok Tepé, gave of Skobeleff's siege to the officers of the department. He had shared the whole of the fighting, and narrated in a most graphic manner the more telling incidents of the desperate conflict, which, under any general less brilliant than Skobeleff, would have probably ended disastrously for the Russian army.

On the arrival of General Soboleff, I stated that I had been very pleased with the assurances I had received from the personages I had met, and that there remained only one thing now to give a finishing touch to my mission—namely, a run to Askabad and back. "Impossible," said Soboleff, in a tone that showed clearly his mind was made up. He is very much opposed to Englishmen visiting

The Policy of being so very humble. 191

any part of Central Asia, even Khorassan, which is Persian territory, and I found that it was of no use trying to shake his decision. Russia may throw out explorers in front of her in Central Asia, but Englishmen must not haunt the Persian frontier. For instance, I have just mentioned that Lessar, the engineer who surveyed the route for the railway to Sarakhs, has set out to investigate the region between Sarakhs and Herat. It has been represented to me that he would like to go to Herat itself, and as he is very enterprising and courageous, he may disregard his orders to the contrary. Russia does not see that we have any right to be offended if she sends her explorers running about the region between Akhal and Afghanistan, but she holds that she has a right to complain if we do the same. This is a little too much.

Of course Russia can allege that she never sends travellers prying about India, and therefore may resent the intrusion of English visitors in her territories in Central Asia. During the last quarter of a century she has sent only four travellers to India, and none of these have written anything that has survived the customary rapid decay of ordinary current literature. In 1881 Colonel Venukoff published an interesting list of the whole of the Russian travellers (323 in number) who had explored Asia in the course of the previous twenty-seven years, i.e. from 1854 This showed at a glance what parts of the continent had attracted the attention of Russia most, and may be inserted here.

	TRAVELLERS.
Western Turkestan, or the basin of the Caspian Sea and Turcomania	84
Eastern Siberia, without the Amoor and Maritime Province	54
Mantchooria, Mongolia, and Djoungaria	45
The Amoor and Maritime Province	41
Western Siberia without the steppes	37
Transcaucasia and Asiatic Turkey	22
Kirghiz steppes of Orenburg and Siberia	17
China proper	15
Persia and Afghanistan	14
Corea, Saghalien, Japan, and the Kurile Archipelago	13
Eastern Turkestan and Thibet	11
India and Ceylon	4
Indo-Chinese Peninsula	3
Arabia and Beluchestan	0

The majority of these have been despatched under the auspices of the Russian Government. Every Russian advance has been followed by the thorough scientific exploration of the territory annexed, and the despatch of pioneers into the unconquered country in front of it. Thus, at the present moment, Russia is preparing to survey the whole of the new province of Akhal, while caravans are making their way to Merv, and

Lessar and his associates pushing on to Sarakhs and the region beyond stretching up to Herat. This process will probably go on until India is reached.

Formerly England paid great attention to the exploration of Central Asia; and Afghanistan, Bokhara, and Persia were overrun by travellers and agents, like Burnes, Abbott, Fraser, and a score of others. Recently, however, the successive English Governments have done their utmost to restrain travellers from stirring out of India; and every effort has been made to keep English officers from penetrating to the remoter parts of Afghanistan. I do not see what gain is derived from this policy, as it is not reciprocated by any corresponding action on the part of Russia. In a word, it is a policy that simply plays our interests into Russia's hands, and leaves the intervening territory between Turkestan and India to be dealt with and influenced by her as she pleases.

At the same time it is impossible not to notice the extraordinary indifference manifested by the Royal Geographical Society towards Central Asian travel. Whatever opinions may be entertained in regard to Russia's advance in Central Asia, all Englishmen are agreed that we ought to be kept well informed as to what she is doing there. It is one of the duties of the Geographical Society to make known to the public the progress and the results of foreign research. Now the proceedings of the Russian Imperial Geographical Society are almost entirely taken up with accounts of exploration along the Russian frontier in Asia. A vast amount of information is periodically published, dealing with these researches, which, for want of a translator, lies dormant in the Russian language. The charge I formulate against the Royal Geographical Society is this, that it makes no attempt to avail itself of this mine of wealth for the benefit of the public, nor yet in any way encourages the dissemination of information dealing with the Central Asian region. If the truth must be told, the society spends the whole of its time upon Africa and the North Pole. Africa, I will admit, is a very important region, and we have great interests there, but those interests are not so pressing as those in Central Asia. As for the North Pole, of what profit will be the discovery of that Arctic mystery, if we lose Herat, "the key of India?" The Russian Imperial Geographical Society—which is not so governmental as is commonly believed—has one great feature that gives it its popularity in Russia. It is deeply patriotic. It has always at heart the interests of the empire. Its fundamental principle is, that the exploration of the Russian empire and the adjacent outlying region should precede the investigation of distant countries. It holds that if travellers are to be encouraged at all, Russian ones should certainly have the preference. Towards young explorers and struggling authors it displays a spirit of kindly appreciation and readiness to assist, which one looks for in vain in our own society; and when a traveller distinguishes himself, like Prejevalsky has done in Thibet, it gives him a greeting on his return, such as puts to shame the chilliness and the cliquishness of the English association.

As, in making my request, I was well aware of the disinclination of the Russian Government to allow Central Asia to be explored by English travellers, I was not very much disappointed at Soboleff's refusal. In its policy of keeping Central Asia dark the Russian Government is the principal sufferer; just as the general, who keeps away newspaper correspondents from his army, loses the whole of the lustre a graphic writer like Forbes can impart to great achievements. If Central Asia were thrown open to Englishmen, Tashkent and Askabad might be visited by Russophobes, but they would certainly be reached also by Russophils. A single work by a Central Asian Mackenzie Wallace would more than repair all the damage done by successive " Rides to Khiva."

For Colonel Burnaby and Eugene Schuyler the Russians have no love. "The Ride to Khiva" and "Turkistan" have sealed Central Asia to English-speaking travellers for years, and there is little chance of the Russian portals of that region being opened again till the Russo-Indian Question is at rest; which will not be for some years yet. I have never been able to understand why Schuyler's "Turkistan" should be regarded so unfavourably by Russians. Annenkoff denounced it strongly during one of my conversations with him. Yet, taken on the whole, Schuyler makes out a wonderfully good case for Russia in her conquest of Central Asia, and speaks more disrespectfully of English policy than he does of Russian. The chief causes of the offence he gave Russia were his disclosure of the administrative corruption in Turkestan, and his denunciation of the Yomood Turcoman massacre.

As regards the first there is nothing he writes in his book, which in any way approaches the guiltiness brought home to Adjutant-General Krijanovsky a year ago, and for which a few months ago that governor-general of Orenburg was ignominiously expelled the Russian service. The Russian province of Turkestan was a development of the province of Orenburg; it was formed to a considerable extent by the bureaucracy presided over by Krijanovsky. If the parent province of Orenburg was saturated with corruption, misrule, and oppression to an extent that angered and amazed Russian society—which is used to all this sort of thing—and compelled the Tsar to abolish the whole administrative structure of Orenburg at a stroke, besides disgracing the Governor-General and the Minister of Crown Domains, Prince Lieven, as the only means of cleansing the Augean stable, what kind of government might we expect to find in Turkestan—its offshoot? A good tree does not bring forth evil fruit, nor does an evil tree bring forth good fruit. Mr. Schuyler simply recapitulated in his work Russian charges made by Russians themselves against the Turkestan administration, and these are constantly being substantiated by fresh allegations in the Russian press.

With regard to the Yomood massacre, everything that has been published of the Russian mode of warfare since 1876 has strengthened his case against General Kaufmann. The massacre itself has been surpassed by Lomakin's bombardment of women and children at Dengeel Tepé in 1879, when the Cossacks drove the fugitive families of the Tekkes back into the fortified encampment, to be there mown down by hundreds by the guns.[1]

While Soboleff and myself were talking, an officer brought into the department an English blue-book on Afghanistan, which was no doubt being employed in the compilation of the Russian official account of the war. When he had finished consulting Soboleff and had gone away, the latter asked me what points I had discussed with Skobeleff. I mentioned the Slaughter of the Eight thousand. "The killing of the women caused a deal of comment in England," I said. "You hanged people at Cabul," he rejoined. "After a trial," I replied; "but our generals did not kill women and children."

An officer who was present during the pursuit following the assault at Geok Tepé, told me a few days ago that the Cossacks slashed the women to pieces as they ran shrieking before them, or dropped on their knees imploring mercy; and that the babies, falling out of their arms on the sands, afterwards died of cold or starvation. Many of the women and children were subsequently brought in; but the officer told me several hundred women at least were killed by the Cossacks, and that most of the children left on

---

[1] "The Disastrous Russian Campaign against the Turcomans" gives a circumstantial account of this massacre.

the sands at night were found dead the next morning.

"It was war," said Soboleff, smiling and shrugging his shoulders, in reply to what I said; "in war women get killed as well as men."

"Our generals do not kill women," I retorted, and there the matter dropped. It is one that will be fully treated in my forthcoming work on "Skobeleff's Siege of Geok Tepé," and it is upon the Russian evidence and defence adduced that Humanity will base its opinion.

I may mention that another officer, who was present at the siege, told me recently that he considered the total of 8000 exaggerated. He asserted that Grodekoff had counselled the slaughter, on the grounds that our blowing away of the Sepoys from the guns in India during the Mutiny had struck terror into the natives, and raised our prestige. I pointed out that the Indian army was enraged by the dishonouring of the English women by the Sepoys. "The Tekkes butchered sixty of our prisoners in Geok Tepé," he replied. This was the first Russian admission of this massacre I had heard. O'Donovan telegraphed the news home, but Skobeleff does not mention it in his official report. I urged that there was no resemblance between the two cases. In the recent wars both the Zulus and the Afghans massacred some hundreds of our troops, but we did not retort by slaughtering women and children. The officer, however, did not see anything in Skobeleff's slaughter of the 8000 Turcomans after the capture of Geok Tepé to provoke criticism.

Mr. Gladstone extenuated and did his best to explain away the Yomood massacre. I leave it to him for the moment to deal with the slaughter at Geok Tepé. By ignoring the Lomakin massacre he left it to be inferred that he treated it as a matter of course. The same is the case with the slaughter at Geok Tepé.

It is because I have such a great personal regard for Skobeleff, that I myself sincerely regret that any women and children should have been killed at all by the Russian troops after the capture of that fortress. I also should like to ignore the slaughter; but, claiming to be impartial, I have no right to suppress this feeling, although it pains me to have to express it.

CHAPTER XII.

PROFESSOR MARTENS AND RUSSIAN INTERESTS IN HERAT AND AFGHANISTAN.

The position which the various Russian authorities on Central Asia occupy to one another—Influence exercised by General Soboleff and Professor Martens—The bargaining feature of Russian policy—"The catspaw of the wily Gortschakoff" —How Martens' brochure on Central Asia came to be written—His opinion that England ought not to have Herat, and that we ought to keep out of Afghanistan— Lord Hartington's declaration of English policy—Baron Jomini's threat—Proposition to turn Herat into an Asiatic Switzerland—Russian claims to Afghanistan—A red rag to English Russophobists—Necessity for deciding upon a clear and consistent policy for England to pursue in Central Asia—England much to blame for the Central Asian agitation—Professor Martens and Sir Charles Dilke's declaration anent the evacuation of the Akhal Tekke region —The secret Cabul correspondence—Kaufmann's policy in Central Asia—General Stolietoff in disgrace.

ST. PETERSBURG, March 18.

My interview with Professor Martens to-day was attended with the most important expression of opinion regarding Afghanistan and Herat, that has yet marked my conversations with the eminent

Russians controlling the course of the Central Asian Question. As was pointed out to me a few days ago by a Russian personage of weight, Skobeleff and Grodekoff have dropped out of the race as regards Central Asia, and, practically speaking, exercise no influence over Russian policy in that region. Should a fresh war with the Turcomans take place, then Skobeleff and Grodekoff would again come to the front; but, as things now are, Russian policy in Central Asia is guided by M. de Giers, the head of the Russian Foreign Office, General Soboleff, the head of the Asiatic Department of the General Staff, and Professor Martens, Professor of International Law at the St. Petersburg University, author of two well-known brochures on Central Asia, and member of the Imperial Council dealing with Foreign Affairs.

Of course the Tsar has his own opinion on Central Asia, and General Ignatieff is too ambitious and too clever not to influence Russian policy in that region, and make it subservient to his Eastern policy; but both of them take counsel, more or less often, from the three persons above mentioned, and cannot but be more or less affected by the views they express. M. de Giers possesses great weight from the fact of his having been some time Minister at the Persian Court. General

Soboleff is equally influential, owing to his knowledge of Turkestan and his mastery of English operations in Afghanistan. In General Miliutin's time, his influence was limited by the intimate knowledge which that able Minister also possessed of Central Asian affairs, and his strong and unswerving convictions on the subject. But the present Minister of War, General Vannovsky, knows nothing of Central Asia, and Soboleff is therefore supreme. As regards Martens, he is member of the Council that meets at the Foreign Office from time to time to discuss foreign affairs, and, from what I have gathered from his own lips, and those of other people, he exercises an influence which daily grows stronger, thanks to his complete knowledge of the past and present of English policy in Central Asia. His reputation in this respect was made by a brochure on Central Asia, from an international-law point of view, which he published in 1879,[1] and which was regarded at the time by Central Asian experts in England as a decoy-duck sort of expression of opinion, put forward by the Russian Government through the private and non-official medium of

---

[1] La Russie et l'Angleterre dans l'Asie Centrale, par M. F. Martens, Professeur de droit international à l'Université impériale de St. Pétersbourg. Gand, Imprimerie L. S. Van Doosselaere, 1879.

the Professor, to assert certain claims that would excite indignation and be repelled if announced officially. No Government knows better than the Russian Administration that, the more you ask the more you stand a chance of getting conceded to you. In Russia, nothing is bought without prolonged bargaining, and the system of demanding a great deal in the hope of getting something beyond a fair and proper price, is too familiar to every one not to influence the high and mighty individuals who constitute the ruling forces of Russian diplomacy. In his pamphlet, the Professor claimed the Hindoo Koosh for the future frontier, instead of the Oxus, and treated Herat as a very questionable annexe of a neutral Afghanistan. These pretensions excited an outcry; and I plainly told the Professor, as we sat talking in his handsome and well-equipped library in the luxurious suite of rooms he occupies in the Mokhovoi Street, that he had been called a "catspaw of the wily Gortschakoff" by a section of the English press.

This was after he had already explained to me how he came to write his brochure on Central Asia. In excellent English he said:—" I had gone to Baden for a month, and at that time was not connected with the Foreign Office. My bookseller in London—Trübner—obtained for me the blue-books on Central Asia, and after I had read them I wrote my brochure. The Russian Government knew nothing of its publication, and I myself had never heard previously Prince Gortschakoff express personally his views on Central Asia. What I said was simply what I myself thought. I published it at my own expense, and it will not surprise you as an author to learn that I lost by the transaction. When it was finished I sent copies to Prince Gortschakoff, General Miliutine, &c., and received most gratifying letters from them, expressing their concurrence in the views I had expressed. I could show you those letters to prove the accuracy of what I state," waving his hand towards his writing-table. This, I said, was unnecessary. I quite believed him, I added, reflecting internally that I should be sorry to cast a slur upon his frankness and honesty by demanding to see the proofs. " After it appeared, a Mr. Campbell wrote to me, asking permission to translate it into English, and thus it reached the English public. It is only within the last few months that I have been appointed member of the Council of Foreign Affairs; and this is only one of a series of similar appointments I hold at the other Ministries. If I lost it, or resigned it, my emoluments as Professor at the University of St. Petersburg, &c., would still render me quite independent of Government support." This altogether agreed with what I had been informed by a very old Russian friend of mine, who knows him well, and described him to me as one of the most prosperous *savants* in Russia. At the same time he allowed me to see, during his conversation, that even before being made Councillor at the Foreign Office, two or three months ago, he had shared in and expressed opinions at the deliberations there. He was exceedingly frank, and stated many facts I should like to be able to make public.

He argued that Russia could not help advancing in Central Asia, owing to the provocation of the nomads, and justified those advances by many arguments which I myself have already approved of. He said it was folly to retire after conquering Asiatic territory—an opinion which every Russian holds, and which reflects upon the policy of our own Government in evacuating Candahar. He thought the new Persian frontier a permanent one, but admitted that any restlessness among the Merv Tekkes would lead to a Russian occupation of Merv. I thereupon made use of his own arguments, and proved to him, in a manner he did not attempt to controvert, that the turbulence of the Sarik Turcomans, and of the Afghan Djemshidi and Hazare tribes would infallibly lead

Russia from Merv to Herat. In arguing this point with Russian military men they had said—and particularly Annenkoff—" Well, take Afghanistan, and, by controlling the Afghan tribes living between Herat and Merv, prevent a Russian advance upon the Key of India." But Professor Martens declared to me, in reply to a pointed question I put to him, that England would not be able to annex Afghanistan *without Russia's permission*, or, as he more delicately put it, " without informing her first of her intentions;" *while, as to Herat, he said that Russia would view an English occupation of the place with displeasure.*

He would not allow that we enjoyed supremacy in Afghanistan; nor yet that we could regard it as a second Bokhara. He said Afghanistan was an independent State, and a neutral one; and, with reference to Lord Hartington's declaration last year, that " England would not allow any Power to interfere with the internal and external affairs of Afghanistan,"[1] which I quoted to show

[1] It is to Mr. E. Ashmead-Bartlett, M.P., who has rendered many services to the Central Asian Question, that the credit belongs of evoking this important opinion. In reply to a speech he made Aug. 1, 1881, the Marquis of Hartington said : "The extension of Russian territory along the northern border of Persia raises a question of the integrity of Persia which cannot be indifferent to us, and the near approach of Russia to the borders of Afghanistan is not a matter of indifference to us. The present Government have admitted as plainly as any other that the integrity and independence of Afghanistan is a matter

what our Government thought of Russian pretensions, he said that the declaration was contrary to the views which Russia and England had diplomatically expressed upon the matter previous to the Marquis's speech. He would not agree that the Afghan war had cancelled those views. "Herat," he said, "is quite as important to Russia as to England. If it is the 'key of India,' it is also the key of Central Asia. If we were there, we could threaten you in India: if you were there, you could threaten us in Central Asia."

This opinion was expressed also by Baron Jomini, one of the Under-Secretaries of State at the Russian Foreign Office, to Lord Dufferin in 1879. Writing on the 16th of July in that year, he states that Baron Jomini said to him: "Although we don't intend to go to Merv, or to do anything which may be interpreted as a menace to England, you must not deceive yourself, for

to them of vital importance, and that they do not intend to permit interference by any foreign power with the internal or external affairs of Afghanistan. (Hear, hear.) If Afghanistan were under a settled form of government, it might be indifferent to us whether Russia or any other country extended to the very borders of Afghanistan. But that is not the case of Afghanistan. It has not, and perhaps it never may have, what we recognize as a settled form of government. There could be no doubt that, if Russia advanced towards the borders of Afghanistan, a state of things might ensue, which would not be of advantage to the good relations between this country and Russia."—Hansard, vol. 264, pp. 430—434.

the result of our present proceedings" (i.e. the operations of General Lazareff for conquering and annexing Akhal), *will be to furnish us with a base of operations against England hereafter, should the British Government, by the occupation of Herat, threaten our present position in Central Asia.*"[1]

Professor Martens would not admit that Herat was as much a part of Afghanistan as Cabul or Candahar, and thought that Persia ought to have it. On my pointing out what a rotten State Persia was, and how completely it was under Russian control, he said that if Russia occupied Herat, she would make Persia her enemy. My strong dissent from this led him to propose that Herat should be made into a sort of Switzerland, on the buffer state system, although he had previously expressed his disbelief in the possibility of keeping up Afghanistan as a buffer between the two empires. I held that such a project was impossible with Asiatics, but he continued to maintain that England should keep her hands off the place under any contingencies.

As I gathered from him, he maintains Russia's right to annex all the territory up to the Afghan frontier, if the nomads provoke her to advance; he holds that Russia should also have Afghan Turkestan, i.e., the country between the

[1] Blue-Book, Central Asia, No. 1 (1880), p. 100.

Oxus and the Hindoo Koosh; he considers that Herat ought not to be treated as an Afghan possession; and, finally, he insists that the rest of Afghanistan should be looked upon as a neutral independent State, in the existence of which Russia has as much interest as England. It is needless to point out that these opinions cannot but be so many red rags to English Russophobists, and that, much as the Professor desires a reconciliation between England and Russia, a cessation of the Central Asian agitation is impossible while they are maintained. I myself would allow Russia to annex up to Afghanistan, but I would give her to understand that that country is English territory, and must not be looked upon as less our property than Mysore or Baroda.

I used to think that the claims put forward by the *Golos* and *Novoe Vremya* asserting Russia's right to treat Afghanistan as a neutral State, and Herat as apart from Afghanistan, were merely expressions of Anglophobe feeling. It has surprised me to find them seriously maintained by a person of such weight as Professor Martens. All this, however, constitutes a matter which may be dispersed by amicable discussion. It is better that the Professor's opinions should be contested in a friendly spirit, than that people should fall into paroxysms of Russophobia over them. At the same time, it would be well perhaps, if the Government made up its mind what English policy ought to be in Afghanistan, and intimated its views to Russia on the points raised by the Professor. We often accuse Russia of shifty evasions; but let us remember that she has to deal with series after series of English statesmen, who do not know their own minds, and have no intelligible policy to present to the consistent officials of the Russian Foreign Office. I believe a careful review of the Central Asian Question would reveal, that Russia has been frank and plain enough in explaining her policy to us. Her complaint is, that we have always met this with carping criticism, while never attempting to reciprocate her action by explaining to her our own policy. That would have been a difficult matter. Russia knows her own policy in Central Asia, and we know it. But she does not know England's policy in Central Asia, for the very simple reason that England does not know it herself.

Excluding this phase of our conversation, everything the Professor said was eminently satisfactory. He is a young-looking man, with a German head, very frank, clear in his views, and dispassionate. He earnestly insisted that Russia had no plan for invading India, that she did not move onwards with a view to attacking us there;

and urged that all our alarm on that score was groundless. In regard to Sir Charles Dilke's famous declaration, during the Candahar debate, he said it was regrettable the English Government should have allowed the House of Commons to labour under a misapprehension as to Russia's retirement from Akhal. Such an idea was never entertained by her. Sir Charles Dilke ought to have frankly solicited the views of the Emperor, instead of accepting assurances from Berlin.

With reference to the Secret Cabul Correspondence, which he had in his library with other blue-books, he defended Russia, on the ground that it was difficult to control the actions of a Governor-General at such a distance from Tashkent. Kaufmann did not change his hostile policy with the change of policy at St. Petersburg. He took a local, narrow view of what he ought to do. General Stolictoff, he admitted, was treated with disfavour on his arrival at Livadia from Cabul, and is now on the retired list. On taking my departure, he gave me the same assurances regarding Russia's friendship towards England I have received from every person I have conversed with in this country, and declared that if both nations only knew each other's aims and actions better, all hostility between them would disappear.

CHAPTER XIII.

COUNT IGNATIEFF ON "MISREPRESENTED RUSSIA."

Count Ignatieff at home—A Tuesday reception at his official residence—Curious commingling of cocked hats and sheepskins—Waiting to see the Minister—Ignatieff's mode of dealing with place-hunters—Worked to death—His attitude towards newspaper correspondents—How he humbugs them—A second interview with his Excellency—His cabinet—The disclosure of the Anglo-Russian Agreement—His opinion of Lord Salisbury and his inquiry as to the cause of his enmity—"We were such friends at Constantinople"—Ignatieff on the cause of the war with Turkey, and the Treaty of Berlin—Austria and the Southern Slavs—Russia misrepresented by Europe—Ignatieff's indignation at the European press for trying to make him out to be a fool—Russia did not provoke the occupation of Bosnia by Austria—Ignatieff's admiration of Mr. Gladstone—His view of a Russian occupation of Constantinople—"Russia the victim of English party misrepresentations"—The Jewish outrages—The Russian Government unable to prevent the expulsion of Jews—Something worse than a Parliament—Ignatieff as a reformer—The manufacture of official Russian news—Ignatieff and Lord Salisbury's portrait.

St. Petersburg, March 21.

Ascertaining that on certain days in the week the Leading Minister of Russia, General Count

Ignatieff, receives every one at his official residence, I decided that, instead of applying direct by letter for an interview, I would call upon him with the rest of the world, and thereby enable myself to judge of his accessibility. Accordingly, I presented myself this morning at a few minutes before ten at his house on the Quay of the River Fontanka, an ordinary-looking building, which formerly contained the Third Section—the dreaded title of the Chancellerie of the all-powerful and oppressive secret police, abolished during the benevolent *régime* of the much-admired Loris Melikoff. Quite appropriately the building faces the gloomy Palace in which the Emperor Paul was murdered, and which is now used by the administration of the military engineers.

The first feature that struck me in connexion with Ignatieff's residence was the utter absence of those precautions to ensure safety, which even Melikoff did not disregard. A desperate assassin would experience no more difficulty in placing himself alongside Ignatieff, than a murderer would alongside the person of any of the Cabinet Ministers in England. Outside the principal entrance there was no guard whatever, and a policeman could be seen only in the distance, chatting with some washerwomen on the Quay. Inside the hall were three or four hall porters, of the ordinary description, and a non-commissioned police officer of enormous stature—quite a giant, in fact, but having the harmless aspect of a dove. This individual, stooping down from a few inches of the lintel of the hall-door, to place himself on a level with ordinary humanity, informed me that I was considerably too soon, and said that I had better call again between half-past ten and eleven. On my doing so, I was at once politely disrobed by the attendants, and, without any questions being put to me as to my name and the purport of my visit, I was conducted up a few stairs to a door on the left, which was opened for me to enter.

Inside I found a large and spacious room, at one time evidently parted into two by folding doors. Drab curtains, looped against the wall, now took the place of these, and gave plenty of space for the circulation of the forty or fifty individuals who were waiting to see the Leading Minister of Russia. These were disposed on comfortable drab rep chairs along the walls, or were leaning against intermediate tables or convenient corners. A more curious crowd of callers could not have been found at that hour in any part of Christendom. There were colonels and majors in full dress, and ablaze with military millinery and decorations. There were civilians in court costume—white trousers and dark tunics, with enormous gold bands across the breast, dimming with their glitter the many decorations and medals, of which every Russian, with any pretensions to respectability, would seem to possess at least a score. There were other civilians, not possessing place or rank, in dress coats and white kid gloves. Mingling with these were peasants, or *moujiks*, in coarse, homespun coats, or greasy sheepskins, with huge boots that had never been blacked, and bore the aspect of a navvy's after a hard day's work in clay-cutting. Their coarse and uncombed hair was in keeping with the frowzy caps they carried in their hands, or deposited alongside the gilded and gorgeous cocked hats on the tables. To keep their letters or petitions clean, they held them between pieces of coarse brown paper, which served the purpose of the Russian leather portfolios of the richer applicants present. The peasant class crowded near the entrance door, where the gloom dealt tenderly with their shabbiness. The upper class congregated more towards the windows in the second half of the room, overlooking the river Fontanka. But there were representatives of both classes in each room, and they mixed with each other and with such nondescripts as a French governess, a Tartar merchant from Kazan, a German woman of the landlady type, and a plump Finnish nurse, with none of that air of superiority on the one hand, and "I-am-as-good-as-you" assertion on the other, which is a characteristic of any commingling of the leisured and working classes in England.

Two rooms adjoined the one in which the petitioners were assembled. One, nearer the entrance door, contained the adjutants, ushers, and orderlies of the Minister; the other, overlooking the river, was carpeted and fitted up with sofas and easy chairs, and led immediately into General Ignatieff's apartments. A few minutes after my entrance, an usher came up to me, and, without attempting to speak Russ, asked at once in French if I had any petition to present. I gave him my card, and said I simply wished to see the Minister. A quarter of an hour later a gendarmery orderly addressed me, and inquired, in Russ, the object of my visit, saying that some explanation would be required. I therefore wrote, under my name, "the Special Correspondent of the *Newcastle Chronicle* solicits a few minutes' conversation with his Excellency." This was carried off to the adjutants' room, and there subjected to a scrutiny and discussion by most of the officials present, after which they all indulged in a prolonged stare at me; one individual, in civilian dress, being so little satisfied with this that he came out and traversed the waiting-room twice, in order to survey me from various points of view—from my nose to my toes, and from either wing of my dress coat. After this there was a prolonged pause, during which secretaries with portfolios and officials of various ranks were shown into Ignatieff's room, and shown out again, no effort being made, however, to dispose of the petitioners. Very few arrived after half-past ten, most having presented themselves between the time I first called and the time indicated by the hall porter for me to call again. Two hours passed slowly away, during which the petitioners fidgetted about wearily more or less, watching an adjutant in full Circassian uniform, with a row of cartridges across his breast and all manner of silver trappings about his person, who dodged at intervals between the adjutants' room and the Minister's, showing persons in and out, in obedience to the tinkling of an electric bell.

Shortly before one, the head usher singled me out, and bore me off to the room adjoining the Minister's, where he asked me to sit down among a selection of callers in court dress and full military uniform. I thought I was sure now of an early interview, but nearly three quarters of an hour again passed away, during which only two or three persons were favoured with an audience of the Minister. One or two more callers—a country mayor with some huge medals suspended round his neck, and a horribly vain, fat officer, who performed all manner of toilet operations before the mirror between the windows—were added to the number in the room; and while they were explaining the object of their visit to the head usher, I accidentally saw my card lying among some letters in his pocket-book. It looked as though it had not been sent in to the Minister at all. Before I could make any inquiry, however, the door suddenly opened, and Ignatieff stepped into the room. He was in full uniform, and his breast was ablaze with decorations. Russians of rank spend all their life in uniform; they never seem to sigh for lounge suits. From their babyhood upwards they are buttoned up, and buttoned in. Theirs is an existence in uniform.

Everybody rose as the Minister of the Interior entered; and Ignatieff, all smiles and affability, addressed himself to each in succession. He has a face denoting great capacity; although it is occasionally spoilt by a bold and sinister expression, that somehow seems to find its way into all his portraits. He can be wonderfully genial and winning; he can give a look that would shrivel up the heart of a coward or a fool. The greatest charge that has been brought against him is, that he is unscrupulous; but, how far are English statesmen clean-handed on that score? Look at some of Gladstone's recent unscrupulosities, to say nothing of certain episodes in Salisbury's career. The charge is one that can be raised against most great men; and it is a question whether Ignatieff is worse in this respect than many who detract him. In appearance, he looks more to advantage sitting than standing. His legs appear to have acquired an Oriental twist during their prolonged residence in the East.

Many of the persons in the room were place-hunters. To one of these the Minister said, almost affectionately, as he shook him by the hand, "Well, show me a vacancy, and I will see what can be done for you."

"But I cannot indicate one," said the man.

"What can I do, then," rejoined Ignatieff. "I cannot make you one. Look out for a vacancy, and then tell me."

"But I have been waiting five months," retorted the place-hunter, desperately.

"What's to be done," demanded the Minister. "Look here, now, have a talk together," and, drawing him towards the head usher, he passed on to the next applicant.

The Minister soon came along the line to me,

handing over petitions to one usher, place-hunters to another, and dismissing the rest with a word and a smile. I uttered my name. "I am well acquainted with it," he said, in English.

I continued, explaining the object of my visit, and added that I saw he was too busy to see me to-day, and that I should be glad if he could appoint a regular interview before my return to England.

"I do not know," he replied. "I have so much to do—from six o'clock in the morning till two o'clock in the morning. It is very difficult. But come to-morrow morning."

"At what o'clock, your Excellency?"

"Ten o'clock."

"I shall then be able to have a short conversation," I said, knowing how much Russians dislike to give a plain refusal, and fearing a repetition of the weary waiting of to-day.

"I do not know," answered the Minister; "I hope so." He then passed on to the next person in the line, and I came away.

Count Ignatieff, unlike many statesmen, has the reputation of being always obliging to newspaper correspondents. He does his best to conciliate the representatives of the foreign press here, although there is hardly one who has a good word to give him in their communications. Against any grievance he may nourish on this score they may set their own, that when they go to him with awkward questions he sends them baffled away, and that he is only frank with them when he summons them to him to express some opinion or other he wants communicated to Europe in an impersonal form.

* * * * * *

St. Petersburg, March 22.

On presenting myself this morning at the Count's residence, I found no row of carriages waiting outside, as was the case yesterday, and was informed by the hall porter that "his Excellency did not receive to-day." Stating that General Ignatieff had personally appointed an interview, I sent in my name, and in a few minutes was asked to proceed to the waiting-room, where there were only two persons waiting for an interview, and an adjutant of the police. Before long, an official in a dress coat, with his breast profusely decorated, was shown out of the Count's room, and in advance of any one else I was at once ushered into it. The room is a very large one, well-furnished, and decorated with oil paintings. The Count was sitting at a writing-table in the middle of it. He rose as I entered, and advancing, shook hands with me, and asked me to seat myself in a chair at the opposite side of the table. He was in plain uniform, without any decorations. I could not help noticing how much better he looks in a chair than out of one, in the same manner that Circassians and Turcomans only appear at their ease when in the saddle. He speaks English well, is very earnest, and both of us being intent upon the topics under discussion, I was unable to divert my eyes and attention from the Count a single moment during our forty minutes' conversation, to take in the surroundings, except once when he pointed out to me a portrait of Mr. Gladstone upon the wall.

"In England," I said, "I write for eighteen newspapers and journals upon Russia and Central Asia, but at the present moment I solely and exclusively represent the *Newcastle Chronicle*." I stated this on account of the many reports which had been circulating in the Russian press respecting myself and the objects of my journey, and which I had been compelled to contradict.

"I have read in the *Novoe Vremya*," rejoined the Count, "about your interview with General Tchernayeff."

"Which was very badly reported," I said. "A correct account will reach Russia soon. The main object of my journey has been, to ascertain Russian opinion regarding the Central Asian Question, and—"

"I have nothing to do with that," interrupted Ignatieff. "That question concerns other people; but can you answer me one question—Are you the Mr. Charles Marvin that disclosed the Salisbury-Schouvaloff Memorandum?"

"Yes; it was believed at the Foreign Office it would be published in the *Times* the next morning. I published it in the *Globe* overnight."

"Ah, what terrible havoc that caused," said the Count. "What a disturbance there was through that. I remember that well."

"It did no harm to Russia. The regrettable part of the affair was the injury it did the Conservative party in England."[1]

---

[1] I narrate this passage in the conversation simply because it actually occurred, not from any desire to flaunt the subject. At the same time I may here repeat what I wrote in 1878, before I had entered upon the literary phase of my career, that there is nothing in the disclosure of the Anglo-Russian Agreement that of itself occasions me any regret. The summary I published in the *Globe* of May 30, in the belief that the full text would appear in the *Times* the next morning. This belief was borne out by evidence at the trial. As I had not been enjoined to secrecy, and was under no restriction of confidence, indirect or direct, or even implied, Mr. Vaughan, the magistrate, saw nothing in this act but "indiscretion." Lord Salisbury denied the authenticity of the summary. To re-establish the reputation of the *Globe* I considered then, and I consider now, that I had no other alternative than to publish the full text. Mr. Vaughan censured this act, but ignored the provocation. That provocation, I hold, justified the act. But whether it did or whether it did not, there was nothing in the transaction which I would

"Tell me this," continued Ignatieff. "Why is the Marquis of Salisbury so bitter against me?"

"I do not know Lord Salisbury's private sentiments," I replied.

"But your own opinion," said the Count, eagerly. "You know we were such great friends at Constantinople. We were constantly together. We reciprocated each other's sentiments. I liked him very much—he is a clever man—and now he is quite against me and Russia."

"There is one impression in England," I answered, "and that is this, that Salisbury allowed himself to be made a tool by you at Constantinople, and again by Schouvaloff previous to the Treaty of Berlin. I do not say Salisbury shares this impression, but if he does, you will understand that a clever man does not like to be used as a tool by another."

"But I do not understand why he should be so bitter against me. I never wanted a war with Turkey. It was quite against my wish. It was not Russia's fault that there was war. If there had been a European demonstration—a naval

expunge from the record of my career. The disclosure of the Anglo-Russian Agreement, in common with my three years' attention to the Central Asian Question, is but a minor episode in my life. The past will lose its prominence by what comes hereafter.

demonstration against Turkey—which we wanted—there would have been no war. But after the refusal of the Protocol it would have been impossible for Russia not to go to war. I do not see why the Marquis of Salisbury should be angry at this. As to the Treaty of Berlin, that was a Treaty made by Europe, not by Russia. Russia is not responsible for what arises from that. The Treaty of Berlin was made by persons who did not know the Balkan Peninsula geographically. They drew the frontier-lines on the map anyhow. I said to myself the morning after the signature of the Treaty of Berlin, as I read it—'This will not last.' And you see the troubles that have arisen from it, and will arise. In Bosnia and Herzegovina, for instance. If my plan had been followed for giving to Montenegro all the country containing people like her own, there would have been no revolt. The people are mountaineers, and difficult to govern; the country is poor and rocky; the Montenegrins would have been the best to manage it."

"What do you think will be the result of the struggle? Will there be a Congress?"

Ignatieff shrugged his shoulders. "It is a matter between Austria and Europe, not between Russia and Austria. Austria, by the Treaty of Berlin, was allowed to occupy the country to make peace, but she has made war. She has thus broken the Treaty of Berlin. But that is between her and Europe, not between her and Russia. I do not understand why Russia is attacked by the European press. It is not the fault of Russia. What has Russia done to cause the revolt?"

"An impression prevails in England," I replied, "that Russia fomented the insurrection. It has been said that she has sent money and arms to the insurgents. I do not say that I believe this. I simply tell you the causes of the feeling against Russia in this matter."

The Count interrupted me impatiently. "They always misrepresent Russia. They see Russia, they see me, in everything. Skobeleff goes to Paris and makes a speech, and they say I sent him there to do it. They say I caused this revolt. Why? For what reason? Do you think Russia would impel these poor people into war, when there was no chance of their succeeding. There are people who will believe anything, but you are a clever man, Mr. Marvin, and will understand this—there are three elements in the revolted provinces: the Orthodox, the Roman Catholic, and the Mussulman. The principal element was the Orthodox. The two latter have not joined in the revolt, the Orthodox has done so and has had its power destroyed. Is that to the advantage of

Russia? The Press have said many things about me, but they have never yet tried to do what they have been recently attempting. They have never tried to prove me to be an imbecile. I may be many things they say I am, but I think I have a right to resent that they call me a fool."

"The revolt was spoken of as a symptom of a general Panslavist movement," I said.

"Pan-slavism!" exclaimed Ignatieff, "Russia has sympathy with the revolters through similarity of race and religion, but tell me—What provoked Pan-slavism? Pan-germanism. It was the idea of Pan-germanism that brought about Pan-slavism. But see how it is misrepresented. Bulgaria would not unite itself to Servia, nor yet Servia to Bulgaria. Both are patriotic, but only for themselves. It is the same with the Slavs in Austria. They are the faithful subjects of the Emperor. Yet Russia is charged with a design to make all these and others, who will not unite to each other, unite under herself. And Russia is charged with inducing Austria to enter Bosnia in order to drive the Slavs into her arms. Why should she do this? No, it was not Russia who did this. There was a man who did this—I will not tell you his name. This man did this to weaken Austria. It was he who did this, not Russia."

I inferred that he meant Bismarck. He said nothing to me, however, to warrant this inference, I therefore leave it open.

"See there," he continued, pointing to a portrait in a prominent position on a wall, between the two windows overlooking the river Fontanka and the gloomy palace beyond, in which the Emperor Paul was strangled. "That is Mr. Gladstone. I admire him very much. It is the only portrait of a foreign statesman that decorates my room." The portrait was a recent engraving representing Mr. Gladstone in a standing position, with his hands clasped before him.

"But Mr. Gladstone is apparently not helping the Slavs very much. What is your opinion of his policy?"

Ignatieff shrugged his shoulders. I could see he was not disposed to answer the question. He turned it off by repeating again what he had already said, and what was evidently the main point he wished me to insist upon in public. "It is not a matter between Russia and Austria, but between Austria and Europe. Russia has quite enough to do with her home affairs. Europe made the Treaty of Berlin; it is her business to see to it."

To get some expressions of opinion on Central Asia from him, I said: "The Russophobes in England state that Russia is annexing territory in Central Asia, and taking up a powerful position on the Persian frontier, in order, by threatening India, to be better able to take Constantinople."

"Why should we do that? We could have occupied Constantinople twice already—in '29 and again in '78. We were close outside it in '78. We could have entered it, if we had wished. It was not the 10,000 troops you brought from India to Malta that prevented us occupying Constantinople then." He said this with great significance and earnestness, pointing his finger towards me to enforce attention to what he said.

"The contention is, that you are seeking to occupy Herat, in order the more readily to be able to gain Constantinople."

"If you adopt a policy hostile to a country," replied Ignatieff, "that country has a right to resort to all manner of means to protect itself. I do not understand why the Conservatives are the enemies of Russia; they were once always her friends."

"And may be better friends still than the Liberals," I said, and thereupon traced the bad feeling against Russia which the present Government has occasioned, by deliberately permitting the House of Commons and the public to erroneously believe during the course of the Candahar debate that Russia meant to give up Askabad and retire to the Caspian. When I had finished, he said: "Russia is the victim of party misrepresentations in England. You know yourself, Mr. Marvin, what the nomad is? How could Russia retire from Akhal? Whatever we do in Russia never gives satisfaction—the Jewish outrages, for instance."

"But the reports published are so circumstantial that it seems difficult to controvert them."

"There are the reports of your consuls," rejoined Ignatieff.

"But these have not given satisfaction. For instance, it is pointed out that the consuls questioned the Jewesses in the presence of men, as to whether they had been dishonoured. What woman would have cared to state her case under those circumstances. The reports of the refugees are extremely circumstantial—are they all false?"

"If you wish," rejoined the Count, "I will draw up for you what reports you like on these outrages, circumstantial in every detail. It is not difficult to do that."

"Then your excellency would have me believe that no women have been outraged, as alleged."

"Yes; it is not the character of Russians to commit such outrages. They are not like the people of southern climates. The Russian soldier does not outrage women."

I may here remark that every Russian I have yet met since my arrival here has expressed his disbelief in the dishonouring of the Jewish women. This, however, does not disprove the reports published in England. A mere belief is not a sufficient answer to a circumstantially recorded fact. As was pointed out to me by an English resident a few days ago—"If you allow a mob to rob and beat for twenty-four or forty-eight hours with impunity, every facility is given for the roughs to insult females of a different race and religion, and you can well imagine what an English rough would do under similar circumstances."

"If the Jewish Committee in London," I said, "sent agents to Russia, would every facility be accorded them to make a searching inquiry?"

"Most decidedly," answered Ignatieff. "They could then judge as to the accuracy of the reports."

"But there is one thing that seems at least established," I continued, "for nearly two days the authorities made no effort to quell the riots at Warsaw."

"It was some time before the authorities could deal with the riots," he answered, "and if the troops had fired and killed many of the rioters and Jews in the street crowds, Russia would have again been blamed. If Russia goes to the right Europe blames her for not going to the left, and if to the left, then for not going to the right. The Jews constitute a community by themselves. They have their own customs and habits, and will not conform to those of Russia. They are a state within a state. How can we deal with such a foreign element?"

"But the complaint is, that you will not allow the Jews to enjoy the privileges of other Russian subjects, that you will not let them be as the rest of the subjects of Russia."

"If you have lived in South Russia, you know what the Jew is," replied Ignatieff. "He is dirty, he dresses differently from anybody else, he forms a society of his own, and he oppresses the people. As I pointed out to a deputation that waited on me some time ago, respecting the expulsion of Jews from certain towns and territories—How can I make the people accept you, if you do your best to make them hate you and cast you out? The rural communes and town assemblies say you shall not live with them—shall I send an army and compel them to let you reside in their midst? To do that, I should have to send a battalion of soldiers at the back of every Jew. Look at England. When I was there in '57, a Jew could not sit in Parliament, and even now a Jew cannot be a judge. If this be so in a Constitutional country like England, how shall we deal with the popular feeling in Russia?"[1]

Turning round in his chair he said then, wearily, "I have much to do now. From six o'clock in the morning till two o'clock in the morning I am occupied with work. People say—'I would like to be in power, to be a Minister.' I tell you, that if the Emperor sent for me in five minutes, and said I could retire from being a Minister, I would do so gladly—with pleasure. We have so much to do in Russia with internal affairs; yet they say Russia wants war."

"But at least you are not bothered by a Parliament," I said.

"I have something worse than a Parliament. I have fourteen departments to see to, and they are all exacting and want to take up the whole of my time."

Mentioning that the immunity of his *régime* from Nihilist disturbances had occasioned some surprise in England, where it had been believed his reactionary policy would occasion outbreaks, he replied: "Why so? I have made reforms, and am making them now. I have always been of a

---

[1] The reader will remember that the Count's apologetic statements about the Jews were shortly afterwards followed by the frightful excesses at Balta and other large towns in South Russia, which surpassed the previous outrages at Warsaw and Kieff, and by the expulsion of Jews from Moscow.

Liberal tendency. I promoted the liberation of the Slavs in the Balkan Peninsula."

He then accused the press of Europe of always misrepresenting him, and said, smilingly, of the newspaper correspondents at St. Petersburg: "They surprise me. They gather information somehow—in the cafés—and telegraph it as official." I laughed at this, and seeing by a movement of his chair that he wished the interview to close, I arose at the same time as himself. In conducting me to the door, he paused to point at Mr. Gladstone, and as he shook hands said: "But I have also a portrait of the Marquis of Salisbury —a cabinet photograph." Then opening the door, he added with a smile, " But I do not show that ! "

CHAPTER XIV.

A SECOND INTERVIEW WITH SKOBELEFF, AND A SURVEY OF THE RUSSO-INDIAN QUESTION.

General Skobeleff and his Paris speeches—His admiration of General Roberts and his march from Cabul to Candahar—His opinion of long and short service—A campaign conducted by young men—His view of the Channel Tunnel; of the English army; of our native forces in India; and of our frontier policy on the borders of Afghanistan—England's ability to engage in a European war—Her chances in 1878—Russian opinion of Austria and the Austrian army—Skobeleff's mission—Russia compelled to advance in Central Asia—Her designs against India—The new frontier beyond the Caspian—Russia and the occupation of Merv—Prospective annexations—Double movement upon Merv—Russian claims upon Herat and Afghan Turkestan—How to deal with them—Divergences of opinion in Russia upon the Central Asian Question—One mode of dealing with Annenkoff's Indian railroad in the event of a war—Calming effect of Russian assurances—No Sir Henry Rawlinson in Russia—The rival merits of English and Russian policy in Central Asia—Our shiftless mode of dealing with frontier tribes—List of frontier wars—Duplicity of Sir Charles Dilke—Gladstone the deceiver, not Russia.

St. Petersburg, March 23.

With a short account of a second and final interview with General Skobeleff to-day, I will

bring to a close the series of letters on the Central
Asian Question, and append a brief summary of
my impressions of Russian views of Russian policy
in the East. In the course of our conversation
the General expressed a hope that I would not
involve him in any of those unpleasantnesses,
into which he has been dragged through the
exaggerated reports of foreign interviewers, and
taking this to mean that he did not wish me to
repeat the more candid part of his talk, I will
only note those expressions of opinion which are
of interest to the English public, without being
calculated in any way to prejudice the utterer.
At the outset I asked him if I might put to him
several questions in regard to his recent Paris
speeches, which he could refuse to answer, separately or in all, as he liked; and to this he said,
" Certainly, I will honestly tell you whether I
care to answer or not." I will not repeat what
these questions were, but to one of them, " Were
you sent by General Ignatieff to Paris to deliver
your speeches there?" he replied, " No, most
decidedly not," and he added that I was at liberty
to publish this answer if I chose. Respecting
another point of controversy, as to whether he
was reprimanded or not, on his return, by the
Emperor, no information is obtainable at St.
Petersburg. I have found every one's mouth

closed on that subject, and can only state as my own impression, that if Skobeleff was reproved at all, the reproof was conveyed in a very gentle manner; and that, if anything, he stands higher in the Emperor's estimation than he has ever done since he returned from Geok Tepe. If I add that the general enjoys the best of health and spirits, and that he is more than ever the idol of the army and the people, it will be seen that his journey to Paris has done him no harm to speak of.

Referring to Central Asia, he said that he had followed the whole of our operations in Afghanistan. "For General Roberts," he continued, "I have a great admiration. He seems to me to possess all the qualities of a great general. That was a splendid march of his from Cabul to Candahar. I think more highly of him than I do of Sir Garnet Wolseley, but there is this to be said of all your generals—they have only fought against Asiatic and savage foes. They have not commanded an army against a European enemy, and we cannot tell, therefore, what they are really made of."

On my describing the controversy between Roberts and Wolseley, in regard to the Long and Short Service Systems, he said: "I myself prefer young soldiers to fight with. We take our soldiers at twenty-one; and I think two years, or three at the outside, is quite sufficient to fit them for war." There is, of course, a very great difference between the strong and robust youths of twenty-one, mainly drawn by Russia from the peasant class, and the boyish " weeds " of inferior physique that drift into the English army. Sir Frederick Roberts would probably share Skobeleff's views, if he had to deal with Russian soldiers. It is noteworthy that Skobeleff likes to surround himself with young officers. The recent brilliant campaign against the Turcomans was essentially a war conducted by young men. There was hardly a grey head in the force.

Mentioning Sir Garnet Wolseley's objections to the Channel Tunnel, he said—" If I were an Englishman, I do not think I should like to see the tunnel constructed. The possibility of 2000 or 3000 of the enemy treacherously seizing the English end, deserves to be seriously considered." He went on to say, in regard to the English army, that he thought we ought to have compulsory conscription in our country. I pointed out the impossibility of carrying this into effect, and observed that we had a vast reserve of military power in India, which a Government like that of Russia would know better how to make use of than our own. "I doubt it," he replied. "I do not think much of the native army in India. We have also a vast native reserve—Tartars, Circassians, and so forth—but we do not draw upon them beyond a certain point. Asiatics cannot be trusted against European troops." I referred to the Indian troops brought to Malta during the Turkish War, and said it would have been interesting to have seen how they would have comported themselves in the presence of a European army. "It would have been interesting," he replied; "but you did not use them, and we therefore do not know what they would have done. The best criterion of the quality of the native troops of India is, the fact that India should allow itself to be dominated by only 60,000 European soldiers."

Discussing the shiftless English policy of incessantly sending punitive expeditions against the frontier tribes of India, which, according to our present system, have to be repeated every few years, he observed that he considered it a very bad one. "In dealing with savage tribes," he said, "the best plan is, to fight as rarely as possible; and when you do fight, to hit as hard as you can. By incessantly attacking them, you teach them the art of war. Your policy is the same as that which we pursued in the Caucasus, and has had similar results. Prince Bariatinsky, however, replaced it with a fresh policy. Wherever he advanced, he stopped and made roads to the point, and fortified it. In this manner, in course of time, we were able to put down the lawlessness of the tribes."

He seemed to be very dubious as to the possibility of England engaging single-handed in a European war. Reverting to the Turkish campaign, he expressed an opinion that if we had helped the Turks in 1878 we should not have succeeded. "We were quite ready for you in May; we were as well-armed as you were, and we had received new artillery for the army. If there had been any attempt to sever our communications, we had two years' supplies in the country; Austria was watched by 400,000 troops, and I do not think that even if she had joined England we should have been beaten. All depended, however, upon the attitude of Germany, whether she would adopt a policy of neutrality— of honest neutrality—or not. This applies, however, only to the state of affairs in May. After the typhus epidemic in July, when we lost 60,000 men, things altogether changed. You would have had a better chance of winning then."

He did not appear to entertain a very high opinion of the Austrian army. "Half the troops are Slavs," he said, in the course of some critical remarks on the subject. It may be noted that most Russian officers despise the Austrian army, and think that they could make very short work of it and the Austrian Empire also, if Germany only held aloof. Not that they underrate the bravery of the Austrian soldier. They simply share the opinion expressed in a famous *mot* by Prince Gortschakoff, that "Austria is not a State: it is only a Government;" and that under the pressure of the Slavs from without and within, the army and it would go to pieces.

The arrival of some officers on business broke up our interview. In taking my leave of General Skobeleff he gave me, as a souvenir of the recent campaign, the cap he wore during the siege of Geok Tepé, and on the day of the assault of the fortress.

It was recently stated in a letter from St. Petersburg to the *Times*, that Skobeleff regards it as his mission to either fight England in Central Asia, or Germany and Austria in Europe. The same writer also expressed doubts as to whether Skobeleff ever really stated at Paris that he hated war. This latter sentiment, however, he expressed to me several times in our interview, using the same words, "I hate war," which he was affirmed to have employed at Paris. As to his alleged mission, I have already stated that my own impression is that he is quite sick of Central Asia, and has no wish to go there again. He has no desire to fight England in that region, and seems to share the opinion held by almost every Russian I have met since my arrival here, that the region is not worth England and Russia fighting about. I have been struck with the unanimity with which Russians of all classes disclaim the existence of any designs upon India, and the earnestness with which they advocate a suppression of the Central Asian controversy. Whatever may be the sentiments expressed from time to time by the Russian press, there would appear to exist here none of that Anglophobia, matching the Russophobia so rampant in England. The opinion that Russia cannot but advance in Central Asia when attacked by nomad tribes, and that the only sound policy in dealing with such tribes is to permanently occupy their country, is held by every one I have met, and is justified by such opposite authorities as Ignatieff at St. Petersburg and Prince Krapotkin, the Nihilist leader, in London. But, in expressing this view, every one earnestly denies that any desire exists to disturb us in India, and questions the possibility of Russia doing us any serious harm there. I may add that these views are not expressed merely by the statesman and generals I have conversed with, but also by Russians of other ranks; some of whom were close and intimate friends of mine during my residence in Russia from 1870 to 1875, and whose assurances I am able to accept without any reserve.

Russia says that she has no designs upon India, and does not seek to meddle with us in any way there. This applies to a period of peace. If we went to war with her in Europe she would naturally attempt some sort of demonstration against us in Asia, and it is upon this point that Skobeleff has expressed opinions, which will probably allay some of the alarm prevailing as to the possibility of invading India. These opinions, however, largely apply to the present condition of things in Central Asia. Affairs may change in that region, and it is necessary to point out what those changes may be.

Russia denies that she has any designs upon Khorassan, and maintains that the new frontier may be regarded as a permanent one. I have already expressed an opinion that Russia was exceedingly moderate in choosing her frontier, and that she displayed an appreciation of Persian interests and Persian susceptibilities which, to say the least, entitle her to respect. I am inclined to accept her assurances that no alteration will take place in the frontier, so far as concerns the immediate future, even in spite of the complications with the nomad tribes at the mouth of the

Atrek. This opinion applies to what may be termed the exclusively Persian portion of the frontier. So far as concerns the country east of Askabad, open to Turcoman raids, I entertain an impression, while accepting her assurances that she does not wish to advance, that changes may in course of time take place in that quarter. A deal depends upon the attitude of the Turcomans of Merv. They are quiet at present, and have just given a good reception to a Russian caravan, despatched by Gospodin Konshin, from Askabad. But they may resume their raids, and if they do Russia will certainly occupy Merv.

A glance at the map will show that between Gyaoors, the final outpost east of Askabad, and the river Oxus, Russia possesses at present no frontier. There is a probability that she will seek by degrees to secure one there. It seems almost certain Bokhara will be annexed when the Emir dies. This will bring Russia into direct contact with Afghanistan and with the Ersari and other Turcoman tribes dwelling between the Oxus and Merv, and owing allegiance to the Emir. She will probably seek to impose some sort of administration over these tribes, and this will bring up her Turkestan wing very close indeed to Merv. There will then be only a small gap left, composed of Merv, separating the Caucasian and

Turkestan ends of the Russian Asiatic frontier. The temptation will be great, when this event comes to pass, to induce Merv to accept a Russian protectorate and complete the chain; and whether a protectorate be adopted or not, the fact of the establishment of constant communication between Askabad and Bokhara by way of Merv will give Russia supreme influence in that region.

In occupying Bokhara, Russia will come into direct contact with Afghan Turkestan, which General Soboleff and Professor Martens, both very influential men, hold ought to pass under Russian influence, or, in plainer language, ought to be annexed in the event of any partition of Central Asia. Neither of those personages wishes to see Herat continue under the influence of England, and it must be pointed out that the annexation of Bokhara will render possible conflicts with Afghan tribes south of the Oxus, which may draw Russia by degrees close up to Herat; this, too, without any actual design on her part. I consider it a regrettable circumstance that Russians are not unanimous in accepting England's claim to exclude their influence from every part of Afghanistan. So long as any desire is expressed to withdraw Herat and Afghan Turkestan from our influence, and pretensions are put forward to dispute our right to control both in the event of any partition of Central Asia, the uneasy feeling prevailing in England cannot be expected to disappear.

But, as General Annenkoff said to me last Sunday on this point, while I was discussing with him and Gospodin Serbriakoff, the able constructor of the Bender-Galatz war railway in 1878, the possibility of continuing the Transcaspian line to India—" These are opinions, not threats." He continued : " You cannot but see, Mr. Marvin, that we are not all agreed upon every point of the Central Asian Question. Professor Martens says, England ought not to have Herat. I say, Take all Afghanistan, take Herat. Let us have no quarrelling. Let us be friends. Why war ? If we must do something with our spare money, let us make the railway to India— you from Sibi to Herat, and we from Askabad to Herat. But we will not fight ; we must not fight. Why war in Central Asia ? Let us have the railway, if you please, but no war."

" But your very railway excites alarm. When it is finished, there exists a fear that it will be very easy for Russia to invade India. Your very project has promoted excitement, not allayed it."

The general laughed good-humouredly. The idea of 100,000 troops being conveyed along a single line of rails to India without any impediment on the way struck him as very comic. Gospodin Serebriakoff added: "But you know this invasion could be easily prevented. It requires engineering skill to make a railway, but any savage can pull it to pieces again. England could easily rip up the rails and prevent an invasion. But, as General Annenkoff says, why should we always be discussing the possibility of war in Central Asia? Why not change the topic and discuss the possibility of peace? We wish you no harm in India, and if the railway were made and we were neighbours, we should know more of each other and become friends. Russia has no ill-feeling whatever against England."

If Professor Martens is really the earnest advocate of reconciliation I take him to be, there should be no difficulty in inducing him to amend his opinions as to the exclusion of English influence from Herat and Afghan Turkestan. But, irrespective of this, if English statesmen do their duty honestly towards our Indian Empire, and do not sacrifice its interests to party considerations, as has been done too often in the past, it should not be difficult to effectually dissipate the Professor's opinions, by developing the Ameer's power—or our own—to such a degree in Herat and Afghan Turkestan, as to render those opinions no longer tenable. In that case, the Central

Asian Question would be reduced to very simple proportions. A large amount of the constant uneasiness prevailing in England regarding the Central Asian Question arises from the fact that Russia, being a fortnight nearer Herat than we are, renders the "key of India" more within her reach than our own. Had we been in possession of Candahar, there would have been less ground for this uneasiness, and I could have counselled its partial disappearance. As it is, it is useless to give advice where there is no likelihood of its being accepted.

At the same time it is impossible, I think, for the public mind not to be calmed by the reassurances which Skobeleff, Grodekoff, Annenkoff, Tchernayoff, and other eminent Russians have given in regard to the alleged designs against India. Be it noted that these men do not constitute a clique, but represent individually various phases of Russian thought. Collectively they form the entire group of Russian authorities on Central Asia, if we include Colonel Kostenko, now in Kuldja, and who has often expressed to me by letter the sentiments held by Skobeleff and Annenkoff; and Colonel Venukoff, at present a political exile at Geneva, who is equally remarkable for his lack of Anglophobia. Their expressions of goodwill towards England, and their earnest disclaimers of any designs against India, are not to be lightly treated, I think. If we exclude the views of Soboleff and Martens, their advocacy of a suppression of the Central Asian Question is accompanied by no terms; and even those two outsiders do not take up a position that would render it impossible for them to modify their opinions. To speak plainly, there is no Sir Henry Rawlinson—or even the ghost of a Sir Henry Rawlinson—in Russia. There exists no Anglophobia in Russia to match the Russophobia in England. This of itself is a striking fact, for, as a Russian officer put it to me a few days ago, " England has certainly done its utmost to make us her bitter enemy; yet you find us without feeling against her, and desirous of being her friend."

Thus, should we find Russia effecting no fresh serious advances in Central Asia in the immediate future, I think an effort ought to be made to reciprocate the expressions of good feeling which have been made during the last few weeks by the leading Russian authorities on that region; and, at the same time, it would be well for Englishmen to ask themselves whether their own policy in Asia does not need amending. Every Russian holds—and Russia having been dealing with the problem 300 years ought to know what she is about—that the only satisfactory way of pacifying nomad tribes is to occupy their country out and out. This is an opinion I myself shared long before I came to Russia, and which I have not modified since. It is held not only by myself, as an English writer on Central Asia, but by many of our ablest Indian authorities, who unite in denouncing our costly and stupid mode of dealing with the frontier tribes of India. Of course, one must not shirk the consequences of holding such an opinion. If England adopted the Russian policy towards the north-west tribes of India, she would probably be compelled to over-run and annex by degrees the whole of Afghanistan. This would blot out Central Asia, and render England and Russia neighbours—a far smaller evil than the continuance of their present attitude of being almost foes to one another in that region. So long as any lawless and savage territory lies unabsorbed between the two empires, there can be no disappearance of the Central Asian agitation. It is a question whether the cost of absorbing Afghanistan would not be repaid over and over again by the growth of a better feeling between England and Russia.

If such a policy would be costly, it should be remembered that it would be effective. It is doubtful whether, systematically and carefully conducted, it would be more expensive than the present system, which consists, it should also be remembered, of efforts thrown away. Our present policy is all loss; with a forward policy there would be a certain amount of gain. The Afghan tribes would be no more difficult to bring into order than those of the Punjab.

Since 1849 we have sent, guided by our present policy, no less than twenty-five expeditions against the tribes on the north-west border of India.

	Date.	Offending Tribe.	Commander.	Casualties. Killed.	Wounded.
1	1849	Swatees of Lundkor	Colonel Bradshaw, C.B.	9	45
2	1850	Afreedees of Kohat Pass	Sir Charles Napier	19	74
3	1851	,, ,,	Captain Coke	11	25
4	—	Vazeerees of Miranzai	,, ,,	1	18
5	—	Momands	Sir C. Campbell	3	19
6	1852	Swatees of Black Mountain	Colonel Mackeson	3	17
7	—	Utmankhel	Sir Colin Campbell	14	48
8	—	Vazeerees of Kafir Koti	Captain Nicholson	23	5
9	1853	Bori Afreedees	Colonel Boileau	8	33
10	—	Sheoranees	Brigadier-Gen. Hodgson	5	42
11	—	Kasranees	,, ,,	11	31
12	1854	Momands	Sir Sydney Cotton	2	16
13	—	Afreedees	Colonel Craigie, C.B.	9	39
14	1855	Orakzais	Brig.-Gen. N. Chamberlain	10	23
15	1857	Bozdar Beloochees	,, ,,	12	49
16	—	Narinjee	Sir S. Cotton	6	36
17	1858	Sittana	,, ,,	6	28
18	1859	Cabul Khel Vazeerees	Sir N. Chamberlain	2	19
19	1860	Mahsood Vazeerees	,, ,,	93	286
20	1863	Umbeyla	,, ,,	238	908
21	1868	Black Mountain	Sir A. Wilde	20	109
22	—	Bazoti	Major L. B. Jones	11	44
23	1869	,,	Colonel C. P. Keyes, C.B.	8	33
24	1872	Dawar	Brig.-Gen. C. P. Keyes, C.B.	3	16
25	1878	Afreedees	,, ,,	18	78
			Total......	545	2041

This list is complete up to the late Afghan war. It excludes the half-a-dozen small expeditions that have been conducted since. Surely, no one, looking at the total of killed and wounded, can affirm our present frontier policy to be a cheap one. These expeditions represent in the aggregate enough expenditure of power to have brought the whole of Afghanistan beneath our rule. All has been thrown away.

If we may rely upon the Russian lists of casualties, the entire conquest of Central Asia, excluding the recent siege of Geok Tepé, has been accomplished with fewer losses than have marked our thirty years' fruitless campaigning against predatory tribes in the north-west frontier of India.

A final word about Russia's recent operations in Central Asia. Before coming to St. Petersburg I completed arranging the materials for my new work on Skobeleff's siege of Geok Tepé; and the Russian military matter, with the parliamentary and blue-book information, compiled during a year of labour, bore out conclusively that Russia always said that she meant to annex as far as Askabad—even two years ago, in Lord Salisbury's time; that Skobeleff never intended at any time to advance on Merv, as repeatedly announced by Mr. O'Donovan; that he was not recalled in disgrace; and that she never gave any assurance to England that she would fall back upon the

Caspian, as the House of Commons was misled into believing by the Government during the Candahar debate. All this has been substantiated by information forthcoming here, which has further confirmed the moderate and non-aggressive character of the new frontier beyond the Caspian.

Speaking then as an "alarmist writer" (as I have been called), and as impartially as any man can, I am compelled to admit that there has been no ground for those bitter charges against Russia of broken promises, duplicity, fresh advances, and so forth, which have filled the English press for some weeks past, and have been so prominently promulgated in the *Times*. I brought this opinion out with me to Russia to test. I have found nothing here to shake it. I have seen nothing, either in English or Russian print, to cause me to alter my view. So long ago as July last year I affirmed that Russia had broken no promise in annexing Akhal,[1] and the charge, therefore, cannot be brought against me that my visit to Russia has in any way converted me from a Russophobe to a Russophil. I would rather any charge be made against me, than that I should be thought to be of the latter class, with the hateful odour of the Atrocity agitation sticking to the title.

[1] *Army and Navy Magazine*, "Russia's new Province in Central Asia."

As last July, so now, I am compelled with equal candour to avow that if there has been any duplicity in connexion with the Central Asian Question during the last two years, it rests more with England than with Russia, and that it is to be found in the conduct of Sir Charles Dilke and the Marquis of Hartington in wilfully causing the House of Commons and the public to believe during the Candahar debate that Russia meant to fall back upon the Caspian, when nothing had been put forward by Russia to justify any such erroneous impression; and was contrary to her own declarations on the subject. Had not Russia been made the victim of misrepresentation, for English party purposes, there would have been none of the recent unjust outcry against her in England. It is not to the honour of Mr. Gladstone that it should have been his own cabinet which has inflicted on Russia a great wrong, nor to the credit of the Russophil Liberals that none of them should have attempted to expose it.

APPENDIX.

RUSSIA'S NEW PROVINCE IN CENTRAL ASIA.

THE Central Asian Question has entered upon a fresh phase. The eyes of vigilant politicians are no longer fixed upon Tashkent; they are directed towards Tiflis. For the moment Turkestan has lost the interest it used to possess for Englishmen. The policy of the apoplexy-stricken Kaufmann, or his assistant Kolpakovsky, no longer occasions uneasiness. The "great game" of Central Asia has shifted from Turkestan to the Caucasus, from Tashkent to Tiflis, and from Samarcand to Geok Tepé. By the annexation of Akhal Russia has formed a strategical wedge beyond the Caspian, threatening the security of Meshed and Herat. By establishing a powerful garrison at Askabat, under the control of Major-General Grodekoff, of Ride to Herat notoriety, she has prepared England for the ultimate occupation of Merv. Finally, by undertaking, in the event of any further Kurdish disturbances, to invade Persian Azerbijan and Turkish Van, she has displayed clearly enough where the next extension of the Transcaucasian territory may be looked for.

The conquest and incorporation of Akhal has immensely improved Russia's position in Central Asia. When General Skobeleff proceeded to the Caspian in May last year,

[1] *Army and Navy Magazine*, July, 1881. By the Author.

Russia's prestige was at a very low ebb. In the words of General Annenkoff, the constructor of the Transcaspian Railway, the disastrous defeat experienced by Lomakin the previous autumn had "shaken the power of Russia throughout Central Asia; the Turcomans raided to the very outposts of Krasnovodsk and Tchikishlar, the Kirghiz of Manghislak were mutinous, Persia treated Russia coolly, and the Chinese prepared to take Kuldja by force." Skobeleff enjoyed *carte blanche* as to the forces he should employ to conquer the Akhal Tekkes—an undertaking which General Tergoukasoff, Lomakin's successor and Skobeleff's predecessor, had just reported would take three years at least to accomplish—but it was *carte blanche* with serious limitations. From Turkestan he could receive little or no assistance, all the garrisons having been denuded to swell the force concentrating in Kuldja to repel the Chinese; at Tiflis he could not count upon the undivided attention of the Viceroy, who was busy preparing to assemble 6000 troops at Naktchevan, to put down the Kurdish horde of the Sheikh Obeidullah, and the general state of Europe was such that Russia might at any moment be involved in war with Turkey over the growing Dulciguo, or other chronic questions, arising from the decrepit condition of the "Sick Man."

Skobeleff arrived at Tiflis in May. His staff he sent on to Tchikishlar, *viâ* Baku, himself taking the road to Krasnovodsk, *viâ* the Daghestan port of Petrovsk. The day of departure from Tiflis the Grand Duke Michael sent Colonel Grodsky to Khiva to arrange for a column to manœuvre in the direction of Merv, to distract the attention of the nomads. Proceeding first to Krasnovodsk, Skobeleff found General Petroosevitch, the Governor, busily superintending the arrangements for constructing the railway from Michaelovsk to Kizil Arvat. Skobeleff had no need to reconnoitre the country near Krasnovodsk, having spent some months there in 1870; the Atrek, however, was new to him, and he accordingly visited in succession all the Russian forts, stretching from Tchikishlar to Douz-Oloum, controlled by General Mouravieff, who had recently had several skirmishes with the redoubtable leader of the Akhal Tekkes, Tekme Sardar. A few days sufficed to complete arrangements at Tchikishlar for the despatch of troops to the front, and then taking ship again Skobeleff coasted along the Caspian to Fort Alexandrovsk, where he reorganized the garrison, and started off a column into the steppe to meet 5000 camels he had telegraphed to Krijanovsky to send him from Orenburg. On his return to Tchikishlar he marched with the assembled troops up the Atrek, and on the 23rd of June occupied, without opposition, the Akhal Tekke fortress of Bami, the connecting point of the roads running from Krasnovodsk and Tchikishlar to Merv, viâ Geok Tepé. Twenty days were spent in fortifying Bami and strengthening the two lines of communication with the Caspian, after which Skobeleff set out with 1000 bayonets to have a look at Geok Tepé, and see what force would be needed to reduce it to submission. The reconnaissance was a brilliant success. Five days' march brought him to Geok Tepé; he obtained a good survey of the Tekke stronghold; and then returned to Bami, with the enemy at his heels, but losing only a dozen men killed and wounded during the operation. The reconnaissance convinced him that Geok Tepé was no easy nut to crack, and it speaks volumes against the prevailing notion that Skobeleff is impetuous, rash, and foolhardy, that he should have settled down patiently at Bami for more than six months, spending the time in maturing his preparations for the siege. During this period he concentrated the whole of his energies, and those of his subordinates, upon the conveyance of munitions of war to the front, making no response to the raids of the Tekkes, and turning an equally deaf ear to the instructions of the Viceroy Michael to hurry the campaign to a close. When everything was ready he marched to Bami, regularly invested Geok Tepé with 8000 troops, and after a harassing and bloody siege of twenty-three days' duration, successfully reduced the place by storm. A few days later, Askabat and Gyaoors were occupied, and the Akhal Tekke campaign practically came to a close. Well planned, well executed, brilliantly successful, and accomplished without any disaster, it crushed every spark of independence and resistance out of Akhal, and left Russia absolute mistress of the whole of the country from the Caspian Sea to the mouth of the Tedjend.

In some respects the supremacy which fell to Skobeleff was not very dissimilar from that which Robinson Crusoe enjoyed on his desert island. Russia was mistress, simply because there was no one left to contest her rule. After the fall of Geok Tepé the Akhal Tekkes fled to Merv, and Russia was left to exercise sway over the oasis in Imperial solitude. Before long, however, they began to turn back, and at least 20,000 had returned to Akhal when Tekme Sardar, the hero of the Geok Tepé defence, rode into Askabat one morning and submitted to General Grodekoff. This completed the subjugation; and a sort of truce which Skobeleff, with the aid of Tekme Sardar, was able to strike up with the Merv Tekkes, gave Russia leisure to decide calmly what she should do with her conquest.

Four courses were open to her: to evacuate the country, to establish a protectorate with Tekme Sardar as responsible ruler, to hand it over to Persia, or, finally, to annex it. None of the first three courses would bear examination. Had Russia retired from Geok Tepé, as we injudiciously did from Candahar—in nowise tricked by Russia into so doing, as has been falsely alleged, but misled by Gladstone's watery sentiment—the Tekkes would have been encouraged to resume their former mode of life, and, after a while, the Turcoman scourge on the north-east Persian frontier would have been as bad as ever. Such a policy as this—of keeping marauding tribes in order, or disorder, by periodical punitive expeditions—prevails on our Indian border, and is quite in keeping with our shiftless mode of ruling our splendid empire, but it is too costly, to say nothing of being too ridiculous, for the Russians to adopt. The experience of 300 years has demonstrated clearly to Russia, that it is cheaper in the long-run to absorb disorderly frontier tribes, than to attempt to repress their turbulence, as we vainly do in India, by the alternate use of the rupee and the rocket. When pacified, the Cossack helps to subjugate the Caucasian, the Caucasian in turn assists in the conquest of the Turcoman, and the Turcoman on his part will be fit, in a few years, to put down the Afghan.

The second course—to make Tekme Sardar ruler of the Akhal Tekkes, and then to return to the coast—had this fatal objection: the tribesmen of Akhal had never been accustomed to recognize any authority; each man was equal, and the leaders simply exercised influence, which is very different from administrative authority. Hence, on the departure of the Russians, the Akhal Tekkes would have simply ignored the powers delegated to Tekme Sardar. The third course—to allow the Persians to occupy the oasis—was hardly to be thought of at a moment when the Shah was imploring the Tsar to help him against the Kurdish rabble from Van, and when his troops were frightened to show their noses outside Astrabad, for fear of the Turcomans. Such a ridiculous compromise between evacuation and annexation, by supporting Persian rule in Akhal by the aid of the Berdan and the rouble, could have only been considered worthy of adoption by statesmen of the Duke of Argyll order.

On every ground the total absorption of Akhal was the best course for the Tsar to pursue, and it is not surprising that it should have been adopted with a thoroughness that startled the Gladstone Government. A glance at the map will show that Russia had pressing need of a scientific frontier from Turkestan to the Caspian, to round off her Central Asian possessions and keep the border tribes in order. It is unnecessary to go back to old controversies and argue whether Russia was right or wrong in establishing a footing in the Transcaspian region at all —Alexander III. had to face the fact that Russia *did* hold certain loosely connected points along the Caspian coast, and again on the Oxus, and the problem to solve was, to establish such a connexion between the two as would keep the Transcaspian highways and settlements clear of the Tekke robber. The annexation of Akhal assisted largely in the solution of the problem, since it gave her a scientific frontier for half the distance from the Caspian to the Oxus, and a potential claim to the remainder. It is not surprising, therefore, that the Tsar rejected the timid suggestions of the English Radicals to fall back on the Caspian, and annexed the conquered Tekke territory to the very limits of the region penetrated by Skobeleff's troops.

The annexation of Akhal has provoked a strong feeling

of mistrust and hostility in England, but for the prevalence of this Russia is not in any way responsible. The absorption of Akhal has been a card she has been playing openly for many years. So long ago as 1879 General Lazareff said to the Central Asian correspondent of the *Daily News*, "I have sent to the Tekkes to tell them that I mean to annex their country; and have warned them that if they intend to fight they had better get ready at once. I mean to subjugate and annex the country. If circumstances compel me to go to Merv, to Merv I shall go."[1] Nothing could be more explicit nor plainer than this, and the same frankness characterized the subsequent statements of the diplomatic authorities at St. Petersburg. Pressed by the English ambassador, Russia repeatedly declared she would not go to Merv if she could help it, but she candidly admitted that circumstances might arise compelling her to march thither. For instance, if, in the recent campaign, the Merv Tekkes had taken a larger share in the operations, and had killed General Skobeleff, no consideration would have prevented Russia from seeking revenge by blowing down the stronghold on the Moorgab. This was the kind of "circumstances that might arise," that M. de Giers and Baron Jomini constantly impressed upon Earl Dufferin. As to Akhal, Russia repeatedly intimated to England in 1879 and 1880 her intention of establishing a post somewhere in the Kopet Dagh, at Bami, or Geok Tepé, for the purpose of overawing the marauding Tekkes. Thus, when the Candahar debate took place last March the English

---

[1] "The Disastrous Russian Campaign against the Turcomans," p. 56. More recent military operations and diplomatic negotiations will be found in "Merv, the Queen of the World; and the Scourge of the Man-stealing Turcomans." W. H. Allen and Co.

Government had the strongest possible reasons for knowing that Russia would not surrender Akhal, whatever sacrifice she might make in regard to a forward move on Merv. So far as Merv was concerned, the siege of Geok Tepé had so exhausted Skobeleff that he was not in a fit position to undertake a second campaign. This was known to the Government, as will be seen on a reference to the latest Central Asian blue-book. The question thus narrowed itself as to whether Russia would annex Akhal or not, and one of the most powerful points which the Opposition had in favour of the retention of Candahar was, the menace which the continued occupation of Geok Tepé and Askabat would offer to the security of Meshed and Herat.

This point was broken down by the Government in a manner which lays Sir Charles Dilke open either to a charge of political dishonesty—to put the matter mildly—or to a want of sagacity, damaging to his reputation as a statesmen. At the very outset of his speech, on the 24th of March, Sir Charles said:—" The very first act of the new Emperor has been to recall General Skobeleff, and to put a stop to the whole of the undertakings which that general has been carrying on in Central Asia." This was accepted by the Ministerial party, and by the public and press generally the next morning, as being tantamount to an announcement that the Tsar had decided to evacuate Akhal, and fall back upon the Caspian.

Certain members, however, refused to believe that Russia had cast aside, in a moment, a policy she had been pursuing for 300 years; and Lord George Hamilton expressed their incredulity clearly, the following day, when he said: —"Great stress has been laid by the Under-Secretary of State on the recall of General Skobeleff; but, what does he mean by the word 'recall'? Has the Under-

Secretary any authority to state that General Skobeleff has been displaced from his command because the Emperor of Russia disapproves of the expedition he is conducting?" This provoked from Lord Hartington the statement that "The Opposition seem to think that the announcement made by Sir Charles Dilke, with regard to the policy of the present Emperor of Russia, and the order which has been given for the recall of General Skobeleff, has been made by the Russian Government for some political purpose connected with this debate. I do not think my hon. friend attributed any very great importance to Sir Charles Dilke's statement—('Oh, oh!' from the Opposition)—*but he thought it was one, and I think it is one*, which is satisfactory to the House. And it may be an additional satisfaction to the right hon. gentleman to know that the information did not reach her Majesty's Government from the Russian Government, or from her Majesty's ambassador at St. Petersburg, but from a totally independent source." The result of this declaration was, that the Opposition attack completely broke down, and, in the belief that the relinquishment of Candahar would be followed by the evacuation of Geok Tepé, the House gave the Government a large majority.

Before long, however, it began to be seen that Skobeleff was very slow in returning home, and rumour accredited him with curiously ambiguous activity in the direction of Merv. The Beaconsfield Administration had made it a point to maintain a special consul at Astrabad, a newswriter at Meshed, and a military agent—Major Napier—on the Turcoman border, to keep it informed as to Russia's operations on the Atrek; but these praiseworthy precautions had been discarded by the Gladstone Government, and hence Sir Charles Dilke could say nothing to allay the public alarm. On the 13th of April—that is to say, twenty days after his declaration in the House—a telegram to the *Daily News*, from its well-informed correspondent at St. Petersburg, stated that Skobeleff was at Kelat, halfway between Geok Tepé and Merv. This provoked even the *Daily News* to indignation. In a powerful leader, it said that Sir Charles Dilke's declaration had been so "opportune that some scepticism was expressed, not, of course, as to the good faith of the Under-Secretary for Foreign Affairs, but as to the real motive and conduct of the Russian Government. The communication, of which Sir Charles Dilke was the organ, did not, we believe, come to our Foreign Office straight from St. Petersburg. It reached it through the friendly intervention of the German Ambassador." The following day a telegram arrived, that the leading Akhal Chief had submitted, and sworn allegiance to the Tsar. The indignation of the *Daily News* at this knew no bounds. In another leader it said:—"The telegram cannot by any ingenuity be reconciled with the statement which was made by Sir Charles Dilke. That statement was to the effect that the Emperor had recalled General Skobeleff, and had put a stop to the operations which the General had been conducting. General Skobeleff has not been recalled. On the contrary, he has completed the operations which he was conducting. These operations are indeed announced as closed, but as closed only because of their completion. If this can be regarded as in any sense a fulfilment of the pledge to the English Government, we can only say that those who so regard it must be very easily satisfied. The Emperor's orders, if they were ever given, have been in part simply disregarded—in part, were mere wasted breath. If the expedition has come to an end, it is the

Tekké Chief, by submitting, and not Alexander III. by ordering retirement, who has put an end to it. The unavoidable construction of the news is, moreover, as we have already pointed out, that Russia has definitely assumed the sovereignty of Akhal. We do not think that this either can be said to be a fulfilment of the famous pledge. It may be necessary to repeat that dissatisfaction with the apparent construction put by the Russians on their undertaking has no necessary connexion with a belief in the importance of the subjugation of the Akhal Tekkés. Those who saw in the presence of Skobeleff at Gyaoors, and at the Tedjend, a reason for the holding of Candahar, and those who saw in it no such reason at all, may, it ought to be possible to say must, agree that such a termination of the Russian expedition as appears to be indicated in this telegram, is, in fact, a distinct violation of the pledge implied in the communication of the Emperor's intentions. The view that the presence of Russia on the north of Afghanistan in no way necessitated the occupation by England of the south of Afghanistan, has been the view consistently expressed in these columns. Nor is that view now departed from. But it may be worth while to consider what Russians would have said of us if, after announcing that General Hume was to be recalled, and operations at Candahar put an end to, we had sent General Hume back, and had discovered that the putting an end to operations was compatible with the steady continuation of occupation. When a great Sovereign allows it to be asserted that he has recalled a general on the 24th of March, it is not fitting that that general should be acting apparently with full powers on the 9th of April."

It is easy to raise a howl against Russia to cover minis-

terial blundering, but it is not so easy to prove Russia to
have been really in the wrong. Before discussing this,
however, let us ask how it was that in a matter affecting
the most vital interests of our empire Sir Charles Dilke (in
all this business Earl Granville seems to have been treated by
both parties as a nonentity) should have contented himself
with the second-hand whispers of a German functionary,
instead of obtaining a clear explanation from the Emperor
himself. Surely England has not yet descended to such a
depth of grovelling self-effacement and ignominy that her
statesmen are frightened to put a plain question to a
Nihilist-stricken potentate? In omitting to demand a
frank declaration of policy from the Tsar himself at such
an important juncture, and in staking so much on the
verbal communication of a German intermediary, the
Gladstone administration was guilty of a breach of statecraft which has few parallels in modern times. As regards
the communication itself, it would be difficult perhaps to
detect where the error lay, if there was any error. Each
of the three parties concerned, the Tsar, the German
Ambassador, and Sir Charles Dilke, might impute the
misunderstanding to each other. In the absence, therefore, of any precise official information, we have no right
to fix the blame on Russia. Frankly, I would sooner
impute trickery, if there has been trickery, to Sir Charles
Dilke or other members of the Gladstone cabinet, than I
would to Alexander III. There is more unscrupulosity of
speech and action perpetrated in the faction-ridden House
of Commons in one session than there is by Russian
diplomacy in a century.

For more than two years Russia had so frankly and so
frequently declared her intention of annexing Akhal, and
all her actions had so clearly led up to the consummation

of this policy,' that I find it difficult to believe that the Tsar was guilty of wilfully, or even accidentally, giving rise to an impression that he meant to abandon his conquests. The more probable supposition is, that the English Government wanted a weapon to break down the powerful Opposition attack, and, in the trickish manner peculiar to Parliamentary politicians, placed on the Tsar's words a forced construction purely their own. But let us take Sir Charles Dilke's declaration on its own merits: "The very first act of the new Emperor has been to recall General Skobeleff, and to put a stop to the whole of the undertakings of that general in Central Asia." There was nothing in this to imply an intention to evacuate Akhal. All that was said was that Skobeleff was to come home, and that a stop was to be put to the operations—reconnoitring and other—he had been conducting in the direction of the Tedjend. Russia has kept her word. Skobeleff has come home, and the undertakings he had in hand have been entirely brought to an end.

But, either with "intent to deceive," or from a fatal stupidity which it seems almost impossible to ascribe to statesmen reputably possessing among them a natural share of common sense, the Gladstone Government still allowed the world to see that they clung to the belief that the Russians would fall back upon the Caspian. They resented every attempt to disturb them in their Fool's Paradise. When, on the 28th of April, Mr. Cowen, M.P., asked whether Sir Charles Dilke could give any further information respecting the alleged abandonment of the forward policy of Russia in Central Asia, the Under-

[1] The *Daily News* made the admission that the telegrams for two years from its St. Petersburg and Central Asian correspondents had pointed to ultimate annexation.

Secretary replied, "The statement I made on a former occasion is correct. General Skobeleff has been recalled, and the military operations have terminated;" adding triumphantly, in a manner that crushed the suspicions of the House and provoked loud Ministerial cheers—"Eight battalions of Skobeleff's troops are now on their way home."

The same day I received a copy of the official Tiflis journal, *Kavkaz*, confirming what Sir Charles Dilke had said, but nullifying its effect by adding, "*the troops are being replaced by fresh ones!*" I forwarded this to Mr. Cowen, but such was the reputation which the Under-Secretary enjoyed in the House for honesty and sagacity, that the member for Newcastle very properly preferred letting matters take their course for a few days to stirring up the troubled waters again with unpleasant questions. An interval then elapsed, during which Skobeleff started home, leaving garrisons at every point between the Caspian and Askabat. On the 14th of May the uneasiness of the public found expression in a question put to Sir Charles by Mr. Stanhope, receiving the rejoinder, "that there has been a stop put to the forward movements of the Russian army. In fact, so far from advancing, it has fallen back since the date of the Candahar debate (Hear, hear)." Fallen back to where? It was a pity there was no one in the House to "floor" the Government with this sledge-hammer query. The Russians had not fallen back an inch. *Previous to the debate* they had made some reconnoitring movements with cavalry in advance of Askabat, but these had ceased before the 24th of March. When Sir Charles made his famous March declaration, the Russian advanced guard was quietly camped at Askabat; it was there when Sir Charles made his dogmatic reply to Mr. Stanhope, in May. It is there now.

Two days after this reply Skobeleff arrived at St. Petersburg. Two days later the ukase was issued incorporating Akhal. In this manner General Lazareff's declaration in 1879 was carried into effect; and the intention of Russia to establish a permanent hold upon Akhal, expressed over and over again by M. de Giers, was finally realized. With respect to the two years' diplomatic campaign regarding Akhal, I find it difficult to formulate any charge of wrong-doing against Russia. In annexing Akhal she broke no promise, she violated no diplomatic understanding. Because we were foolish enough to give up Candahar to an obese sensualist, and resign a valuable province to anarchy and disorder, we had no right to expect Russia to follow suit at Geok Tepé. Of all the courses open to Russia for the disposal of her conquest, annexation pure and simple was the best. The only serious objection to it was that it was contrary to the sentiment of England, and was calculated to provoke a fresh outburst of animosity; but the sentiment was a false one, and did not deserve to be respected, while in regard to the animosity, Russia has grown so accustomed to seeing herself howled at by England (nothing ever comes of the howling, be it noted), that a consideration of this insignificant character could hardly be expected to influence her Central Asian policy.

It is curious, as illustrating the apathy of England to her Imperial interests, that the annexation of Akhal should have provoked no public controversy. The *Daily News* ignored it altogether, finding this the safest way to conceal the blundering statesmanship of the Gladstone Government. When Mr. Ashmead-Bartlett inquired on the 10th of June as to the extent of the Russian advance, Sir Charles Dilke felt himself sufficiently in harmony with the indifference of the public to Central Asian affairs to reply, that "Her Majesty's Chargé d'Affaires at St. Petersburg had been informed that the territory described as the Transcaspian territory was the Tekke oasis, but they had no information as to its limits." When Mr. Bartlett revealed his knowledge of the Turcoman region, by asking the simple and sensible question whether "the whole of the Tekke country, including Askabat, was comprised in the annexation," Sir Charles Dilke replied, in the *blasé*, *Cui Bono* manner he seems to have picked up from the Marquis of Hartington, that "when those limits were known, the request might be complied with, but at present the Government did not know the exact position of the country occupied by the Russian forces." Such an astounding exhibition of Jack-in-Office ignorance must have struck many admirers of "Greater Britain" (and there are few who do not delight in that clever work) with painful surprise. If English statesmen will not be at pains to know what is transpiring in Central Asia antagonistic to our interests—and I presume we are all of us, either Liberals or Conservatives, interested in Russia's forward operations in the direction of India—what confidence can we place in the security of our Eastern Empire? As regards the position of Skobeleff's troops, full details had been published by the Russian newspapers; and hence, England having an Embassy with paid translators at St. Petersburg, the Government had no excuse for remaining in ignorance of it, while with respect to the "exact position of the country," so much had been published of late on the matter[1] in English, that here again the Government had no ground for indulgence.

[1] The two works previously referred to give the amplest details regarding Akhal and the contiguous region.

Appendix.

But this ignorance of Russia's operations in Asia, affected or otherwise, was nothing more than part and parcel of a policy having for its aim the withdrawal of England from all affairs outside our Indian border. Russia is to be allowed to close round Afghanistan and Persia unhindered; she is to be permitted, from the new base of operations afforded by the oasis of Akhal, to lay her plans for the absorption of Khorassan. Persia is to be suffered to become a second Khiva. Such a yard-measure policy may lead to diminished budgets—and diminished trade—but England will find after a while, that if an Empire is worth having at all, it must be governed in an Imperial manner, and not by the petty principles that prevail in a parish workhouse. England could do very well without a certain section of the Liberal party, but it is open to doubt whether she could get on as she does without India.

HAS ENGLAND LOST HERAT?[1]

HAVE the Russians made such advances in Central Asia that we may be said to have practically lost Herat? "Certainly not," is the general answer; "we still enjoy advantages over our rival, being as close to Herat as he is, in spite of our withdrawal from Candahar, and being able, moreover, by our large resources in India, and our superior communications with Afghanistan, to anticipate any occupation of the city, or, at any rate, to send against it a force that would easily wrest it from any Russian raiding party that had captured it by a *coup de main*." Is this impression of the security of Herat founded on facts? What will be said if proof be forthcoming that the Russians are in every respect very much closer to Herat than we are; that they could occupy it with a force from the Caucasus in a fortnight less time than an English army from India; and that, moreover, they are completing a few links in their communications which will enable them next year to invade Herat from Odessa in six weeks less time than we could send a force from England to the menaced city, and even, if the line to Askabat be completed, with the same army of invasion reach Candahar at the same time as our troops? Such facts seem so startling, that they need to be subjected to careful investigation before accepting them as a basis for political argument.

[1] *Army and Navy Magazine*, November, 1881. By the Author.

The position which India occupies with regard to the English foreposts on the Afghan frontier has its counterpart in the relations between the Caucasus and the Russian forts along the border of Khorassan. India is the basis of any English operations against Afghanistan, and the Caucasus of any Russian. These two bases may be well compared before discussing the relative ability of England and Russia to aid them with fresh resources.

First, as to which of the two bases could despatch an army in the shortest time to Herat. Sukhur, on the Indus, from its position in regard to the Indian railway system and the port of Kurratchee, may be appropriately selected as a point of concentration for the English army in India, while its counterpart will be found in the port of Michaelovsk, in the Caspian. It is obviously an impossible matter to decide, in the absence of any Russian data, which of the two countries would be the readiest with their preparations at the starting-point. But the proximity of the principal Caucasian military depôts to Michaelovsk affords a strong reason for believing that a force could arrive there from Vladikavkaz, Baku, and Petrovsk, in quite as little time as it would take for an English column to assemble at Sukhur.

From Michaelovsk to Fort Bami extends the Transcaspian railroad and tramway, corresponding with the line from Sukhur to Sibi, at the entrance to the Bolan Pass. From Bami to Askabat is easy marching, which has to be compared with the extremely heavy journey from Sibi, across the Bolan, to Quetta. After this a third stage runs direct from each forepost to Herat.

The Russian railway beyond the Caspian already extends to Kizil Arvat, if not, indeed, beyond; while the Decauville portable railroad, for which locomotives are provided, but which is only worked by horses, traverses the oasis of Akhal as far as Bami. Very shortly the railway will be finished to Bami, and the tram will then run from Bami to Geok Tepé. From Port Michaelovsk to Fort Bami the distance is 190 miles. From Sukhur, on the Indus, to the Bolan at Sibi is 133½ miles. The difference of fifty-six and a half miles would mean three or four hours more railway travelling for the Russians than for the English; but as the Transcaspian railway is on a larger scale than the Sukhur-Sibi one, the real difference is not so great as to demand particular notice in the calculations we have in view.

From Bami to Askabat is 100 miles; from Sibi to Quetta eighty-five miles. The former traverses country as grassy and as level as Hyde Park the whole of the way,[1] and is not intersected by rivers of any size. Water, forage, and fuel exist in abundance along the route; and, at the usual rate of marching in Turkestan, a Russian army would arrive at Askabat from Bami, without severe exertion, in about six days. On the other hand, the shorter distance between Sibi and Quetta consists of such difficult country that an army cannot cover it in less than eight days, and arrives at its destination in a distressed condition, after undergoing an amount of wear and tear in traversing the Bolan, which a Russian force would escape. There would thus be a difference of two days in favour of Russia on reaching the foreposts.

From Quetta to Herat, viâ Candahar, is 514 miles; from Askabat to Herat, viâ Meshed, is 370 miles. This difference of 144 miles would be as good as ten days'

[1] The country is fully described in " The Russian Campaign against the Turcomans," and " Merv, the Queen of the World." W. H. Allen and Co. 1881.

march to Russia, and raises the amount in her favour to twelve days. But a careful examination of the country and its resources between Askabat and Herat, and between Quetta and Herat, shows that the Russians would be able to traverse their section two or three days quicker than we our own. In this manner Russia would be able to enter Herat, under the existing arrangements, a fortnight in advance of any English force hurrying forward from India to save it from seizure.

But there is another factor which must not be overlooked in any calculations. England, in marching upon Herat, would have to traverse hostile Afghanistan, and perhaps might have her progress arrested several days by resistance at Candahar. At any rate, she might expect tribal troubles most of the way. On the other hand, Russia would move through friendly Khorassan, traversing Persian territory up to within two or three marches of Herat, and, in this intervening sparsely-populated district would experience none of those tribal difficulties we should encounter even before we got to Candahar. It is difficult to gauge precisely the gain that would accrue to Russia through experiencing no political delays and tribal resistance *en route*, but it might very easily amount to a week in her favour, and, in that case, would give her a superiority of three weeks in a march upon Herat.

Russia might also make a move upon Herat by the shorter and more level road *viâ* Sarakhs, but her flank would be exposed to the attack of the Merv Tekkes for a long distance, and she would require a large number of troops to guard the communications. Once an alliance with the Tekkes, however, is effected—by no means an improbability in the immediate future—this shorter road can be safely utilized, and a further advantage gained over India.

Another point must also not be overlooked. The Russians in Central Asia march with one camel to every three men. In our advance, in 1879, upon Candahar, we employed one camel and one camp-follower to every Anglo-Indian soldier. This excess of transport of an English army operating from India of three times over and above that of a Russian force operating from the Caucasus, together with an extra army of servants as large as itself, is insisted upon by Indian military writers as a necessity,[1] although Russians take a very different view of the matter, and regard it as one of the great advantages they should enjoy over ourselves in any rapid war operations in the country lying between Turkmenia and India.

The army of the Caucasus consists of 150,000 men on a peace footing, and double that number when mobilized on an outbreak of war. It is composed mainly of Europeans, whose constitutions are kept in excellent condition by the magnificent climate of the Caucasus. Their loyalty and their bravery are beyond doubt. Against them would be matched the army of India, consisting of 65,000 European troops, whose constitutions had been to a certain extent weakened by residence in a hot climate; 125,000 native troops, whose loyalty could not be absolutely guaranteed; and 381,000 troops belonging to the native princes, whose fidelity, Russia thinks, could not be relied upon at all. A military expert alone could decide which army would be the

---

[1] "Analyzing the table given of the Candahar force, and straining the question as you will, there is only one result, viz. that for every fighting-man you must have one follower and one camel.'
—Le Messurier's "Kandahar in 1879."

stronger, but it is not too much for a civilian to affirm that, at the very least, the inferiority would not lie to a very marked extent with Russia. In this manner we see that the Caucasus, possessing military resources presumably not very inferior to those of India, could despatch to Herat an army as large as any India could furnish, in fourteen days less time than ourselves, requiring only one-third the transport, enjoying happy immunity from a horde of camp-followers, and probably experiencing a further gain of a week, in consequence of our having to move through a hostile country to arrive at the Key of India.

But there is one other great advantage Russia possesses which throws all the foregoing into the shade. The extent of this can only be ascertained by instituting a comparison between the time it would take to aid India with English resources, and that which Russia would require to reinforce the military strength of the Caucasus.

The voyage from England to Kurratchee occupies on an average about twenty-five days. Between Kurratchee and Sukhur exists railway communication. To traverse this section would add another day to the journey. In this manner it would take twenty-six days for England to reinforce the Indian army operating against Herat from Sukhur, of which twenty-five would be passed by the troops on a highway open at any point to the attacks of the enemy's cruisers. Against Russian cruisers the Indian troopers journeying from Portsmouth to Kurratchee might probably be safe; but what would be the result of a Russo-French alliance? Our relations with France in Africa are not so satisfactory that our statesmen can afford to dismiss such a combination from their calculations.

Without going beyond her usual arrangements, Russia has assembled 65,000 troops in the Odessa district, for the autumnal inspection, during the last few weeks. This will give some idea of the force that Odessa alone could despatch, on an emergency, to the assistance of the Caucasus, to say nothing of other points in proximity to the Black Sea. With the Russian railway system stretching to Odessa, to Nicolaeff, to Sebastopol, to Mariopol, to Taganrog, and to Rostoff, the Czar has it in his power to assemble on the shores of the Black Sea and Sea of Azoff a force for the assistance of the Army of the Caucasus, as large as any we could hope to despatch from England to India. There is very little doubt that he could assemble an immensely more powerful army than we could; but the moderate estimate we have made will answer our purpose quite as well as any larger one.

From the points we have mentioned, troops could be conveyed across the Black Sea to Poti and Batoum in forty-eight hours. Poti is twelve hours' distance from Tiflis by rail. The branch line connecting Batoum with the Tiflis-Poti railway is under course of construction, and, when finished, will give Russia two ports of debarkation on the Caucasian coast. For the present she would use Poti.

Between Tiflis and Baku there is also another line of railway under course of construction. This will be finished by next year, when Russia will be able to convey troops across the Caucasus, from the Black Sea to the Caspian, in very little more than a day. As it is, the 400 miles between Tiflis and Baku alone take thirty-seven days to traverse. From Baku to Michaelovsk the steamboat journey occupies two days. Thus, the present conveyance of troops from Odessa to Michaelovsk occupies forty-two days, as compared with the twenty-six days required to convey reinforcements from Portsmouth to Sukhur, leaving a balance of sixteen days in our favour. This, however, does not wipe off the superiority enjoyed by the Russians in any movement from their forepost; while, directly the important link between Tiflis and Baku is finished, the advantage will be altogether on the side of Russia. She will then be able to send troops from Odessa to Michaelovsk in five days, and enjoy a gain over the despatch of military forces from Portsmouth to Sukhur of three weeks.

In this manner, as soon as the Tiflis-Baku railway is finished, Russia will be able to despatch troops from her home provinces to her Transcaspian base in three weeks less time than we can send reinforcements to India; she will enjoy a further superiority of a fortnight in marching those troops from Michaelovsk to Herat, over an English column marching towards the same destination from the Indus; and, unless Afghanistan becomes friendly to ourselves and Khorassan hostile to Russia—both events improbable—she may count upon another week's grace at Herat, while tribal attacks and complications delay us on the road. Russia will, consequently, be in a position next year to occupy Herat, with an army from Odessa, in six weeks less time than we could hope to do with troops from England.

More than this. She will be in a position to march an army from Odessa almost as far as Candahar before troops can arrive there from England, and if she completes the rail from Bami to Askabat, 100 miles, even reach it at the same moment as our soldiers.

The accompanying march-routes will demonstrate this:

Russia to Candahar on the completion of the Tiflis-Baku Railway, 1882.

	Days.
Odessa to Michaelovsk	5
Michaelovsk to Askabat	7
Askabat to Herat, *viâ* Sarakhs [1]	20
Herat to Candahar	24
Total	56

If the Russians complete the Transcaspian railway to Askabat next year, as contemplated, the journey from Michaelovsk to Askabat will be abridged to a day, thus making a despatch of troops from Odessa to Candahar feasible in fifty days.

England to Candahar.

	Days.
England to Kurratchee	25
Kurratchee to Sibi	2
Sibi to Quetta	8
Quetta to Candahar	15
Total	50

It has been pointed out that during the twenty-five days' voyage from England to India, the troops would be liable to attack from the enemy's men-of-war and cruisers. Russia would experience a similar danger only during the two days' voyage from Sebastopol or Odessa to Poti. But any war between England and Russia would probably be of an all-round character. No other power but ourselves would fight for the preservation of Constantinople from Russia. By a sudden move Russia, with the assistance of the armies of Bulgaria and East Roumelia, might

---

[1] Calculated at fifteen miles a day. Kaufmann marched a force for two months at this rate in 1880, arriving at Kuldja in splendid condition.

establish such a hold upon the Bosphorus as would keep the Black Sea free from English cruisers. We, on our part, could adopt no similar movement to protect our extended line from England to India from hostile attack.

But supposing the Black Sea entered, and the communications between Odessa and Poti severed, Russia would only have to fall back upon two other lines, which she already uses for Transcaspian operations, and which will not be superseded until the Baku-Tiflis railroad is finished. One of these extends from Vladikavkaz, at the head of the Russian railway system in the Caucasus, by road to the Caspian port of Petrovsk; and the other from Tsaritzin, at the head of the railway system on the Volga, by water to Michaelovsk.

The latter merits particular notice, because the journey from Tsaritzin to Michaelovsk can be effected in a week, and Tsaritzin lies nearer to Russia's inner resources than Odessa. With an improved organization of the steamboat traffic, the journey could be accomplished in five days, which would be as quick as the journey from Odessa to Michaelovsk on the completion of the Baku-Tiflis railway. Russia has thus two good routes to Afghanistan, of which one is perfectly secure from attack, as compared with our single and easily assailable line from England to India. An alternative one is the route mentioned above, from Russia by railway to Vladikavkaz to the Caucasus, and thence to Petrovsk, on the Caspian, by road. From Vladikavkaz to Petrovsk a railway has been long projected. When this is carried out, the Vladikavkaz route will be as good as the other two. At present, it takes quite sixteen days for troops to get from Vladikavkaz to the Transcaspian coast, which makes it considerably shorter than the existing incomplete Odessa-Michaelovsk communication, but eleven days longer than the latter will be next year.

The recent Russian advance upon Askabat, and the retirement of England from Candahar, have been partly the cause of the superiority, present and prospective, which Russia enjoys in despatching an army to Herat; but a greater cause is to be found in the improvement of the communications between the Russian home provinces and Central Asia. When the Russian forepost was at Michaelovsk, the Cossack was 670 miles from Herat, *viâ* Askabat and Meshed; while the sepoy at Quetta was only 514 miles distant; thus leaving a balance of 156 miles in our favour. Had we permanently occupied Candahar as a counterpoise to the Russian occupation of Askabat, we should have been within 369 miles of Herat, as compared with the 370 miles intervening between Askabat and Herat, *viâ* Meshed, or a little over 300 *viâ* Sarakhs and the valley of the Heri Rood.

But we threw away Candahar, and fell back upon Quetta, with a result that we deliberately placed 514 miles between ourselves and Herat, although we knew Russia had permanently taken up a stand within 300-370 miles of the place.

We did this, recklessly ignoring the fact—which none of the eminent authorities who expressed their opinions in the Blue-book this year on the Retention of Candahar ever once referred to—that Russia, by the rapid construction of railways between her advanced posts and her base, was acquiring an advantage over ourselves which we could not possibly hope to recover. Only extraordinary improvements in the propulsion of steamers, which no statesman can take into calculation, can abridge the twenty-five days' journey between England and India to any appreciable extent. Russia, on the other hand, by merely completing a railway link between Tiflis and Baku, *which was commenced previous to the evacuation of Candahar*, diminishes at a stroke the journey between the great military depôts on the coast of the Black Sea and the Transcaspian region from forty-two days to five!

With Russia thus so much nearer Herat than we are, so much better able to occupy it than ourselves, and actively completing communications which will place her home troops six weeks nearer Herat than our own—can we conscientiously regard the key of India as more within our power than within the power of Russia? Is the August declaration of the Marquis of Hartington, that England "will not allow any foreign power to meddle with the internal or external affairs of Afghanistan," a sufficient protection to Herat against its inevitable seizure by Russia, in advance of ourselves, by a larger force, on any declaration of war? It is believed to be an understood thing that we should treat an open Russian advance upon Herat as a *casus belli*. Has it ever occurred to our statesmen that Russia might adopt the same course against ourselves in the event of an English advance upon the place?—Russia being so bitterly averse to an English occupation of Herat. Whether we accepted her challenge or she ours, the advantage would rest with her all the same. It would be within her power to be the first to enter the "key of India." Such being the case, is it too much to ask ourselves the question—Has England lost Herat?

THE RUSSIAN FLEET IN CENTRAL ASIA.[1]

OF recent years little has been published about the operations of the Russian fleet in Central Asia, although, in the interval, the Aral steamers have penetrated to the Afghan towns on the Oxus, and bold plans have been drawn up for establishing a waterway between that river and the Caspian. The possibility of war-vessels plying from Cronstadt to Koondooz, and from Astrabad to the Syr Daria ferry near Tashkent, may seem to many minds chimerical, but the true statesman is bound to take notice of every circumstance that may affect his policy. It is known that General Kaufmann and the Grand Duke Michael are warm advocates of the diversion of the Oxus into the Caspian, and we have recent advices from Khiva that General Glukhovsky, a veteran explorer of the Aral-Caspian steppes, has confirmed, from actual official survey, the feasibility of the project. With, however, this particular question we have nothing to say on this occasion, the Russian data dealing with the scheme being too large to be compressed within the limits of two or three pages. What we purpose doing is, to describe the rise, and progress, and actual condition of the marine in Turkestan, that the public may be able to clearly estimate Russia's naval strength to-day in Central Asia. A few

---

[1] *Army and Navy Magazine*, March, 1881. By the Author.

words will then be sufficient to deal wtth the development and scope of the Aral Fleet in the immediate future.

The Syr Daria and Oxus rivers flow almost parallel through Turkestan, and empty themselves at opposite points into the Sea of Aral; the one at the northern extremity, and the other at the south. Until recently the naval operations of the fleet were restricted to the Syr Daria and Aral, and it is only within the last few years that gunboats have essayed to navigate the Oxus as far as the Afghan frontier. The navigable part of the Syr Daria commences at Fort Tchinaz, a ferry ten hours' drive from Tashkent, to which it serves as a river port. The river here is two-thirds of a mile wide, and rapid and yellow. Its characteristics as a mountain stream, narrow, deep, and abounding with rapids, are lost at Tchinaz, and from that point to Perovsky it courses smoothly through an undulating plain, broadening out as it rolls swiftly along, and cutting a tortuous channel for itself out of the soft alluvial soil. On leaving Fort Perovsky it enters a marshy level, and throws out branches on either side that waste their waters on swamps or sands. The chief of these is the Yany Daria, or New River, which runs out towards the Aral, and expires in the desert midway between the mouths of the Oxus and Syr Daria. A short distance below the point where the Syr sends out this useless shoot, the river divides itself into two channels, running through a swamp. One of these is the Kara Uziak, useless for navigation purposes, and the other the Jaman Daria, or Bad River, having a course of 150 miles, a width at places of only 200 feet, a winding channel full of shoals, and a depth of water rarely exceeding three or four feet, and mostly as low as twelve inches. On quitting this swamp the river recovers its volume, and in spite of a rocky bed, is navigable thence to the sea.

In this manner the river may be divided into three sections: from Tchinaz to Fort Perovsky navigable, from Perovsky to Fort No. 2 almost impassable, and from Fort No. 2 to the sea again navigable. In 1856 Captain Butakoff tried to widen a stream connecting the Kara Uziak with the Jaman Daria, so as to increase the volume of the latter, but the channel shoaled up directly water was let into it. In 1860 works were commenced for cleaning out the Kara Uziak for four miles, which operation, it was estimated, would occupy sixty-five men for 180 days, but the undertaking was never proceeded with. In 1862 an attempt failed for increasing the water in the Jaman Daria; and four years later an expedition sent to explore the Kara Uziak reported the cleansing of the channel to be an impossibility. In 1866 a canal was cut from the Syr to the Jaman Daria, above its commencement, employing 400 men for seventeen days, and costing 2471 roubles. Unfortunately it became clogged with sand the moment it was opened, and since then nothing has been done to effect further improvement.

The Aral Fleet may be said to have commenced its existence in 1847, when two two-masted schooners, the *Nikolai* and the *Mikhail*, were conveyed in sections from Orenburg to Aralsk, a point on the Syr Daria near the Aral occupied the same year; and were sent down the river to survey the sea. These vessels did little beyond exploring the mouth of the stream during the short season of 1847, but the following year Lieutenant Butakoff proceeded to the Aral in the *Konstantin*, a much larger wooden vessel, and in 1848 and 1849 completely surveyed the Aral. In 1850 General Obrutcheff suggested the construction of two steamers to patrol the Syr Daria, to prevent the Khivans from crossing the river to pillage the Russian Kirghiz. It was also thought that their rapid conveyance of troops, and the novelty of their appearance, would strike terror into the unsophisticated Central Asian mind, while they might prove of great service in co-operating with the projected expedition against Khiva. Accordingly the *Perovsky*, a 40-horse power steamer, and the *Obrutcheff*, a screw iron barque of 12-horse power, were ordered in Sweden; the former being designed with a movable keel, so as to serve on the Sea of Aral, as well as on the Syr. Their collective cost was 37,445 roubles, which was increased to 49,374 roubles, or 6200*l.*, in conveying them in segments to Central Asia and defraying the expenses of the Swedish mechanics sent out to put them together. Pending their construction, the schooners *Konstantin* and *Mikhail* were employed throughout the season of 1851 in conveying *saksaoul* to the island of the Kos Aral. *Saksaoul* is a species of briar, with close fibre and abundance of knots. Extreme difficulty is experienced in cutting or sawing it, and it mostly breaks into crooked and unmanageable pieces. General Perovsky was so disgusted with this native fuel, that he reported home that it would be impossible to keep the flotilla supplied with it alone, owing to its scarcity and awkwardness for the furnaces. In consequence of his statements, the following year, 180 tons of anthracite coal were sent from the Don, at a cost of six roubles, or fifteen shillings, a ton.

In 1853 the *Perovsky* was launched at Aralsk, and was sent with two transports—the barges No. 1 and No. 2, of 56 tons' cargo capacity each, built by the Kama-Votka Company—up the river Syr to Fort Perovsky, or Ak

Metchet, which had been taken by storm on the 9th of August of the same year by a force of 2000 troops and twelve guns. Experiments conducted throughout the season showed that the *Perorsky* could only make three round trips during the seven-and-a-half months of open navigation, ten or twelve days being needed for the journey up the river to the fort, and seven or eight for the voyage down the stream, tugging two barges. When anthracite was burnt, the journey to Perovsky and back cost 2500 roubles; when *saksaoul* only 520. The Russians, therefore, decided to use *saksaoul* alone, especially as immense quantities had been discovered in the advance of the military forces up the river. As the water-carriage per pood (36 lbs.) was three copecks, or a penny, when briar-fuel was used, and forty-seven copecks when the stores were conveyed by road, it was decided to develop the Syr Daria flotilla, and make use of the stream as much as possible for transport purposes. The experiments brought out clearly the defects of the two pioneer steamers; the *Perovsky*, drawing three or four feet of water, constantly getting aground in the Syr, owing to its excessive draught, while the little *Obrutcheff* had such feeble engines that it could not tug anything against the stream.

In 1860 an order was given to the Windsor Works, at Liverpool, for two new steamers, of corrugated iron, with flat bottoms and paddles at the stern; one, the *Syr Daria*, to be of 20-horse power, and the other, the *Aral*, to have engines of double that motive force. Both were conveyed from Orenburg to the Aral in sections, on the backs of camels, and were put together by Russian mechanics at the newly-established naval station at Kazala, fifty miles higher up the Syr than Aralsk. On being tried in 1862, neither gave satisfaction, their skins being thin and fragile, and their machinery so badly designed that ten per cent. of the steam was lost in passing from the boilers to the engines, on account of the excessive distance between them. Thanks to these defects and their great draught, the *Aral* could only carry 216 tons instead of 540 tons, when steaming at three miles an hour, while the *Syr Daria* failed to convey more than 172 out of a projected cargo of 216 tons. Alterations to the engines, however, subsequently improved both vessels, though they have never fulfilled the expectations of their designers. In company with these two steamers came, from Liverpool, a corrugated iron floating pontoon-dock, a barge, and six iron shallops, and were followed by three iron barges from the Kama-Votka Works. The dock cost 34,300 roubles, or 4300*l.*, and was made in two divisions. When it was launched at Kazala the current of the river was found to be so strong, that the structure ran a risk of being carried away by the floods in spring and autumn, the repairing seasons at the river port. The dock, therefore, was never used, and in 1873 was cut up into four large ferry-boats. The English barge, No. 4, did not obey its rudder, and was not employed for many years, until at last a more energetic dockyard chief at Kazala rectified the defect. The Liverpool-built shallops were attached to the steamers and barges. As to the three barges constructed at the Kama-Votka Works, ninety feet long, with two masts and sails, they also drew three-and-a-half feet of water when carrying sixty-three tons of freight, and were thus extremely inconvenient for service on the shallow Syr. Two causes may be assigned for these successive failures: bad design and carelessness in putting the vessels together. For the former, the Russians were exclusively to blame, while, as regards the latter, censure can be only mitigated in one instance, when the Swedes put the *Perovsky* and *Obrutcheff* together at Aralsk, under Russian supervision.

In the meanwhile Russia had been pushing on with her conquests up the river Syr. The excellence of the channel above Perovsky encouraged her to advance further along the stream, and in 1864 Tchernayeff occupied Tchinaz, at the head of the river navigation, and the following year stormed Tashkent. This advance led to a further strain upon the Aral flotilla, to meet which the *Samarcand*, of 70-horse power, was ordered of Cockerill, in Belgium, together with two more iron barges, Nos. 6 and 7. This steamer was launched in 1869, and, notwithstanding the thinness of its plates, has proved the most successful vessel of the fleet. Since 1873 it has done inestimable service in exploring the river Oxus, and proved its value a few weeks ago in ferrying Colonel Kouropatkin and his Samarcand contingent across the stream to Tchardjui, thus enabling him to join without delay Skobeleff's army at Geok Tepé.

Three years previous to the launch of the *Samarcand*, the Russian authorities in Turkestan had finally given up all thoughts of improving the Jaman section of the Syr Daria, and now decided to divide the river into three sections, employing the large steamers to run on the navigable reaches, and connecting them by a service of shallow boats traversing the Jaman swamp. This system involved all the disadvantages attending a shift of cargo twice during the journey from Kazala to Tchinaz, but it enabled the authorities to take advantage of the longer period of navigation in the upper part of the river. In the Tchinaz-Perovsky reach the open season is from the middle of March to the end of October (o.s.); in the Jaman swamp from March 25th to the middle of September; and in the Kazala section from March 25th to the 20th of October.

For service between Tchinaz and Perovsky the steamer *Aral* was assigned; between the outlet of the Jaman channel and Kazala the *Syr Daria* and *Perovsky*. To connect the two, and traverse the Jaman Daria, where there is usually only a foot or so of water, and no more than four feet during the three to six weeks' floods in June and July, the Government caused a fresh steamer to be built in 1870 at the Kama-Votka Works. This, the *Tashkent*, was to have drawn only eighteen inches of water when heavily laden, but proved to be very much deeper, and was almost as great a failure as the rest.

Since 1870 no more steamers have been added to the Aral fleet, and only one or two barges. In an accompanying table will be found full particulars of the vessels, together with their respective armaments. Writing from Kazala a few months ago, a naval officer, belonging to the dockyard, thus described their actual condition: "The *Perovsky* is twenty-seven years old, and is the best liked of all the gunboats. Its boilers, however, can only last another year, its under-water parts are completely rotten, and its engines are worn out with hard work and old age. The *Aral* and *Syr Daria*, seventeen years old, are a little better, but still their days are numbered. The *Samarcand*, a youngster of twelve, is the pearl of the fleet. She goes well, and defies her great defect of excessively light constitution. The *Tashkent* is a tiny craft, altogether spoilt by engines of the most wretched description."

From the tabulated statements given—the latest obtainable from Tashkent—it will be seen that Russia's marine in Central Asia consists of six steamers, nine transport barges, seven large iron ferry-boats, ten iron long-boats for the various river forts, and twelve iron and four wooden shallops belonging to the steamers and barges. The barges carry guns as well as the steamers, the latter having thirteen altogether, and the former nine between them.

THE ARAL FLEET.—STEAMERS.

Name of Vessel.	Horse-power.		Displacement in Tons.	Dimensions in Feet.			Armament.	When and where built.
	Nom.	Ind.		Length.	Breadth.	Draught.		
1. Perovsky .	40	93	157	107	22	3	One 4-pr. and two 9-pr. howitzers.	1853, Mutual Works, Sweden.
2. Obrutcheff .	12	18	—	70	9	2½	None.	Do. do.
3. Syr Daria .	20	41	66	88	18	2½	One 9-pr. bronze howitzer.	1862, Windsor Works, Liv'pool.
4. Aral . . .	40	92	149	105	24	3½	Two 9-pr. do.	Do. do.
5. Samarcand .	70	213	167	150	22	2⅔	Two 4-prs., two 36-lb. howitzers, and two 6-lb. carronades.	1866, Cockerill, Belgium.
6. Tashkent .	35	—	86	105	24	2	One 9-pr.	1870, Kama-Votka Works.

THE ARAL FLEET.—TRANSPORTS.

Name of Vessel.	Cargo capacity in Tons.	Displacement in Tons.	Dimensions in Feet.			When and where built.
			Length.	Breadth.	Draught.	
Barge No. 1. .	56	96	99	18	3½	1855, Kama-Votka Works.
,, No. 2. .	,,	,,	,,	,,	,,	Do. do.
,, No. 3. .	60	102	94½	18	3½	1860 do.
,, No. 4. .	30	38	64	17	1½	Do. Windsor Works, Liverpool.
,, No. 6. .	121	165	120	20	3½	1855, Cockerill, Belgium.
,, No. 7. .	,,	,,	,,	,,	,,	Do. do.
,, No. 8. .	130	226	126	26	3½	1871, Kama-Votka Works.
,, No. 9. .	,,	,,	,,	,,	,,	Do. do.
,, No. 10. .	185	305	140	29	3⅔	Do. do.

THE ARAL FLEET.—MINOR VESSELS.

Description.	Displacement in Tons.	Dimensions in Feet.			When and where built.
		Length.	Breadth.	Draught.	
3 Iron Ferry-boats .	34	70	20	2	1859, Kama-Votka Works.
2 ,, . .	30	38	17	2	1873 and 1877, made from Pontoon Dock.
2 ,, . .	25	30	20	2	1872 and 1875, do.
2 Iron Long-boats . .	8¼	35	12½	2	1854, Nijni Novgorod.
8 ,, ,, .	5	26	7½	2	1859, Kama-Votka Works.
8 Iron Shallops . .	1½	25	6	1½	1871, do.
4 ,, ,, .	1	20	5	1½	1862, Windsor Works, Liverpool.
1 Wooden Shallops .	1	20	5	1½	1866, Kazalu.

The *personnel* of the fleet consists of fifteen staff and superior officers, fifteen engineers, 322 seamen, and 275 riflemen. The seamen are armed with breechloaders, boarding-pikes, and Colt revolvers. Nearly every one can swim. The Aral Fleet is subject to the Russian Admiralty only as regards the appointment of individuals to it; in every other respect it is under the control of the War Office. The officers and seamen are drawn from the whole of the navy, and serve a specified period in Central Asia. Formerly they only received home-service pay for serving there, but within the last few weeks a reorganization has taken place, resulting in their pay being placed on the same footing as that of men serving in the Pacific, or twice as much as they formerly received. Service on the Syr is by no means child's play. In the summer the heat is intense, and blisters the feet of the seamen employed on the decks of the steamers and barges. In the Jaman swamp enormous numbers of mosquitoes abound, rendering it imperative for the crews to wear veils. Extreme caution has also to be observed in touching the *saksaoul*, which usually swarms with scorpions and phalange or stinging spiders.

Great difficulty is experienced as regards fuel. From the mouth of the Syr to Utch Kayook, 1100 versts, *saksaoul* is used, costing from Kazala to Perovsky ten copecks a *pood*,[1] and higher up the stream four copecks. This is piled at the water-edge at intervals of fifty versts. Between the mouth of the Syr and Utch Kayook there are twenty-three of these *saksaoul* depôts. The requirements of the fleet have told so much on the briarwood supply, that last year the steamers had to stop repeatedly

[1] One hundred copecks make a rouble, the fluctuating value of which may be calculated at half a crown. A pood is 36 lbs.—$62\frac{1}{56}$ go to a ton. A verst is about two-thirds of a mile.

for want of it. In the autumn, however, some shafts were sunk at Ak-Djar, ninety miles above Kazala, and thirty tons of coal extracted. This will be tried on board the *Tashkent* in the spring, and if it prove satisfactory the Russians will be able to dispense altogether with *saksaoul*. Beyond Utch Kayook, as far as Tchinaz, coal is already in use, being brought from some mines near Tashkent. In this section of the river there are six coaling depôts at intervals of ninety miles, and eleven wood depôts at intervals of fifty. Coal costs the Russian Government thirty-two copecks a pood, or 2*l*. 10*s*. a ton, and wood ten or twelve roubles the fathom, weighing forty poods.

The dockyard is situated at Kazala, a small fort on the river-bank, 3115 versts from St. Petersburg, 937 from Tashkent, and 595 from Fort Petro-Alexandrovsk, in the Khivan oasis. The river Syr is yearly wearing its way towards the north, tearing down every flood vast quantities of earth along its right bank, on which Kazala, Perovsky, and other Russian forts are situated. It is thus menaced with destruction. In the winter the ice at Kazala is over a yard thick. The steamers then are kept on shore, alongside the scattering of shanties forming the dockyard. A branch establishment is maintained at Fort Petro-Alexandrovsk, where there is a repairing yard and barracks for 100 seamen.

When the fleet was first established hopes were entertained that the transport of private merchandise would, in course of time, cover the expenses of the steamers, but these have never been realized. In 1865 upwards of 218 tons of private freight was carried; in 1866 this had increased to 318 tons, and in 1867 to 404 tons; but the following year the amount fell to fifty-six tons, and during the last decade the quantity has been so insignificant that it has not figured at all in the official returns. The causes of the falling off are the extreme slowness of water-transport, the difficulties of navigation, and the usual large accumulation of Government stores at Kazala in the spring, when, as might be expected, private interests are sacrificed to the necessities of State. In 1869, the Government contemplated turning the Aral fleet into a private concern, and the Lebed Company, one of the principal steamboat corporations on the Volga, was induced to send two agents to Central Asia, but their report was so thoroughly adverse to the project that it has only been taken up afresh within the last few months. At the present moment the steamers are employed chiefly in conveying Government stores and troops. The busiest season yet experienced by the fleet was in 1874, when 3000 tons of military stores and 4480 passengers were conveyed during the summer by the steamers. The average yearly transport is 1200 tons of goods and 2000 passengers.

The great drawback to the river service is its excessive slowness. The vessels always stop at night during a voyage, and constantly stick on shoals during the day-time. Until the season of 1880, when a new and energetic commander arrived at Kazala, the captains were wont to perform their voyages ashore, posting ahead of the vessels a good distance, and enjoying several days' holiday in the bosom of their families at Perovsky, while the steamers crawled lazily after them. When the vessel had approached within a few miles of its destination the captain would go aboard, and again assume command. From Tchinaz to Perovsky, 800 miles, the voyage occupies eight to fourteen days with the stream, and twelve to twenty days against it. The very broad margin left for the date of arrival is due to the constant delays occasioned by grounding, or bad weather, or deficiency of fuel. From Perovsky to Fort No. 2, through the Jaman swamp, a distance of about 200 miles, the voyage occupies two or three days with the stream, and three to six against it. A similar period is required to cover the identical distance between Fort No. 2 and Kazala.

The cost of the various vessels of the Aral fleet has been as follows:—

	Roubles.
Steamer Perovsky	37,445
,, Obrutcheff	
,, Syr Daria	16,000
,, Aral	30,080
,, Samarcand	78,700
,, Tashkent	35,000
Floating dock	34,300
Two iron long-boats	2400
Eight ,, ,, ,,	6400
Twelve iron shallops	6000
Four wooden ,,	400
Barge 1	16,428
,, 2	
,, 3	8000
,, 4	6000
,, 6	29,304
,, 7	
,, 8	41,400
,, 9	
,, 10	23,500
Ferry-boats	not known
Total	371,357

Adding one-third to this amount for the transport of the vessels in segments to the Syr Daria, and including the cost of the ferry boats, we attain a total of half a million roubles, or 63,500*l*., as the cost of establishing the Aral Fleet.

The annual expenditure of the Fleet is 123,000 roubles. Of this amount 53,000 roubles may be struck off as representing the freight-value of the passengers and stores transported, leaving a dead loss of 70,000 roubles, or nearly 9000*l*.

At present the fleet suffers from the indecision of the authorities regarding its future. Colonel Kostenko, of General Kaufmann's staff, is of opinion that the fleet ought to be bodily transferred to the Oxus; or else turned over to a private company, subsidized by State, and the *personnel* removed from Kazala to Fort Petro-Alexandrovsk, where it could take charge of a fresh set of gunboats. The original duty of the fleet—the extension and preservation of Russia's influence on the Syr—has completely disappeared. The Cossack outposts long ago left the river behind them, and the stream to-day is as free from danger of native attack as the Volga or the Neva. On the other hand, the Oxus still lies outside the control of the Cossack, and the waterway is menaced with so many perils from predatory Turcomans and Kirghiz, that no regular traffic can be maintained on the river.

The advantages of the Aral fleet were signally displayed in 1878, when the steamers ferried across the Syr Daria, at Tchinaz, the Tashkent column, which subsequently marched to Djam, on the Bokharan frontier, with the intention of invading Afghanistan, perhaps India. Last autumn the *Samarcand*, with barge No. 9, conveyed at one trip 500 troops from Kazala to Petro-Alexandrovsk for service against the Turcomans, and later on proceeded to Tchardjui, where it ferried across the Oxus Colonel Kouropatkin and the Samarcand contingent. Communications having been thus established between Bokhara and Akhal, we may expect to see a further development of these naval operations on the Oxus. Rumours already prevail of the intention of the Government to establish a regular gunboat service on that river, and if the number of vessels ordered proves to be small, it will only indicate that the Governor-General shares the faith of every recent Russian explorer in the possibility of establishing a waterway between Khiva and Krasnovodsk.

While, therefore, England can afford to regard with a certain amount of indifference the decrepit fleet existing in the Aral, she cannot altogether ignore the political results involved in a transfer of operations, on a more vigorous scale, from the Syr Daria to the Oxus. Small though it has always been, the Aral fleet has done good service in extending Russia's influence in the valley of the Syr Daria, and might achieve, if renovated, still greater results on the more navigable river watering Afghanistan and Bokhara. Now that Kouropatkin has broken the ice of Bokharan exclusiveness, by marching a contingent from Samarcand to Geok Tepé, we may expect to witness a sensible increase of Russian activity in the Oxus region. This will create a need for more steamers; these steamers will carry the Russian flag to the Afghan border; and, by their means, Russia's influence, as advocated by Kostenko and Sobeleff, Kaufmann and Skobeleff, will be extended to Balkh and Maimene, and other strategical points of the true Indian frontier. At present England, with lazy complacency, merely regards the Oxus as a possible Indo-Turkestan frontier. Russia, on the other hand, is earnestly seeking to establish herself beyond the Oxus, in the very passes of the Hindoo Koosh. On this account, the operations of the Central Asian Fleet may probably serve as a good test of her future intentions. If we see more steamers following the *Samarcand* to the Oxus, and fresh vessels arriving from Russia to run from Khiva to the Afghan border, we may assume with tolerable certainty that the time is not far distant when the Cossack will be quartered at Balkh and Maimene, and the old plans carried out for seizing and occupying Herat.[1]

[1] Since writing the above the *Samarcand* has disappeared from the fleet, having foundered during the ice flow on the Syr Daria. Nothing has been done to recover or replace it since, nor has any attempt been made to revive the Aral fleet.

LETTERPRESS ACCOMPANYING THE MAP ON THE RUSSO-PERSIAN FRONTIER.

CHARLES MARVIN'S MAP OF THE NEW RUSSO-PERSIAN FRONTIER IN THE TRANSCASPIAN REGION, AS DEFINED BY A CONVENTION SIGNED AT TEHERAN IN DECEMBER, 1881.

Issued to both Houses of Parliament, February 25, 1882.

The issue of a sketch-map showing the new boundary of the recent Russian conquests beyond the Caspian was suggested to me by the following "Note of the Day," published in the *Globe* of February 20, 1882:—

"WHEN WILL IT BE READY?

"On the 10th of June last year, Sir Charles Dilke, replying to a question put to him by Mr. Ashmead-Bartlett, with respect to the annexation of the Akhal Tekke region by Russia, stated that a map of the district acquired would be prepared by the Intelligence Department, and laid before the House. On the 27th of June, replying to Viscount Sandon, the Under-Secretary of State for Foreign Affairs promised that Her Majesty's Chargé d'Affaires at St. Petersburg should be instructed to send home any map that might be published in Russia, showing the boundaries of the annexed territory, and that this should be placed in the library of the House of Commons. A month later, in answering a question put by Mr. E. Stanhope, Sir Charles

Appendix.

Dilke said that the map would be ready before the end of the Session. On the 9th of August he promised Viscount Sandon that the moment any information arrived, whether in the form of a map or not, it should be laid before the House; the maps possessed by the Government did not give the names of all the frontier points, and he thought it would be a difficult matter to construct a new map. Since then more than six months have elapsed, or eight months since the first promise was given, and no map is yet forthcoming. What is the cause of this extraordinary delay? Is it possible that the English Embassy at St. Petersburg, the Foreign Office at home, and the Intelligence Department at the Horse Guards, cannot between them construct a rough map of the Perso-Turcoman region, showing the Persian frontier and the alleged encroachments upon it? It is only the other day we gave an account of the Topographical Department at St. Petersburg, which has got in store over a million maps of various countries of Europe in readiness for any war. Russia, uncivilized as she is, can produce maps by the hundred thousand, while England cannot produce even a sketch-map in eight months. The statement that it was difficult to construct a map last August was absurd, since General Petroosevitch's map of Akhal and Merv had been published some months earlier by W. H. Allen and Co., publishers to the India Office, and this contained the information lacking in previous maps. We hope some member will put a question again to Sir Charles Dilke on the subject, and that he will not be content with the mere promises that fall so readily from the glib Under-Secretary's lips."

The map made use of is General Petroosevitch's, and

the frontier-line is traced in accordance with the information contained in a letter from Teheran to the Russian *Official Journal,* giving an account of the negotiation of the convention. This letter states frankly and accurately that by an agreement arrived at between Russia and Persia in 1869, the course of the river Atrek was selected as the frontier. Russia having soon afterwards dominated the country as high up the river as Fort Tchat, no difficulties were raised as far as this point; but beyond, Persia claimed the region north of the Atrek to the Kopet Dagh range, and even Akhal itself. Russia did not ask the Shah to cede any portion of this magnificent piece of territory, except the two settlements of Kara Kala and Nookhoor, trenching upon Akhal, and Akhal itself. As Persia had never exercised any authority over Akhal, from Kizil Arvat to Askabad, Russia rightly refused to admit her claim to it. Regarding the two disputed settlements, lying in or close to the Kopet Dagh, Petroosevitch says: " Both lie far to the north of the Khorassan border. The ruler of Budjnurd says they yearly pay him taxes; Karri Kala to the extent of 300 toomans, and Nookhoor 100, but his statement is more than doubtful. Both settlements lie in close proximity to the line of Tekke fortresses —within twenty or thirty miles of them—while they are situated at a great distance from the settlements of the province of Budjnurd: Karri Kala, for instance, being 188 miles distant, and Nookhoor 135. The people of Karri Kala are Goklan Turcomans, and the people of Nookhoor members of other Turcoman tribes " ("Merv, the Queen of the World," page 302; also page 321). Persia's authority over these points was so very nominal, and they projected so far from her dominions, that, considering the large area north of the Atrek left unclaimed by Russia, she could not well do otherwise than cede them both. This difficulty overcome, the new frontier was soon selected. "Starting from Tchat it runs along the hill-tops and the course of the river Sumbar. Russia was satisfied with retaining for herself only the oasis itself (i. e. Akhal), and the slopes of the mountains (Kopet Dagh), securing the oasis from the south; so that the frontier from the Sumbar runs mainly along the mountain crest, leaving to Persia the Feerooze district. Attaining the valley of the Baba Doormaz stream, the frontier turns to the north, and cutting the road from Gyaoors to Lutfabad, extends in a northerly direction to the desert, leaving the Atrek outside the Russian frontier."

If this be a correct account of the new convention, then it must be confessed that Russia has been exceedingly moderate, and that there is nothing in it at which England could possibly complain.

SKOBELEFF'S PARIS SPEECHES.

THE following is the account of the interview between General Skobeleff and the Paris correspondent of the *Daily News*, which suggested the journey to Russia.

"PARIS, Sunday night, Feb. 19, 1882.

"Ascertaining that General Skobeleff had not really quitted Paris, I called this afternoon and had nearly half an hour's conversation with him. Before we proceeded to talk about European affairs he spoke with much kindness of Mr. MacGahan and other common friends, and was eulogistic of the *Daily News*, which he said had cleared away the Russian spectre that had long oppressed the English mind. At this point I said to him, 'General, you have been interviewed by an editor of the *Voltaire*. An account has been given in *La France* of your answer to the Servian students.¹ Are they both true?' 'I received,'

---

¹ On the 17th of February *La France* had published the following as the text of a speech which Skobeleff had made to a deputation of Servian students, who had called upon him with an address:—" If Russia does not always show herself equal to her patriotic duties in general, and to her Slav rôle in particular, it is because both within and without she is held in check by a foreign influence. We are not at home in our own house. The foreigner is everywhere, and his hand in everything. We are the dupes of his policy, the victims of his intrigues, the slaves of his power. We are dominated and paralyzed to such an extent by his innumerable and disastrous influences that if we are to deliver ourselves from them, as I hope we shall some day or

said the General, 'a journalist from the *Voltaire* and a Servian deputation, but what I said in both cases has been frightfully exaggerated.' I said, jocosely, 'I am glad to hear you say so; for, to be frank, if you talked in the manner it is alleged you did, it would be the duty of M. de Freycinet to send you to join M. Lavroff.' 'No,' answered General Skobeleff, 'you surely cannot mean that.' 'Personally I am against all expulsions, but as the object of the French Government is to keep out of hot water and in peace with the world, I think it would be only logical, had you spoken as you are represented, to request you to leave France.' 'Is that your impression?' he asked. 'Certainly,' I returned. 'I repeat,' he said, 'that the French journalists have terribly and ridiculously exaggerated what I said. I am not come at all to arouse a storm, but to avert one, which can only be done by frank speaking. If I say that a disagreeable fact exists, I am not responsible for its existence.' 'What is the fact?' I inquired. 'Well, that a great war is inevitable if the Austrians go on oppressing the Slavs in Bosnia and the Herzegovina. I hate war. On my honour and conscience, I detest it. Before God I tell you that I do. I have had 21,000 men killed under me in one campaign, and have realized all that is sickening, cruel, odious, atrocious in

other, it can only be done by us sword in hand. And if you wish to know the name of this foreigner, this intruder and intriguer, this enemy so dangerous to Russians and Slavs, I will name him. It is the German. I repeat it, and I beg you will never forget it. This enemy is the German. A struggle between the Slav and the Teuton is inevitable. It will be long, sanguinary, and terrible, but the Slav will triumph. If any one attempt to molest the States recognized by Treaties, thank goodness you will not be alone; if Fate should so decide, we shall meet again on the battle-field side by side against the common enemy."

the military profession. My object, therefore, is to obtain by the truth the results which our people think may be accomplished by war, and which they will go to war to accomplish. If diplomatists will shut their eyes to facts, there is nothing to be gained by what is called diplomatic discretion. The two greatest masters in diplomacy were Cromwell and Bismarck, and they always talked with the frankness of business-men who knew what they wanted, and saw how to get it.' 'Well, what is it Russia wants to get?' I interrupted. 'Nothing for herself,' said General Skobeleff. 'We are a people of idealists. We are capable of great enthusiasm, and love self-sacrifice. What do we see? Our brothers tyrannized over by Austria, who has made her first approach in Bosnia to domination over all the Slavs in the Balkan Peninsula. She was given in trust, and trust only, as the English were given Corfu, the two Slav provinces that she is now oppressing. She has no right to conscribe for her army the young men there, nor to interfere with the religion of the people. A clerical propaganda has been established by her. The Jesuits that were cleared out of France, Austria received with open arms. The Jesuit fathers are dressed up with her connivance as Greek Popes, and go about trying to entice the peasants from their faith.' 'The Jesuits are consistent,' I observed, 'in trying to convert, but is it probable that any European Government would be so foolish as to institute a propaganda, such as you describe?' General Skobeleff declared that nothing was more certain than that all Russia would unite to combat the military clericalism of the Austrians in the States under her protection. Their formula would be 'Hands off.' If Europe insisted on the observation in letter and spirit of the Treaty of Berlin, Russia would be satisfied.

Appendix.

She agreed to that treaty, which was not a good one for her or for the Slavs beyond the Danube; but it secured to the latter freedom from oppression. To be freed from Mahomet and then to be oppressed by the Holy Roman Empire would be intolerable. The Slavs would neither be Turk nor Jesuit ridden. Their determination should be made known to the world, so that diplomatists, who were always for ignoring the truth, should be compelled to face it and so avert war.

"I here said, 'I now understand why the Tsar allows the war-ship to be called after you.' Skobeleff's face appeared to hesitate about his answer.[1] He had read in German telegrams about the christening of the ship. After reflecting an instant he alluded to a reported mission with which he was charged. It was a purely imaginary one. He had no mission from anybody, but had come on his own account to arouse Western feeling against clerical Austria, and to prevent misunderstanding. I asked in what the misunderstanding lay. There was a notion that Slav emancipation would lead to Russian domination. The more free the Adriatic Slavs were, the greater would be their difference from the Russian type.

"In speaking of Germany no rabid antipathy or hostility was disclosed, but there was disappointment evinced at the indifference with which the German Government witness the infractions by Austria of the Berlin Treaty. An idea had taken root at Berlin that Russia had come dislocated out of the war. She had been

[1] Skobeleff must have thought the correspondent was poking fun at him. The German papers had announced that the Emperor had named two "men-of-war" after Skobeleff—one the *Skobeleff* and the other the *Geok Tepé*. As a matter of fact they were only a couple of tug-boats for the Caspian, and the event possessed no significance whatever.

weakened; her finances were disordered; she was undergoing a political crisis; but she had a population of 80,000,000, and the discontent aroused by the demi-results of the Balkan campaign would be cured by another attempt to champion the oppressed Slavs. Germany could not attack Russia without exposing herself to France. I said that the temper of France was now essentially pacific, and that no statesman who avowed a war programme would have the country behind him. France, after Russia and Germany had exhausted themselves, might step in to recover Alsace and Lorraine, but it would be madness for any State thinking of a great campaign to build on an alliance with her.

"I asked General Skobeleff whether I might publish an account of the interview. He said, 'With pleasure; but first repeat to me the conversation that has taken place, in order that I may be sure you understand me.' I did so, and he was satisfied with my recapitulation. He spoke English fluently. It is easy to see that he is a man of tremendous 'go,' impressionable, enthusiastic, frank to transparency. He has intuition and a powerful intellect, and the temperament of a Crusader. He is the Godfrey de Bouillon of the Slav race."

On the 27th, the same correspondent had a second interview. "General Skobeleff returns immediately to Russia. I spent this morning in his company. He is annoyed and disgusted with the 'reckless sensationalism' of French journalists, and cannot imagine, he says, how their exaggeration is tolerated in a capital which is one of the great intellectual centres of the world. It is not possible, he explains, for him to write a letter to any French paper to contradict the reports of the firebrand speeches ascribed to him, he being on active military service. General Skobeleff talked a great deal in my presence to an old friend of his about Panslavism, Nihilism, and Tsarism. He said that Panslavism was made up of affirmations, and had for its basis, faith in God, attachment to the Greek religion, and brotherly love, and for its means of action the political organization which has been growing up for nearly a thousand years. He thought the Tsar was the backbone of Slavism. By this he meant the autocratic function which was interwoven with Greek orthodoxy. There were fanatical Panslavs who wanted to go back into the night of time beyond the Tsars, but he was not one of them. He could not conceive Russia holding well together without the Imperial system. On being asked whether he wanted to extend Tsarism to the sub-Danubian Slav races, he declared that nothing was farther from his thoughts. All he wanted was liberty for them to develop themselves according to their natural instincts and affinities. I could gather from what he said that he would help them in the same spirit as that which moved Lafayette when he went to place himself at Washington's disposal. He believed that the Danubian provinces, if liberated, would stand towards Russia in the same relation in which the United States stand towards England, and that there would be keen commercial rivalry between Varna and other sub-Danubian ports and Odessa. He spoke of the Tsar as being well-intentioned and extremely honest, and said that all the Slavonic peoples owed an eternal debt of gratitude to Alexander II. for having been the first to give a political expression to Slav aspirations. The General looked upon Nihilism as a disease which arose from the German system of education adopted in the reign of Nicholas. It was Hegelism taken up by nervous, impressionable youths;

in a word, Hegelism gone mad. The Nihilists were hostile to all national tradition, made war against every historical association, and would destroy everything in Russia except the soil. General Skobeleff is not going to England, nor has he had any intention of going."

Appendix.

SKOBELEFF ON WARFARE IN CENTRAL ASIA.

TRANSLATED FROM SKOBELEFF'S OFFICIAL REPORT OF THE SIEGE OF GEOK TEPÉ, PUBLISHED IN THE ORGAN OF THE MINISTER OF WAR, *Voenni Sbornik*, APRIL, 1881.

INSTRUCTIONS FOR THE OFFICERS OF THE TROOPS IN THE FIELD.

Fort Samoorskoe, $\frac{18\text{th}}{30\text{th}}$ *December,* 1880.

The troops who took part in the reconnaissances of the $\frac{6\text{th}}{18\text{th}}$ July, and the $\frac{4\text{th}}{16\text{th}}$, $\frac{11\text{th}}{23\text{rd}}$, and $\frac{12\text{th}}{24\text{th}}$ December, are already acquainted with the enemy and the method of operating against him.

At the present time the army in the field has been joined by detachments which have not yet met the enemy. I consider it my duty therefore to make the following remarks.

The circumstances under which we have to operate are as follows: Obstinate fighting is to be expected for local objects. The enemy is brave, and skilful in single combat; he fires effectively, and is provided with a good side-arm, but he operates in individual extended order, or in detached bodies, very little obedient to the will of their chief, and, therefore, unfit, notwithstanding their overwhelming numbers, for combined action and manœuvring in masses.

Circumstances, the distance, and the nature of the theatre of operations, nevertheless force us, who are limited by the small numbers of our troops, to act on the offensive.

The present European fighting formation is here inapplicable, on account of the small numerical strength of our detachments.

In the open field, the brave cavalry of the enemy, mounted on fleet chargers, and wielding the sword skilfully, will continually threaten long extended lines. His infantry masses are not organized, but they consist of men whose spirits have been raised, who are able to use their side-arms dexterously, and who will endeavour to bring the engagements to hand-to-hand fights, and thus equalize the chances of the struggle in their favour.

As a fundamental principle, a close formation is all-powerful in Central Asia.

In operations such as the present, against an enemy defending himself in a position covered by gardens, buildings, and walls, and strengthened by him during so long a time, and possessing for him a special moral significance in consequence of the success gained last year, and because the families and all the property of the defenders are there collected, we shall be obliged to overcome an obstinate resistance in front of each enclosure. We shall finally have to fight a desperate mortal combat with knives and yataghans. An extended and thin formation, in which the troops easily slip away from the hands of their commanders, and get broken into small divided bodies, without connexion with each other, or the will and heart of their commanders, prevents them opposing unexpected appearances of hostile masses with the power of formation, and, what is inseparable from it, the united force of their discipline, fire, and mutual support.

Appendix.

A combination of these principles of fighting, rapid and suitably adapted, forms the basis of our tactics in Central Asia, and permits us, for causes which we understand, to count on victory over so numerous an enemy.

We will beat our opponent by means of that in which he is deficient. We will take advantage of discipline and our rapid shooting arms. We will beat our adversary by a close, obedient, supple, fighting formation; by unanimous well directed volleys; and the bayonet, always terrible in the hands of men united by discipline; and, finally, by a feeling of duty, and by concentration into one powerful body—the column.

Attacks by the enemy's cavalry should be met by a suitable change of front, if that appears necessary, and by volleys at short ranges. I recommend the formation of squares, even of battalion squares, if circumstances permit of it.

Volleys are to be used against an attacking enemy, both cavalry and infantry, when they have come within a range of 600 paces; but it is to be remembered that volley firing is very effective at much greater ranges against concentrated masses, both when standing in the open, or when covered by walls or the parapets of entrenchments. In such cases volley firing may be opened at a range of 3000 paces, raising the sight to the utmost, and aiming at the crest of the parapet, or top of the wall, if the enemy is concealed behind one. This curved fire, useful up to 3000 paces, is not, however, to be permitted for detachments of less than half a company, and requires attentive supervision on the part of the commander of the detachment.

The artillery should be posted as follows :—The mitrailleurs close beside the troops like the former regimental guns, as a very near support for the infantry; all the other guns for a time to be with the reserve, with the object of being employed all together where circumstances show that the effect of the artillery would be increased by the concentrated fire of several dozen guns obeying a single authority. The departure of the artillery from the reserve will be dependent on my orders, and its subsequent distribution, and the selection of objects to be aimed at, will be dependent upon the chief of the artillery. The well-known saying of Suvaroff, that "artillery moves about just as it pleases," must be continually in the minds both of the commanders of the artillery and those units to which it is attached. But all this only refers up to so long as the solemn beating to attack does not resound. At that great and solemn moment the artillery must give itself up entirely to the support of its comrades. Without heeding anything else, it must precede the attacking detachments, and by its fire, always specially terrible at short ranges, shake the heart of the opponent.

All purely technical considerations must be put aside. At the decisive moment the artillery must have its wits, for an artilleryman is not a machine. The artillery must sacrifice itself entirely, if that is necessary for the success of the attack, precisely as the infantry sacrifices itself, without flinching, when attacking an adversary. The detachment covering the artillery must defend it to the last. Opprobrium for the loss of the guns rests not on the artillery but on the troops.

The whole of the cavalry is to remain with the reserve till the moment when circumstances appear favourable for employing it in masses. Our cavalry should not enter into single combat with the numerous horsemen of the enemy, mounted on excellent horses, and accustomed to wield their weapons from childhood. As long as the enemy's horse remains unshaken, or if it is not manœuvring under unfavourable conditions, or pressed against an obstacle or defile, our cavalry is not to enter into a cavalry engagement with it.

The pursuit of fugitive Turcoman cavalry would lead to a useless destruction of the tactical connexion—our chief strength and security. The cavalry, during attacks, is to preserve a close formation, such as cannot be pierced, forming even regimental, squadron, and sotnia columns.

In the attacks rapidity is not so necessary as compactness and order, and therefore the charges, besides being always made at favourable opportunities, should be short, so that the detachment may be well in hand, and that the stroke may be concentrated and heavy; in one word, the basis of the tactical operations of our cavalry against that of the enemy must be extreme prudence and circumspection.

On the other hand, in operations against unorganized masses of undisciplined infantry, such as the Asiatic infantry militia, the attacks of our cavalry should doubtless be resolute; although even here the intelligent boldness of the cavalry must rely on cautious tactics and suitable massing of reserves; in fine, on short charges with lance and sword.

I remind you of the necessity of taking careful measures of precaution during the night-rests near Geok Tepé. The commanders of the outposts should make themselves acquainted with the roads leading to the bivouac, and the points where the enemy is likely to assemble in masses for an attack.

The commander of each unit is to study the ground

situated in front of his detachment; to think over the amount of assistance which he can give to the neighbouring detachment in case of attack; for, I repeat, mutual support has been, and will be at all times, the key to victory. The ground in front must be understood; distances measured. I remind you of my orders, Nos. 68 and 179, of 1879.

To the last circumstance I direct your special attention, for experience in the case of night conflicts has shown how difficult it is to direct a battle in the dark. Every inclination from a straight direction may lead to firing at one's own side, and to confusion. I call special attention to the advantage of arranging signals known to every soldier, and of defining distances accurately Large piles of wood which are kept burning all night, and in rear of which the outposts and ambush-posts are placed in a suitable manner, may be of great advantage. I instruct you not to light piles of wood in the camp without the permission of the commandant, and in case of fighting to extinguish them immediately by throwing earth upon them.

By day a battle may be brought on by a gradual and intelligent application to the operation, of the ground and means at disposal; but at night the circumstances may be such as to render it necessary to make a very great impression at once. This is the reason why in a battle by night, volleys are always to be fired.

It is to be borne in mind, that judging distances at night is deceptive, and it is of the first importance to remind the men to aim low.

    (Signed)   ADJUTANT-GENERAL SKOBELEFF,
     in temporary command of the troops.

CAPTAIN BUTLER'S CLAIM TO THE FORTIFYING OF GEOK TEPÉ.

On the 19th of January, 1881, an article appeared in the *Globe*, from my pen, entitled "Turcoman Travellers." This evoked from Captain Butler the following letter, published January 25th, in which he laid claim to the designing of the fortress of Geok Tepé.

To the Editor of the "Globe."

SIR,—In your issue of the 19th instant appears a very able and interesting account of the various efforts made by different explorers to penetrate the country of the Akhol and Marv Turkmans, and the results, as published, of their various travels. It is not my intention in the present communication to lay before you a history of the past, present, and probable future of our gallant natural allies, the "Turkmans;" for, if they have not signed an agreement with our Foreign Office as our actual allies, ours is the fault and ours the loss. That they are our natural allies no one, I think, will dispute who has studied the position of their wonderful country, forming as it does, the natural barrier—the neutral ground—between Russia on the north and that part of the British empire, Hindoostan, on the south; or who has mixed with them and heard from them their hopes, their desires, their ambitions, and their cravings for free intercourse with other nations, in order to become the great central carriers, the great medium of that immense commerce between Central Asia and Europe which is at present rotting in fertile valleys, and industrious mountain slopes, in consequence of the selfish, brigand, and immoral character of Persia, and the wolf-like appetite of Russia. In this letter I simply wish to point out a few of the very natural mistakes under which my countrymen are labouring with regard to the Turkmans and their country. At starting, I wish to rid my countrymen of the unintentional slight cast upon them as gallant explorers, that so little should have been done by them in opening out Turkmanland. Two at least, Abbott and Fraser, deserve to be classed with the foremost explorers of Continental nations. Most of us are cognizant of the privations endured, the gallant conduct and valuable information conveyed to us by the former; and our gratitude as a nation is due to the latter for his travels on the Perso-Turkman frontier, and for presenting to England a country possessing immense undeveloped riches, and valleys teeming with all the necessaries of life, a country which sooner or later, if Russia is permitted to annex it, will supply her with a formidable army of brave and warlike troopers, better mounted than any cavalry in Europe. Before proceeding, I wish to point out that it is quite an error, both of Colonel Baker's and the public, that Kouschid Khan, of Marv, wrote to him refusing him permission to proceed to Marv. Baker certainly got a letter to the above effect; but to this day he is unaware, I believe, of the hoax played upon him at the time. Great, indeed, will be our individual joy if the gallant officer of whom you speak as starting from India, reaches his destination at Guek Tepé or Marv. He will be as safe riding across Beloochistan and Persia as he would be across England; but that his service to his country will not be readily forgotten by the public, if I am to judge from past experience, I regret not being able to coincide with.

The only two maps published of the Akhol district with any pretence to accuracy, are the Russian Staff Map and our own War Office Map. Both, which I now have before me, are simply worthless and entirely misleading. Both are on the lines of an old map well known in Persia, drawn over a century ago, with a few dots stuck here and there indicating villages through which a few travellers have recently passed. Can our ignorance of the Turkmans and their country be wondered at, when every Government in power in this country recalls every English officer who endeavours to visit Turkomania, and the Persian Government are permitted by the British Legation at Tehran to seize on British subjects when crossing the Persian frontier into Turkman-land, and march them back again into Persian territory? Such has been the suicidal policy up to the present of our representatives at Tehran. Travelling in various disguises in 1878, I was enabled to take a rapid survey of the district about Akhol, and I hold a correct military survey of its neighbourhood. Further, I have before me a plan of Guek Tepé, the original one made by me for the Turkmans, and given to them for the defence and strengthening of that post, before which the Russians had to retreat under General Lomakin, and before which they are now fighting. Should the Russians penetrate further east, they will find two other posts equally well fortified as Guek Tepé, and defended by a gallant band struggling for life and liberty. In order to throw dust into the eyes of sleepy John Bull, the Russians have industriously spread abroad that the land of the Turkmans and everything north of the Atrak (the sources of which I discovered near Meshed) are barren wastes; and that their only reason for marching towards Marv is to inflict punishment on the Turkman robbers. All this is utterly false. They are trying to conquer a magnificent country—a country which will be a source of wealth on the one hand, and which on the other will supply them with a hundred thousand of the best fighting men in the world, out of Europe; a country which any general can feel safe as a base of operations against Afghan and India, and the non-possession of which by Russia in 1878 prevented that Power from marching the columns she had organized for the purpose into India. An ill-timed timidity (as you have mildly put it) on the part of our Government in 1878 prevented my carrying further the survey to Marv; but in truth I can claim with pride that for two and a half years, at least, by constructing the fortifications at Guek Tepé, I have helped a brave and heroic people to retain their liberty, prevent the wholesale outrages and disgrace on the vanquished which followed the campaign of Khiva, and kept back the Russian army from the frontier of Afghan and the occupation of Marv; and my constant prayer is that my friends will act as heroically at the two spots further east I have chalked out for them, as they are acting within the beleaguered earthwork of Guek Tepé. Without in this letter entering into the subject either politically or militarily, I would ask those whom it concerns to weigh well the reports of those who have visited the country and know thoroughly its people and its resources, before they permit a rival Power to seize on Marv—India's gate; for say what they may, if I can maintain a hundred thousand men on the line between the Caspian and Meshed, which the Russians are now trying to seize, and fifty thousand on the line between the Oxus, Marv, and the Moorghab, I am virtual dictator of India. In another letter I will point out how that Power, which holds the above lines, can at any moment, most convenient to itself, dictate such terms to the holder of India as it pleases, in order to carry out any policy it desires in Europe. Before it is too late, again I say, let those whom it may concern— and now it is the British nation—not turn a deaf ear to the gallant fellows who have offered their friendship, their country, and their lives if necessary, in return for a mutual alliance with England, and who are willing to share the penalty.

Yours faithfully,
F. W. H. BUTLER.

January 24th.

CONVENTION RESPECTING THE RUSSO-PERSIAN FRONTIER.

SIGNED AT TEHERAN, DECEMBER $\frac{9\text{th}}{21\text{st}}$, 1881.

"In the name of God the Almighty.

"His Majesty the Shah of Persia and His Majesty the Emperor and Autocrat of All the Russias, acknowledging the necessity of accurately defining the frontier of their possessions east of the Caspian Sea, and of establishing therein security and tranquillity, have agreed to conclude a Convention for that purpose, and have appointed as their plenipotentiaries:—

"His Majesty the Shah of Persia, on the one hand, Mirza Said Khan, Moutemid-ul-Mulk, his Minister for Foreign Affairs;

"His Majesty the Emperor and Autocrat of All the Russias, on the other, Ivan Zenovief, his Envoy Extraordinary and Minister Plenipotentiary at the Court of His Majesty the Shah;

"Who having exchanged their respective full powers, found in good and due form, have agreed on the following Articles:—

"Art. I.—The frontier-line, between the possessions of the Russian Empire and Persia, east of the Caspian Sea, is fixed as follows:—Beginning at the Hasan Kuli Gulf, the course of the River Atrek serves as the frontier as far as Chat. From Chat the frontier-line follows in a north-easterly direction the ridges of the Songou Dagh and Sagirim ranges, thence extending northward to the Chandir river, reaching the bed of that river at Tchakan Kale. From Tchakan Kale it runs in a northerly direction to the ridge of the mountains dividing the Chandir and Sumbar valleys, and extends along the ridge of these mountains in an easterly direction, descending to the bed of the Sumbar at the spot where the Ach-Agaian stream falls into it. From this point eastward the bed of the Sumbar marks the frontier as far as the ruins of Medjet Dainé. Thence the road to Durrun forms the frontier-line as far as the ridge of the Kopet Dagh, along the ridge of which the frontier extends south-eastward, but before reaching the upper part of the Giamab Pass, turns to the south among the mountain heights dividing the valley of the Sumbar from the source of the Giamab. Thence taking a south-easterly direction across the summits of the Misino and Tchoubest mountains, it reaches the road from Giamab to Rabab, passing at a distance of one verst to the north of the latter spot. From this point the frontier-line runs along the ridge of the mountains as far as the summit of the Dalang mountain, whence, passing on the northern side of the village of Khairabad, it extends in a north-easterly direction as far as the boundaries of Geok Keital. From the boundaries of Geok Keital the frontier-line crosses to the gorge of the River Firuzé, intersecting that gorge on the northern side of the village of Firuzé. Thence the frontier-line takes a south-easterly direction to the summits of the mountain range, bounding on the south the valley, through which the road from Askabad to Firuzé passes, and runs along the crest of these mountains to the most easterly point of the range. From here the frontier-line crosses over to the northernmost summit of the Aselm range passing along its ridge in a south-easterly direction, and then skirting round to the north of the village of Keltechina, it runs to the point where the Ziri Kou and Kizil Dagh mountains join, extending thence south-eastward along the summits of the Ziri Kou range until it issues into the valley of the Baba Durmaz stream. It then takes a northerly direction, and reaches the oasis at the road from Gavars to Lutfabad, leaving the fortress of Baba Durmaz to the east.

"Art. II.—Whereas, in Article I. of the present Convention, the principal points are indicated through which the frontier between the possessions of Russia and Persia is to pass, the high contracting parties are to appoint special commissioners, with a view of accurately tracing on the spot the frontier-line, and of erecting proper boundary marks. The date and place of meeting of the said commissioners shall be mutually agreed upon by the high contracting parties.

"Art. III.—Whereas, the forts of Giamab and Kulkulab, situated in the gorge through which the stream watering the soil of the Trans-Caspian province passes, lie to the north of the line which, in virtue of Article I. of the present Convention, is to serve as the boundary between the territories of the two high contracting parties, the Government of His Majesty the Shah engage to evacuate the said forts within the space of one year from the date of the exchange of the ratifications of the present Convention, but shall have the right during the said period to remove the inhabitants of Giamab and Kulkulab to within the Persian frontier, and to establish them there. On its part, the Government of the Emperor of All the Russias engages not to erect fortifications in these said localities nor to establish any Turcoman families therein.

"Art. IV.—Whereas, the sources of the River Firuzé, as well as of other streams watering the soil of the Trans-Caspian province contiguous to the Persian frontier lie within the Persian territory, the Government of His Majesty the Shah engage, on no account whatever, to permit the establishment of fresh settlements along the course of the said streams and rivulets from their sources to the point where they leave Persian territory, and not to extend the area of land at present under cultivation, and under no pretence whatever to turn off the water in larger quantities than is necessary for irrigating the fields now under cultivation within the Persian territory. With a view to the immediate observance and fulfilment of this stipulation the Government of His Majesty the Shah engage to appoint a sufficient number of competent agents, and to subject any infringer thereof to severe punishment.

"Art. V.—With a view to the development of commercial intercourse between the Trans-Caspian province and Khorassan, both high contracting parties engage to come to a mutually advantageous agreement as soon as possible for the construction of waggon-roads suitable for commercial traffic between the above-mentioned provinces.

"Art. VI.—The Government of His Majesty the Shah of Persia engage to strictly prohibit the export from His Majesty's dominions along the whole extent of the frontier of the provinces of Asterabad and Khorassan of all arms and war material, and likewise to adopt measures to prevent arms being supplied to the Turcomans residing in Persian territory. The Persian frontier authorities shall afford the most effective support to the agents of the Imperial

Russian Government, whose duty it shall be to watch that arms are not exported from the Persian territory. The Government of His Majesty the Emperor of All the Russias, on its part, engages to prevent arms and war material being supplied from Russian territory to Turcomans living in Persia.

"Art. VII.—With a view to the observance and fulfilment of the stipulations of the present Convention, and in order to regulate the proceedings of the Turcomans residing on the Persian frontier, the Government of His Majesty the Emperor of All the Russias shall have the right to nominate agents to the frontier points of Persia. In all questions concerning the observance of order and tranquillity in the districts contiguous to the possessions of the high contracting parties, the appointed agents will act as intermediaries in the relations between the Russian and Persian authorities.

"Art. VIII.—All engagements and stipulations contained in treaties and conventions concluded up to this time between the two high contracting parties shall remain in force.

"Art. IX.—The present Convention, done in duplicate, and signed by the Plenipotentiaries of both parties, who have affixed to it the seal of their arms, shall be confirmed and ratified by His Majesty the Shah of Persia and His Majesty the Emperor and Autocrat of All the Russias; the ratifications to be exchanged between the Plenipotentiaries of both parties at Teheran within the space of four months, or earlier, if possible.

"Done at Teheran the 9th-21st of December, 1881, which corresponds to the Mussulman date of the 29th Mucharem, 1299.

   (Signed)   "IVAN ZENOVIEFF."

In forwarding the Convention to Lord Granville Mr. Ronald Thomson, our representative at Teheran, wrote, under date January 23rd, as follows:—

"I have the honour to transmit herewith, for your Lordship's information, translation of the Akhal-Khorassan Boundary Treaty, lately concluded between Russia and Persia, as reported in my telegram of the 4th of January. This translation has been made from the Russian text by Mr. Stephen. Comparing it with the Persian version, I observe that the terms employed in Article V. are not the same in both languages. In the Russian text it is stated that both Governments engage, with a view to the development of commercial intercourse between the Trans-Caspian province and Khorassan, to come to a mutually advantageous agreement for the construction of waggon-roads between the above-mentioned provinces; whereas, in the Persian version of this clause, it is said that, in order to facilitate commercial operations between the Trans-Caspian provinces and that of Khorassan, the two contracting Powers engage, as regards the construction of waggon-roads for the transport of merchandise between the aforesaid countries, to make such arrangements as may be of mutual advantage to them. The Minister for Foreign Affairs has informed me that the Nasseer-ed-Dowleh, who was formerly employed in the Persian Foreign Office, and lately in the Ministry of Justice, will be named Commissioner under Article II. of this Convention for the local demarcation of the line of frontier, on the basis agreed upon in Article I."

GENERAL KAYE ON THE NEW RUSSO-PERSIAN FRONTIER.

THE following letter appeared in the *Broad Arrow* of April 1, 1882, on the new frontier beyond the Caspian :—

"There has been much talk of late regarding the advantages supposed to have been gained by Russia by her operations against the Turcoman tribes, advancing as far as Askabad on the direct road from the Caspian to Merv; and more recently by the treaty concluded with Persia in December last.

"But a perusal of the treaty itself, and an examination of Mr. Marvin's map, comparing it with others of previous date, will quickly show that such is by no means the case.

"Three years since it was stated (see 'Proceedings of Royal Geographical Society,' March, 1879), that the Russians represented their frontier as extending southward to the river Attrek, thus including the northern mountains (Kopet Dagh) and their Passes; but by the recent treaty the boundary-line will leave the river just mentioned at Chat (as maintained previously by Persia in opposing the Russian claims), in a north-easterly direction, and pass along the northern slopes of the mountain ranges. Chikishlar at the western extremity of the frontier-line was in Russian occupation in 1874, and that power has actually gained no territory by her successes over the

Turcomans and her treaty with Persia, nothing save a narrow strip of land, watered certainly by several small streams, but poorly cultivated, intervening between the Songou Dagh and Kopet Dagh ranges, and the desert.

"I do not see any grounds for the conclusion that the Shah of Persia has been outwitted by the statecraft of Russia. On the contrary, the former has asserted his rights of sovereignty over all the valleys watered by the Attrek and its tributaries south of the mountains; he has gained his point, and Russia has yielded. It must be remembered, too, that Persia has greatly benefitted by the action of her powerful neighbour, not only as against the Turcomans of Merv, but also with regard to Khiva, as the depredations of the man-stealing hordes of those petty states had been for long most severely felt by the inhabitants of Khorassan. Therefore, Russia had a certain claim on the goodwill of Persia, and the cession of that insignificant tract between the ranges and the desert is no real loss to her while she retains the more productive valleys south of the mountains.

Both with the robbers of Khiva and the Tekke Turcomans, Russia had as fair cause for quarrel as ever a nation had; but I am sorry that there are so many among us who can see in every movement in Central Asia nothing but a menace to ourselves. And so at first we were told that Merv in the hands of Russia would be a danger to British supremacy in the East. Herat being the key to India, Merv would prove the key to Herat. But growing wiser, next they said that Sarakhs was the key, not Merv; Sarakhs, the starting-point, whence Afghanistan could be more easily approached. And this is true: Merv is of no value at all, for, as Sir Henry Rawlinson (see his paper, 'The Road to Merv,' Pro.

Royal Geographical Society, p. 162) has well proved, an attacking force could reach that place with greater facility by way of Sarakhs than by the direct road across the desert.

"How near to Sarakhs were we told by the alarmists that the Russo-Persian treaty would place the conquerors of the Turcomans? I am afraid to say, an hour's ride, or something of the kind. But the real distance is by the new treaty somewhere about 200 miles. The Obah at Gawars (Gyaoors) seems about the nearest point in the Russian frontier to Sarakhs; and Sir H. Rawlinson gives the distance thus—to Abiverd, seventy miles; to Mehna, forty miles; to Sarakhs, seventy miles.

"But it is scarcely probable that the Russians would take the line from Chikishlar to Askabad as their base of operations for an invasion of Afghanistan. The thin belt of cultivated land through which their road would lie is quite incapable of furnishing food for a force of any strength. Lomakin in 1878 fell back through want of supplies; a caravan from Krasnovodsk was cut off by the Turcomans, while another coming from Bujnoord in Persian territory failed to arrive. Thus, in the first instance, he was forced to retire.

"The Russians ultimately succeeded as far as Askabad, but it was not without the goodwill of Persia.

"I have referred more than once to Sir H. Rawlinson's paper, 'The Road to Merv.' I will here summarize in as few words as possible the leading features of his argument:—

"'The distance from the Caspian to Merv by the Akhal country and Sarakhs, is about 700 miles, and to keep up communications by a line of posts along this interval would be a very serious operation indeed.

"'In the matter of supplies, food could not possibly be obtained in the districts traversed by the Russian columns.

"'With the cordial co-operation of Persia, the occupation of Merv by Russian troops from the Caspian, supported by a column from the Oxus, would be comparatively easy. If Persia were merely neutral, the operation would be difficult, but might possibly succeed; but if Persia were decidedly opposed to the movement, the march to Merv would be impossible.'

"The conclusions at which Sir Henry arrived appear to me incontrovertible; but if true of a march simply with Merv in view, how much more so would they be with Herat as the object? It could not be undertaken, except with the concurrence of Persia.

"That being an acknowledged axiom, it appears to me that Merv and Sarakhs may be thrown out of the question altogether: it is a bad line; and Russia would be going out of her way, if she occupied Merv as a preliminary step. Twelve or fourteen years since the question was much mooted in India, whether the Russians, in the forward movements they had recently made in Turkestan, did not manifest a design to move upon Herat *viâ* Merv and Sarakhs; and I argued then, as I did in a letter to the *Times* in 1877, and as I do now, that the Russians have a far more convenient route open to them (the concurrence of Persia being understood) from the southern shore of the Caspian Sea *viâ* Astrabad, Nishapore, and Meshed.

"The Russians could not attempt the invasion of Afghanistan without making Persia safe—it would be too dangerous to leave in their rear (or on their right flank, should they take the Akhal Attrek line) a doubtful neutral. And, unless comprised, Persia could hardly be reckoned safe. She must be an ally co-operating. Indeed, Russia, with such great designs in view, would require the active friendship of her neighbours; for I have not a high appreciation of her military strength if engaged on a distant expedition. Turkestan, at any rate, could not supply the *corps d'armée*, so troops must needs be transported down the Caspian to Krasnovodsk or Astrabad.

"Should such a contingency ever occur—a Russo-Persian alliance threatening our interests in Afghanistan—we should repeat our policy of 1856, which would, in all probability, speedily break up the *entente cordiale*. But, in February and March last year, I wrote to you at some length explaining what I considered would be the only circumstances under which Russia would offer active annoyance to our Indian Government. At present I took up my pen solely to point out how little Russia had gained by the treaty with Persia. It is the latter state which has asserted its rights, the former which has let go the frontier claimed four years since. The Russ has practised moderation; perhaps our 'scuttling' (as some facetious writer calls it—a very quiet, orderly, deliberate 'scuttle' it was!) from Candahar set him a good example!—Yours obediently,

"E. KAYE,
"Lieutenant-General.

"*March* 22nd, 1882."

THE CENTRAL ASIAN PARTY IN ENGLAND AND RUSSIA.[1]

THE death of the eminent Russian Central Asian critic Gregorieff renders it opportune to say a few words with reference to the actual condition of the party in both countries devoted to the safeguarding of the respective interests of England and Russia in the East. It is some time since any attempt was made to gauge the rival calibres of the Central Asian authorities in England and Russia, if, indeed, any such attempt has been made at all. Yet for more than a quarter of a century the Central Asian Question, in its varied forms, has had its spokesmen in the two countries, and more than one reputation has been entirely made by it. Elsewhere in Europe the controversy, although exciting a certain amount of interest, has led to no individuals giving themselves up very long to it, if we except Arminius Vámbéry in Hungary, and Captain Wahl in France. The latter, however, has simply dealt with the Russian military position in Central Asia in a casual manner, in the course of his larger Russian studies; while the former has so much identified himself with our interests, as to be considered by Germans more or less in the light of a misguided fanatic. Such a reputation is not a pleasant recompense for many a brave word spoken

[1] *The United Service Gazette*, January 21, 1882.

on behalf of England; but even in this country Arminius Vámbéry has got but very little thanks for his trouble.

The first thing that will strike an impartial observer on making a survey of the strength of the Central Asian parties in England and Russia is, the comparative few men in either country who are now devoting themselves to the question. Of earlier Central Asian writers, Captain Trench is dead; Robert Michell is a silent official at the India Office; and James Hutton has written no further books since he issued his admirable "Central Asia from the Aryan to the Cossack," although, in common with Sutherland Edwards, his pen is ever busy in the anonymous columns of the English and Indian press. As for Arminius Vámbéry, he has published nothing of importance on the Central Asian Question, since he met with such a cold reception on his visit to England in 1880; while Sir Henry Rawlinson's voice, with the exception of the solitary occasion of the Candahar controversy a twelvemonth ago, has not been raised for several years. Indeed, during the last three or four years there has been a remarkable dearth of those elaborately-written essays on Central Asia which previously used to appear in the columns of the monthlies and quarterlies. We do not believe that more than three or four magazine articles have appeared on Central Asia since 1879, and these have not been from the pens of the earlier authorities. Several fresh writers in the interval, however, have come to the front, and among these we may mention with pleasure the names of Colonel Cory, Demetrius Boulger, and Charles Marvin. Colonel Cory may be regarded as an excellent spokesman of India in the controversy, although there are chapters in his remarkable work, "The Eastern Menace," which give him an equal claim to pose as an all-round observer of the Central Asian Question. Boulger's attention has been chiefly given to the Chinese aspect of the question, which has lost much of its importance since he wrote his "Yakoob Beg." Nobody, for instance, would re-echo the sentiment expressed in the epoch of the Kashgar mania, from 1872 to 1875, that a Russian occupation of Yarkand or Kashgar should be treated as a *casus belli*. With the development of the new Russian movement from the Caspian, nearly all interest in Kashgar has expired, and in this manner Boulger has become stranded upon a controversy of the past. More happy in this respect is Marvin, whose works, "The Russian Campaign against the Turcomans," "Grodekoff's Ride to Herat," and "Merv," deal with the latest phase of the Central Asian Question, and one that promises to excite undiminished interest until the alignment of Russia and India takes place.

To the authorities we have mentioned above, might be added Burnaby, by right of his "Ride to Khiva;" MacGregor, on account of his "Journey through Khorassan;" Valentine Baker, by virtue of his "Clouds in the East," &c.; but these writers, although the views they have expressed receive great weight, cannot be regarded in the light of "specialists." Besides, if we began to mention them we should have to go further a-field and include Malleson, Sir Rutherford Alcock, and a large number of other persons, who, at one time or another, have said something about Central Asia, but who, like Grant Duff, have "dropped the subject" more or less since. This would involve a similar extension of the survey in Russia, and we should have to mention a number of writers like Grodekoff, who have only expressed their opinion publicly once in their lives. Indeed, we are almost compelled to include such one-book authors as it is, for the Central Asian party is so small in Russia that it barely exists at all. Gregorieff, the Rawlinson of Russia, is dead; Colonel Venukoff has not written a line since 1878, and has practically retired from the controversy; General Petroosevitch was killed at Geok Tepé a year ago, and Colonel Kostenko is too much occupied with his official duties in Kuldja to make any further addition to Central Asian literature. From this list, which is exhaustive, it will be seen that the Central Asian party is in an almost defunct condition in Russia. There are no young writers there to take the place of Gregorieff, or to make up for the silence of Venukoff; Russia has no Marvin, or Boulger. On the other hand, it is a question whether she needs them. While we are fruitlessly wagging our tongues in England, Russia is slicing up Central Asia with the sword. While our Dukes of Argyll waste their time muddling themselves and the public with huge and heavy tomes on "The Eastern Question," Russia's M. de Giers and Baron Jomini silently pursue their course and swallow up province after province. It is flattering, one way, to know that we publish twenty books on Central Asia to Russia's one, and a thousand newspaper articles to every one issued by Russia; but we would sooner have no books and no articles, no Rawlinsons, and Vámbérys, and Corys, and Marvins, if we could have instead such a masterly policy as Russia is pursuing in the East.

THE END.

WORKS BY CHARLES MARVIN.

Published by W. H. ALLEN & Co. Publishers to the India Office,
13, Waterloo Place, Pall Mall, S.W.

"The only work on Merv in any language."—*Newcastle Chronicle.*
One Vol., 450 pages, 11 Maps and Portrait, 18s.

Merv, the Queen of the World; and the Scourge of the Man-Stealing Turcomans. Containing an account of the Turcoman tribes, the history and actual condition of Merv, and the most recent Russian plans for the Invasion of India from the Caspian.

RUSSIAN OPINION OF GENERAL ANNENKOFF.

"In preparing his work on Merv, Marvin availed himself of the latest sources of information, including such Russian ones as Kostenko's 'Turkestan,' and in particular the articles by Petroosevitch, who was killed at Geok Tepé, in consequence of which he describes fully the military life of the Turcomans, the strategical significance of Merv, and the influence Russia will acquire after capturing it."—*Vestnik Europi.*

"Brilliant from beginning to end."—*Morning Post.*
One Vol., 377 pages, 14 Maps and Plans, and 3 Portraits. Price 18s.

The Eye-Witnesses' Account of the Disastrous Russian Campaign against the Akhal Tekke Turcomans. Describing the March across the Burning Desert, the Storming of Dengeel Tepé, and the Disastrous Retreat to the Caspian.

OPINION OF VÁMBÉRY.

"Rarely has an acquaintance with the Russian language been so amply utilized for English political literature as in the present case; for all what you write is totally unknown to the public at large, and political writers, unable to read Russian, must be grateful to you."—*Letter to Author.*

"Every page rich in interest."—*Pall Mall Gazette.*
One Vol., 244 pages, 3 Maps and Plans, and 1 Portrait. Price 8s.

Colonel Grodekoff's Ride from Samarcand to Herat. With his own Map of the March Route from the Oxus to Herat.

OPINION OF SIR HENRY RAWLINSON, K.C.B.

"Colonel Grodekoff knows nothing of commerce, but a good deal of Afghan politics. A very interesting account of a journey from Samarcand, by Sir-i-pul and Mymeneh, to Herat."—*Memorandum on Candahar, Blue Book,* "*Afghanistan* (1881), *No.* 2."

Mounted on Linen, price 2s. 6d.
General Petroosevitch's Map of Akhal and Merv. Translated by CHARLES MARVIN.

Published by Messrs. SONNENSCHEIN, Paternoster Row.

One Vol., 334 pages, Third and Popular Illustrated Edition. Price 2s.
Our Public Offices. Embodying an Account of the Disclosure of the Anglo-Russian Agreement and the Secret Treaty of May 31st, 1878.

LONDON
PRINTED BY GILBERT AND RIVINGTON, LIMITED,
ST. JOHN'S SQUARE.

www.ingramcontent.com/pod-product-compliance
Lightning Source LLC
Chambersburg PA
CBHW020325240426
43673CB00039B/921